Assessing Children's Learning

Second Edition

Mary Jane Drummond

Other titles of interest:

Monitoring, Assessment, Recording, Reporting and Accountability
    (2nd edition)
Planning, Teaching and Class Management in Primary Schools
    (2nd edition)
Professional Values and Practice for Teachers and Student Teachers

David Fulton Publishers Ltd
The Chiswick Centre, 414 Chiswick High Road, London W4 5TF

www.fultonpublishers.co.uk

First published in Great Britain in 1993 by David Fulton Publishers
Second edition 2003
10 9 8 7 6 5 4 3 2

Note: The right of the author to be identified as the author of this work has been
asserted by him in accordance with the Copyright, Designs and Patents Act 1988.

David Fulton Publishers is a division of Granada Learning Limited, part of
Granada plc.

British Library Cataloguing in Publication Data
A catalogue record for this book is available from the British Library.

ISBN 1–84312–040–2

Typeset by FiSH Books, London.WC1
Printed and bound in Great Britain by The Thanet Press, Margate.

Contents

Acknowledgements

I am very grateful to the teachers who generously allowed me to quote from their observations and case studies:

Jenny Colls	Shelagh MacDonald
Maggie Ellis	Jennifer Pozzani
Geoff Fisher	Margaret Prosser
Sheila Gapp	Maxine Purdy
Ann Lawson	Mary Rosenberg
Ann Le Gassick	Michael Tennant

Thank you for helping me to learn about children's learning.

CHAPTER 1

Learning from Jason

In February 1985, a class of seven- and eight-year-olds, in their first year of junior schooling, were taken into the school hall where they sat at individual tables to take a mathematics test (NFER 1984). The headteacher read out the questions, and the pupils wrote the answers in their individual test booklets. One of those children was Jason, aged seven years, six months, who had spent two and a half years in the infant department. There are 36 questions in the test and Jason answered them all. One of the answers was correct, giving Jason a raw score of two, and a standardised score of 81, a 'moderately low score', according to the teacher's guide to the test.

A teacher in Jason's school showed me his test booklet, and I date my interest in assessment from that day. In the analysis of Jason's test performance that follows, we will be able to see some obvious inadequacies in the use of formal group testing as a way of assessing individual children's learning. But I will also argue that the test booklet does tell us some very important things about Jason's learning, and about other children's learning, that must be taken into account in a full understanding of the process of assessment.

Jason's test responses show us, first of all, what he has failed to learn about mathematics. More significantly, they give us an indication of the gap that yawns between what his teachers have taught him and what he has learned. In other words, the test booklet forces us to look critically at the relationship between teaching and learning. Furthermore, Jason's case-study invites us to explore the interplay of the rights and responsibilities of teachers and learners.

But first, what has Jason learned during his eight terms in school? He has learned how to take a test. His answers are written neatly, with the sharpest of pencils. When he reverses a digit and sees his mistake, he crosses it out tidily. He places his answers on the line or in the box as instructed, though he often adds some more digits in other empty spaces, as if he interpreted a space as an invitation to write. (See questions 19 and 22 in figure 1.1.) He has learned to copy numbers and letters neatly and accurately, even though this is not what is being asked of him. (See questions 5 and 6 shown in figure 1.2.)

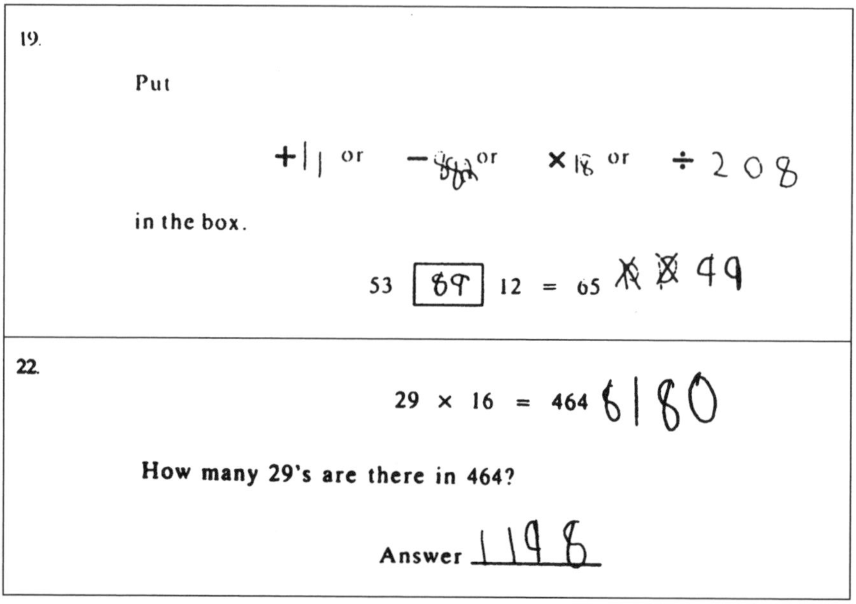
19.

Put

+ or − or × or ÷

in the box.

53 [ ] 12 = 65

22.

29 × 16 = 464

How many 29's are there in 464?

Answer ______

Figure 1.1

In question 5, Jason has been asked to rank the four amounts of money in order, from the smallest to the largest. In question 6, he has been asked (A) who is the shorter of the two children, and (B) by how many centimetres. Jason has simply copied the print from the question into the space provided for the answer.

He has learned to listen and to follow instructions carefully, as closely as he can, though his short-term memory does sometimes let him down. In question 1, for example, he was asked to write in numerals the number two hundred and fifty-two. As we can see, (figure 1.3), he has almost done so, writing two, a hundred, and forty-two. He has learned to stay with a task and complete it. Other pupils in the same class answered only a few of the test questions, leaving many items blank. Others scrawled and smudged their responses: Jason's presentation is exemplary.

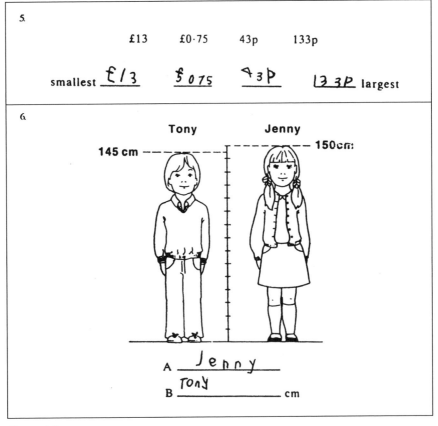

5.

        £13   £0·75   43p   133p

smallest _£13_   _£075_   _43P_   _133P_ largest

6.

A _Jenny_

B _Tony_____ cm

Figure 1.2

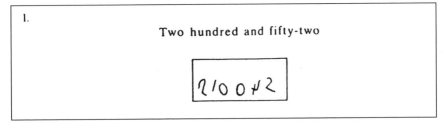

1.

Two hundred and fifty-two

2100#2

Figure 1.3

He has not, it is apparent, learned very much mathematics. He has learned that in a mathematics test, he is required to write numbers, which he does, with one exception. (See question 14 below, in figure 1.11.)

There is no evidence that he has learned the value of the numbers that he writes. So, for example, in question 4, he is asked to calculate the

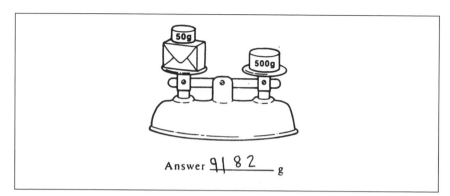

Answer 9| 8 2 ___ g

Figure 1.4

weight of the parcel on the left, if the scales balance (figure 1.4). He has responded by writing four digits in the space provided. I am certain that he has not calculated – or miscalculated – that 9182g + 50g = 500g, or that 500g – 50g = 9182g. He has simply written some numbers in the appropriate place for an answer. He uses the same approach in question 7, question 9, and question 17 (figure 1.5).

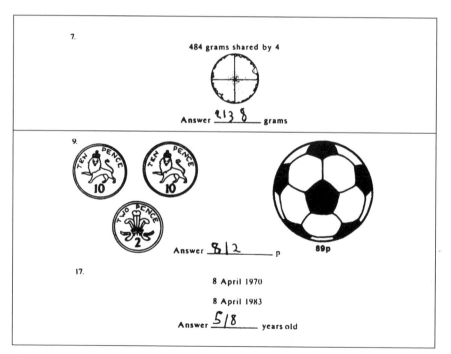

Figure 1.5

Question 7 is a simple division problem; question 9 asks how much more money is needed to buy the football, and in question 17, the pupils are required to give the age of a child born on 8 April 1970 on 8 April 1983. Another child in Jason's class interpreted this question as a subtraction problem; working from left to right he seems to have thought to himself: '8 from 8 is 0, put down 0); April from April is 0, put down 0; 1983 from 1970' – here the answer trails away as the pupil realises he cannot complete the problem.

Jason frequently writes the number 8, and it is tempting to speculate about the reason for this. (See questions 21, 23 for example.) Is it a satisfying number for him to write? Has he recently mastered the art of forming it with a single stroke? Or is it possible that he has noticed the front cover of his test booklet (figure 1.7), and that he has seized on this bold and impressive numeral as a possible clue to what is being asked of him?

21.

Put a ring round each even number.

87   8   11   56   44 8 8

23.

What number is 3 less than 200?

Answer 8 1 8

Figure 1.6

National Foundation for Educational Research in England and Wales

MATHEMATICS 8

Figure 1.7

He uses the same configurations of numbers several times, suggesting that he is not attending to or discriminating between the meaning of the context of the different questions (figure 1.8).

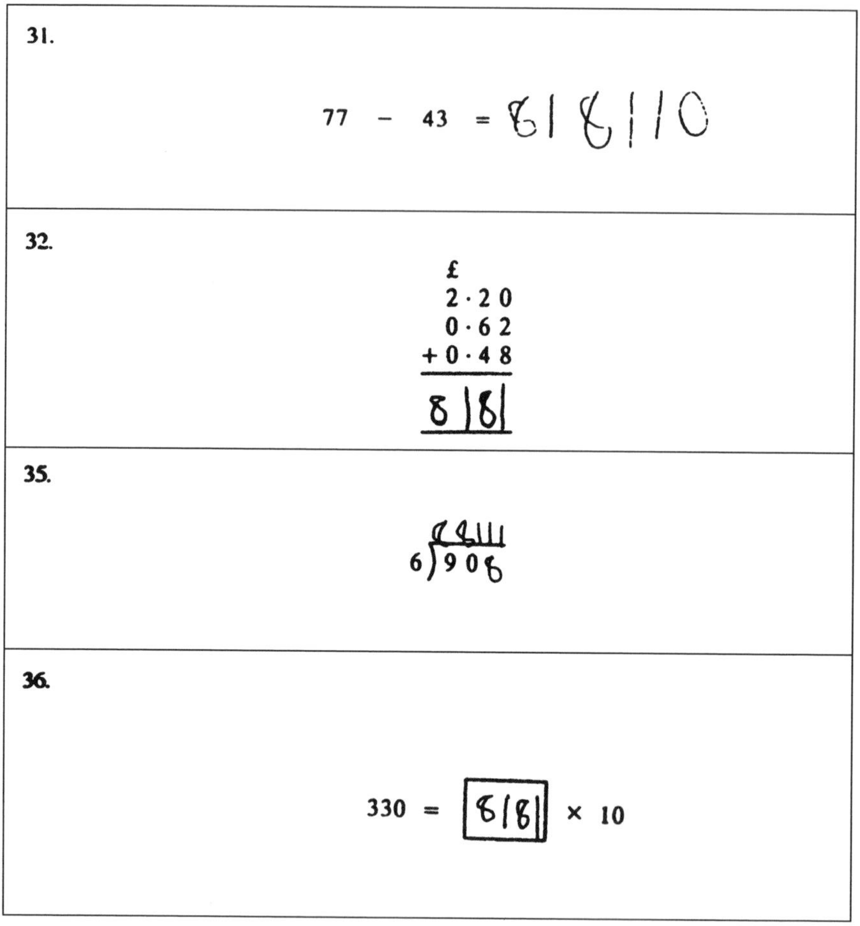

31.

$$77 \ - \ 43 \ = \ 8|8||0$$

32.

$$\begin{array}{r} \pounds \\ 2 \cdot 2\,0 \\ 0 \cdot 6\,2 \\ +\,0 \cdot 4\,8 \\ \hline \underline{8\,|8|} \end{array}$$

35.

$$6\overline{)9\,0\,8}$$

36.

$$330 \ = \ \boxed{8|8|} \ \times \ 10$$

Figure 1.8

But sometimes, it seems, there may be other reasons for his responses; in question 28, for example. It seems just possible here that Jason has read off the length of the rod on the ruler as nearly 8, and interpreted the half-centimetre mark on the ruler as figure 1. How long is the rod? It could be that Jason said to himself '8, and back a bit to this 1 here. 8. Eight. One.' Why has he written it twice? To fill this allocated space?

More convincing evidence that Jason attends to at least part of the content of the question, as he sees it (not as the tester sees it), can be seen

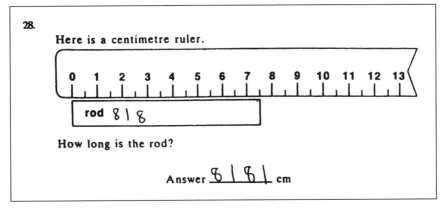

Figure 1.9

in question 34 (figure 1.10). What time does this clock show? Did Jason reflect 'There is the 9, there is the 1; perhaps an 8 for good measure...'? It is at least a possibility.

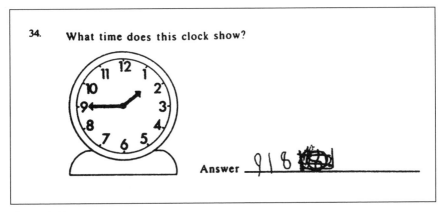

Figure 1.10

Question 14 is more complex. The instruction is: Draw this shape as it will look when it has been rotated one right-angle clockwise. Here I believe Jason makes his first real error, and writes a letter (lower case 'e') before remembering that this is a mathematics test. It is not, at any rate, an impossible or improbable interpretation of what he has done – he will, after all, have seen the capital and lower case letters presented together in just this way in many contexts during his school career. The

one right angle - clockwise

Figure 1.11

rest of his response is more interesting; I suggest that Jason heard the word 'clock' as a significant instruction and, remembering previous class-work on clocks, responded with a sketch of a clock, on which he then duly marked the 8.

In these last two examples, I believe there is substantial evidence that, against what must be, for him, inconceivable odds, Jason is struggling to make sense of the test, and what his headteacher is asking him to do. His mathematical understanding is still too scanty to be of much use to him, but he uses all the other clues he can get. This is, I think, a remarkable achieve-ment, and a tribute to Jason's persistence, to his longing for meaning.

It is also possible to recognise Jason's self-restraint, and his passivity, during what was presumably an uncomfortable experience. He cannot have been feeling relaxed, confident, sure of himself and certain of success, during the test. Or does he not even know what it is he does not know? It seems more reasonable to assume that he does know, very well, that mathematics, and the mathematical tasks his teacher gives him, make no kind of sense at all. And yet he is prepared to sit and comply, as far as he is able, with a string of incomprehensible instructions.

Jason may not have learned much mathematics but he has learned some important rules about being a pupil. Mary Willes' study (1983) of children entering a reception class charts the inexorable process by which children – spontaneous, curious, independent – are transformed into pupils, who know the rules. Her pessimistic summary of the task of the pupil seems to describe Jason's condition all too accurately:

> ...finding out what the teacher wants, and doing it, constitute the primary duty of a pupil.

Willes (1983) p.138

Jason has learned not to resist and rebel when his teachers ask him to do the impossible. Throughout the test he sat at his desk and did as he was told, as far as he was able. It is only in my fantasy that Jason overturns his desk and hurls it at his headteacher, screaming defiance, demanding his rights as a pupil, as a child, as a human being.

When I was first shown Jason's test booklet, the emotional impact on me was very strong. As a result, it has taken me some time to see beneath the surface features of this piece of primary practice to the larger, more abstract issues it exemplifies. Jason's test performance does certainly illustrate inevitable weaknesses in formal group testing, in particular the way in which such tests cannot tell us anything about the processes of pupils' thinking, but only whether pupils arrive at the unique right answer. But there is more to be said. In Jason we see a child who, like all other children, is capable of learning. He *has* been learning, during his three years in school, but much of it is not what his teachers intended. We have little evidence from this test of his learning in the cognitive domain, but we can see how much he has learned about the social conventions of the school – how to keep his pencil sharp, how to stay in his seat, how to take a test, how to be a pupil. In the affective domain, we can see how Jason has learned not to express dissatisfaction or disquiet when meaningless demands are made on him. And yet we can also see signs – small perhaps, but significant – that, in the limited ways left open to him, Jason is still struggling to make sense of what goes on around him in the puzzling world of school.

None of this has come about on purpose; his teachers have not maliciously plotted to keep Jason in the dark, to break his will, to stupefy him with bewildering questions, or to do anything but their best by him. And yet things have gone seriously wrong for Jason. Jason's obedience, his compliance with his teachers' demands, his search for meaning in a largely meaningless world, force us to ask some difficult questions: what is it that has gone wrong? How? And why? I believe that the wrong lies not in his teachers' intentions, not even in their teaching, but in what has been happening to Jason's *learning*. Jason stands as an example, and an awful warning, of what can happen to all children whose learning is not, for whatever reason, the prime concern and central focus of their teachers' attention.

Like all children, Jason has the right to an education in which his learning is seen as of paramount importance – not his difficulties, or his limitations, or his disadvantages, not his successes or failures – but his learning. It is children's learning that must be the subject of teachers' most energetic care and attention – not their lesson plans, or schemes of work, or their rich and stimulating provision – but the learning that results from everything they do (and do not do) in schools and classrooms. Unless there is, at the centre of a school's curriculum, a sustained and unshakable interest in children's learning, there will always be children like Jason who do not learn what their teachers set out to teach them. The process of assessing children's learning by looking closely at it and striving to understand it – is the only certain safeguard against children's failure, the only certain guarantee of children's progress and development.

Jason has the right, like all children, to a satisfying and fulfilling education; children's rights create responsibilities that all teachers are obliged to accept. Paramount among them is the responsibility to monitor the effects of their work so as to ensure that their good intentions for children are realised. The responsibility to assess, to watch and to understand learning, is an awesome one; but the exercise of this responsibility is the only real fulfilment that teachers can know. In the exercise of this responsibility, teachers are powerful agents in children's well-being; the power of teachers to bring about progress and development through their teaching is dependent on their willingness to accept their responsibility for understanding learning.

These three concepts, rights, responsibility and power, give us a clue to understanding the tangle of Jason's predicament. It is possible to see how his teachers' right to teach, drawing on their professional certainties, their good intentions, their well-tried methods, and their published maths schemes, conflicts with Jason's right to learn. We can also see how Jason has accepted his responsibilities as a pupil, including his responsibility to comply with his teachers, who have treated his compliance as a pupil as if it alone were a sufficient and satisfactory outcome of their teaching. They seem to have lost sight of their responsibility to use their power in the interests of learning, rather than simply as an instrument of social control. Jason's quest for meaning emphasises his teachers' responsibility constantly to check whether the world they invite Jason to inhabit as a pupil is one that makes sense to him as a child.

This particular example of a published test that tells us so little about one child's understanding is obviously not an example to emulate. But I believe this brief episode of ineffective assessment has much to teach us about a more effective approach. I am arguing here, and throughout this book, that we will never achieve effective assessment in schools and classrooms if we conceptualise the task as a matter of making pragmatic decisions about formats, formal testing procedures and record-keeping. Trying to understand the place of assessment in education makes moral and philosophical demands on our thinking. The practice of effective assessment requires a thorough understanding and acceptance of the concepts of rights, responsibility and power, lying at the heart of our work as teachers. In searching for ways to make our assessment practices more effective, we are committing ourselves to recognising children's rights, shouldering our responsibilities towards them, and striving to use our power wisely and well.

CHAPTER 2

Looking at Learning: Introductory

In thinking about Jason's test booklet over the years, I have come to see that the key issues in assessment, the most challenging and difficult ones, are moral and philosophical, rather than organisational and pedagogical. Questions of what, when, where and how to assess are of secondary importance beside the more searching question of 'Why assess?' And 'Why assess?' implies 'Why educate?' Effective assessment can only be based on a thorough understanding of our purposes in teaching and of our aspirations for our pupils.

In the chapters that follow I discuss the concepts of rights, responsibilities and power, the concepts introduced in Chapter 1 through the analysis of Jason's test booklet, with reference to two main areas of concern: the interests of children, and the choices made by teachers. The moral imperative for teachers' choices to be made in the interests of children is the starting point for an exploration of the choices that teachers make in the practice of assessment – the choices they do make, and the choices they could and should make. Put at its simplest, the task of the teacher is to work for the interests of children, seeking to understand and articulate those interests, and to serve them well. The right of all children to a worthwhile education imposes on teachers the awesome responsibility of understanding and providing the essential components of such an education. This responsibility entails being able to describe, explain and justify a set of beliefs about what constitutes 'worthwhileness' in primary education, and about what parts of children's learning and development are the teacher's proper concern. So, for example, my own system of beliefs and values has led me to take a wide view of teachers' responsibilities. Teachers are responsible, I believe, for attending to children's spiritual and moral growth, as well as to their physical well-being, to the essential differences between children as well as to what they hold in common, to children's rights to care and loving attention as well as to carefully planned programmes of study, to their right to be treated with honesty, trust and respect, as human beings, rather than just as pupils.

One of the most challenging parts of this immense undertaking is to find ways of assessing children's learning that do honour to their rights and interests, and that enhance the worthwhileness of their educational experiences. The choices teachers make in assessing children's learning must be subject to this one central, inescapable principle: that children's interests are paramount. Assessment is a process that must enrich their lives, their learning and development. Assessment must work for children.

In recent years, especially since the implementation of the 1988 Education Reform Act, the term 'assessment' has come to suggest an objective, mechanical process of measurement. It suggests checklists, precision, explicit criteria, incontrovertible facts and figures. In this book, I will be using the word in a different sense.

When we work with children, when we play and experiment and talk with them, when we watch them and everything they do, we are witnessing a fascinating and inspiring process: we are seeing them learn. As we think about what we see, and try to understand it, we have embarked on the process that in this book I am calling 'assessment'. I am using the term to describe the ways in which, in our everyday practice, we observe children's learning, strive to understand it, and then put our understanding to good use.

In assessment, we can appreciate and understand what children learn; we can recognise their achievements, and their individuality, the differences between them. We can use our assessments to shape and enrich our curriculum, our interactions, our provision as a whole; we can use our assessments as a way of identifying what children will be able to learn next, so that we can support and extend that learning. Assessment is part of our daily practice in striving for quality. This book is based on the view that effective assessment is a process in which our understanding of children's learning, acquired through observation and reflection, can be used to evaluate and enrich the curriculum we offer.

The acts of the teacher in assessment – the responsibility to see, to understand and to put this understanding to good use – are discussed in detail in the chapters that follow. Teachers' choices, the things they actually do, will be examined in the light of the thinking that informs those choices. The emphasis will be on the concepts and values that teachers draw on in assessment, rather than on the physical trappings of their practice, the ticksheets or record formats. Concepts such as happiness, progress, improvement and comparison may be present implicitly, as part of the mental framework that supports teachers' assessment practices, but these concepts are rarely examined critically, in the routines of every day, to establish the part they play in making education more worthwhile for children. Effective assessment – clear seeing, rich understanding, respectful application – will be advanced by a full appreciation of the value-base from which teachers' choices are made.

It is sometimes convenient to think of the process of assessment as a simple three-stage process; the assessor collects evidence, makes judgements on the basis of that evidence, and certain events then follow. This model can be crudely represented as in figure 2.1. In this book each of these stages in the process will be discussed in turn, and later chapters will explore the relationship between the stages, represented by the arrows in the diagram. This plan has the advantage of tidiness, but the disadvantage of suggesting that assessment is a neat and tidy process; it is, of course, no such thing. Assessment is essentially provisional, partial, tentative, exploratory and, inevitably, incomplete. The tension between this necessary incompleteness, and the desire and pursuit of the whole, is one of the reasons why teachers approach the task of assessment with justifiable trepidation. Their trepidation is not allayed by the official insistence, from the top of the educational system, that assessment, as defined by a succession of education acts since 1988, should be both complete and comprehensive. Teachers know better.

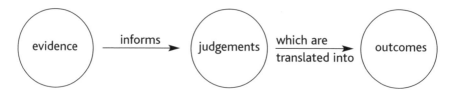

Figure 2.1

There are other tensions. One of these can be seen in the distinction between the expressed purpose of a particular act of assessment, and what the assessors can, if they choose, learn from it. The avowed intention of the assessment may have a narrow focus; there may be a precise question about an individual child to be answered, or the outcomes of a new approach to some specific curriculum area to be ascertained, but the evidence obtained in the process of assessment can always be reread and reinterpreted to tell us more than we thought we were asking. Every enquiry into children's learning, however narrowly framed, will always also have something to say about teaching, about the teacher, and about the whole curriculum, of which the teacher's teaching and the learner's learning are only two constituent parts. Assessment is a process of asking questions about learning that usher in both wider and more deeply reaching (and often more discomfiting) questions about the purposes and outcomes of education. The questions we ask in assessment are members of the extensive set of evaluative questions that we ask when we concern ourselves with the effectiveness and worthwhileness of education as a whole. In a sense, however small a piece of the classroom world we think we are looking at, we are always giving ourselves the opportunity to look critically, or even, sometimes, appreciatively, at a much bigger picture as well.

The case-study material that is used in this book to illustrate and explain the central arguments is no exception to this general rule. Each example has something to teach us about the present and the particular; but its significance does not end there. Each example also has the power, if we choose to respond, to stimulate a more abstract and principled debate. The dictated stories of five-year-old children presented in Chapter 3, for example, illustrate, on one level, the extensive range of imaginative purposes for which these children are using language. But at another level, the material raises questions about the relationship between fantasy and reality in the thinking of young children. These stories suggest the possibility of reconsidering the common practice, in the curriculum of many infant classrooms, of selecting topics and activities because of their familiarity to the children, and their direct relevance to their everyday experience. Similarly, the case-study of James, a child who suffered great distress at parting from his mother each morning, can be seen in two different ways. First, it can be seen to illustrate the possibility of monitoring a child's emotional development, as part of the process of assessing children's learning in all its forms. And, secondly, it can be seen as a challenge to the received wisdom that maintains that it is the business of primary school teachers to ensure their pupils' happiness.

The story of James suggests that perhaps children have the right to be unhappy, and to express their pain and grief. The great educator Korczak (whose work is discussed in Chapter 6) included this right in his idiosyncratic but thought-provoking list of Children's Rights, p. 356: 'The child has the right to respect for his grief. (Even though it be for the loss of a pebble.)' (Lifton 1989).

In the same way, developmental psychologists, such as Margaret Donaldson, whose work is briefly described in Chapter 4, have made it their business to study children's growing cognitive grasp of certain carefully structured problems. But as we shall see, their work has more to offer us: they have revealed unexpected connections between the context of the task and the children's cognitive and linguistic performance. Their work suggests that teachers will do well to examine carefully the context in which their assessments are made, as part of the act of understanding, and not confine their attention simply to what the children say and do.

In schools and classrooms, whenever we set about assessing children's learning, the possibility of these deeper questions, this broader vision, is always there for us to recognise or not, as we choose. Even the statutorily prescribed format of the standard assessment tasks, to be administered at the end of each key stage, may have stimulated some teachers to question their use of group work, or of peer support, or their policy on invented spellings and the use of dictionaries. I am not suggesting that administering a standard assessment task is the most effective way of raising questions about appropriate primary practice; but I do maintain that starting to ask questions about children's learning, however precise or trivial they may seem, is always the start of something big. It may even be the beginning of a life-long enquiry into teaching, learning and the curriculum. Small wonder that teachers are apprehensive about the long-term and short-term effects of their practice in assessment on themselves and on their pupils.

This justifiable apprehension was, of course, enormously increased by the requirements of the 1988 Education Reform Act, which, for the first time, imposed on teachers a programme of statutory procedures to be followed in assessment. Teachers were not slow to realise that, as Blenkin and Kelly (1992) so powerfully argue, 'the central purpose of this programme is administrative and political rather than educational' (p.23). However, in spite of almost universal professional apprehension, expressed throughout the years since 1988, I remain cautiously confident that practising teachers will not readily relinquish the educational purposes of their own enquiries into teaching and learning.

A further tension for teachers can be discerned in the incontrovertible fact that the willingness to embark, however tentatively, on such an enquiry, does not itself guarantee clear sightedness and impartiality, a rounded picture of real life, of teaching and learning as it really is. Like trains at a level crossing, where one train sometimes conceals another from the waiting motorist, the complexity of classroom events may sometimes mean that careful scrutiny by the teacher of one part of the scene may blot out an awareness of other equally important elements of the picture. In particular it seems likely that teachers who are primarily interested in their *teaching*, in their strategies, their goals and their lesson plans, may pay less attention to the extent of the possible gap between their intentions, and the actual outcomes, in terms of children's *learning*. Knowing what one set out to do, and looking for evidence that one has done it, may not help one to see what has in fact resulted from one's good, even exemplary, intentions. Unintended learning is not, in any event, easy to recognise; when it runs counter to the teacher's intentions, it may become virtually invisible.

Looking at learning, it is becoming clear, is not to be undertaken lightly. The very conditions of classroom life, the complexity of classroom events, the interconnectedness of context and curriculum, of teaching and learning, all make it harder for us to look at learning as clearly as we would wish. One of the great pioneers of early childhood education, Susan Isaacs, whose work is discussed more fully in Chapter 4, has an important lesson to teach us here. The experimental school in Cambridge, the Malting House, where for four years Isaacs and her colleagues studied children's learning intently and passionately, was unusual in a number of ways. Isaacs describes the conditions in which her observations took place as 'relatively free'. Evelyn Lawrence, who taught at the school, wrote of it:

> There is no fixed curriculum. The children do what appeals to them at the moment. The work of the educator is to select his material, and at times indirectly to suggest activities, so that the child will of his own accord do things which are useful for his work. Lately one or two of the older children have drawn up rough outlines of their day's work...No child would be forced to keep to his programme if he seriously wanted to depart from it at any time...There is, with all the children, much more active movement than one finds in most schools. In fine weather they are out in the garden for most

of the day, digging, running, carpentering, or climbing . . . The aim of the teachers is as far as possible to refrain from teaching, but to let the children find out all they can for themselves. They are urged to answer their own questions, with the teachers to help them discover where the answers are to be found. Above all, care is taken that their ideas of values shall be their own. They are not told that such and such a thing is good or bad, nice or beautiful, but only that it seems so to some particular person.

Quoted in Gardner (1969) pp.61–5

Isaacs' own words bear out this description; she refers to 'an all-round lessening of the degree of inhibition of the children's impulses' (Isaacs 1930, p.12). There were fewer checks on the verbal expression of the children's views and feelings than is common, and a correspondingly 'greater dramatic vividness of their social and imaginative and intellectual life as a whole'. The materials provided for the children, too, led them to be much more generally active than children in ordinary classroom conditions. More active and more genuinely exploratory: the accounts of the children's investigations into the workings of the Bunsen burners with which their classroom was fitted make primary teachers today turn pale with fright. But the emphasis at the Malting House on the children's freely chosen and self-directed activities was not in any sense a licence for chaos and disorder. On the contrary:

This greater activity in all directions, originated, developed and sustained by the children themselves, was a definite part of our educational aim. And it not only led the children to show us their inner minds with far less reserve and fear than in ordinary circumstances, but through the richer, more varied and more immediate experience of the social and physical worlds which it brought them, it also stimulated and diversified their actual responses. There was, in other words, more for us to see; and we could see it more plainly.

Isaacs (op. cit.) p.12

In the first chapter of this book I demonstrated how little of Jason's thinking and learning there was to be seen in the inappropriate maths test he was given. Let us now imagine Jason as a pupil at the Malting House; what more would there have been for Susan Isaacs and her colleagues to see? How much more plainly would they have seen it?

One aspect of Jason's intellectual life that would, we may be certain, have been fostered there, is his capacity to ask questions. At the Malting House, children's questions were welcomed and valued; the pages of Isaacs' observations are thick with them, even from the very youngest pupils. Phineas, for example, aged three years 11 months, poured out a torrent of questions when looking for the first time at a large picture of a railway station, with a train crossing a set of points and various signals.

> Phineas (3;11) began to ask Mrs I. questions about the picture. 'Why aren't there any coal trucks? Why is it darker there for? Why is it darker in there? I saw a shadow. There is a fire in there. Why is there a fire in there? And there are two men in there. Why are the men there for? Why couldn't you see it (the engine) going on the picture for?' (He asked this exactly the same way three times repeated.) 'What are the railway lines for? What could the puffer do without railway lines? Why aren't there no railway lines here?'(Pointing to the margin.) 'Why couldn't you see the next side for? Why are those funny signals for? What is this round thing for?' (Pointing to the boiler.) 'What are round boxes for?' (Mrs I. was called away then; but he went on talking to Priscilla.) 'What is that man looking at, Priscilla? What are the two colours for?' (pointing to the signal flags.) Then Priscilla went away, and he went to do something else.
>
> Isaacs (op. cit.) p.148

What is remarkable in this extract is not just the thoroughness of this young child's enquiry, both into the actual facts represented, and into the conventions of the two dimensional representation, but also the fact that it is the child who is asking all the questions. It is not the teacher who is asking Phineas to describe what he sees, as in many typical classroom dialogues; it is Phineas who controls his own enquiry, making active efforts to assimilate this new experience. As a result, the teacher, Mrs I, has an enviable opportunity of looking at what Phineas is learning, both about the world and about how to enquire into it. There is more for her to see, and she sees it plainly. If Jason had had this experience, of being encouraged to behave as an active learner, an avid questioner, his mathematical experiences would surely have been more rewarding. We can safely assume that at the Malting House 'a greater dramatic vividness' would have characterised Jason's experiences with numbers, with geometrical shapes, with money, with the whole mathematical world that now seems to be closed to him.

The 'relatively free conditions' of the Malting House curriculum are in startling contrast to the constraints that most primary teachers experience in their over-crowded, under-resourced classrooms. The relative freedom of Isaacs and her colleagues to look at children's learning in ways of their own devising, in ways that matched their central educational purposes, illustrates very clearly one more dilemma experienced by primary teachers today. However much we may aspire to freedom – for the children, for their choices, for ourselves, for our pedagogy and for our assessment practices – that freedom is always, in every school and classroom, substantially curtailed in the interests of everyone else in the institution. There is a constant tension between what might be appropriate for one pupil and what is appropriate for a great many; between the needs of the individual and the group; between the needs of one group or one class, and the whole body of pupils. The sheer physical limitations that have, we believe, to be imposed on our pupils' movements to keep them safe from harm, make it impossible for us to recreate Isaacs' working conditions, and the intellectual and emotional freedom of the 20 children at the Malting House school. But in spite of all these constraints we can, still, I believe, seriously consider the possibility of bringing our assessment practices up to the mark of Isaacs' breadth and clarity of vision: 'There was more for us to see, and we could see it more plainly' – does not Isaacs' achievement set us a goal worth striving for?

Primary teachers commit themselves daily to a life of bewildering complexity and uncertainty; not surprisingly, the inescapable ambiguities, tensions and dilemmas of schools and classrooms awaken in us unfulfilled longings for certainty. When we set about looking at learning, we yearn for the single, simple point of view, for an end to confusion, and a platform of verifiable facts on which to stand. Not surprisingly, we are continually disappointed, but it may be that, in the long term, this disappointment will serve us better than we think.

Erich Fromm's *The Fear of Freedom* (1942) is a psychological analysis of the ills of 'modern' European and American society. Fromm describes the difference between irrational and rational doubt. Irrational doubt is rooted in the isolation and powerlessness of the individual and a negative attitude towards life. It is 'one of the basic problems of modern man' and has dangerous consequences, especially 'the compulsive quest for certainty...(which) is rooted in the need to conquer the unbearable doubt' (p.66). Freedom from doubt, gained by seeking refuge in certainty, is designated by Fromm as 'negative freedom...freedom *from*'. Positive freedom is associated with rational doubt, 'which is rooted in the freedom of thinking and which dares to question established views'. Positive freedom, the freedom *to*...act spontaneously, to think for ourselves, the freedom *to* realise ourselves, does not eliminate rational doubt. The person, adult or child, teacher or pupil, who experiences positive freedom is free to question, to learn, to welcome uncertainty as an inevitable part of growth towards proper understanding of a 'meaningful world'. Fromm's thinking has relevance for us today. He argues that there are many adults in society who are committed, in their search for understanding, to establishing unassailable bodies of fact, to finding a formula that promises absolute certainty. These adults, he concludes, are doomed to negative freedom, to a state of repressed anxiety and overwhelming powerlessness.

This description suggests certain parallels with the lives and philosophies of teachers. In our daily lives we are faced with the possibility of embracing both rational doubt and positive freedom; it is equally possible that we will be tempted to join 'the compulsive quest for certainty' and so will achieve only negative freedom. In our assessment practice, as we look at learning and try to understand it, this alternative may be a very real danger. I am arguing that certainty is rarely achieved in the process of looking at learning. However carefully and questioningly we may look there is always more to see. Given what we know about the effect of context on children's learning, children's language, children's behaviour, there is always more we need to know about the context in which we choose to look at learning. Given what we know about other aspects of the picture – for example, the emotional dimension of learning, and the unintended outcomes of the hidden curriculum – there is always more to know about the whole picture, both its parts and its wholeness.

There is a dramatic example of how, once teachers start looking closely, they learn to see more – and to see it more clearly – in Margaret Meek's *Achieving Literacy* (1983). This is a searching account of the experiences of six teachers working with adolescent non-readers. These teachers made audio-recordings of their lessons with individual pupils, and met together as a group to share and discuss their observations. The audio tapes of the lessons were rich sources of evidence; the group analysed and re-analysed teacher intervention, pupil response and teacher/pupil interaction. But there was still more to see. One lesson was videotaped, and the group watched the video more than once. They saw Jamie, aged 12, who had come for an individual reading lesson with the teacher, Judith Graham. She describes the scene:

> The table before us is mostly stacked with Jamie's books, the two books he has chosen to read, his writing notebooks, my record book, pen and paper. A second copy of *The Magic Finger* is also there. We sit beside each other, which seems friendly. Whilst Jamie initially turns over the pages himself and

presses down the centre of the book, I relieve him of this chore later and hold down the corner of the page as well. When I ask him to write, I thoughtfully produce a pen which I later discreetly remove when he uses it to point at words he reads.

None of this would be evident on an audio tape. Even on the video tape with the sound on one is primarily focusing on the spoken interchanges. But look again at the scene as I have described it. The orderly table in front of us may in fact exclude and intimidate Jamie. Certainly the idea of choice becomes notional as you perceive me 'tidying away' the options I appear so generously to have offered. And my extra copy of *The Magic Finger* – I never open it, seeming to need to follow the same print as Jamie. Is the message one of comforting cosiness or calculated control? The sitting alongside where I can oversee the book at all times could also be construed as less trusting than sitting opposite where I could be an audience. Jamie's reading aloud would then have a real purpose. And leaning back in my chair so that I am slightly out of Jamie's range of vision – does this indicate a wish to minimize the intensity or am I in fact controlling from behind? Does Jamie feel the unseen pressure behind him? My arm resting along the back of his chair may further confuse the message.

Jamie's behaviour with the pages of the book looks promising. We see him flicking through, attempting to piece a story together, using the pictures. As he starts to read he holds the top right hand corner in readiness to turn the page and he enthusiastically rubs along the centre fold. Once the page is turned his reading speed increases noticeably as he senses the progress he is making. Why then do I deprive him later of this aspect of becoming a reader? By the end of the lesson I am doing it all for him thereby increasing his dependence, robbing him of simple competences that may make all the difference to how he feels about himself as a reader. And as an aspiring writer, Jamie surely has his own pen. By pressing mine on him and later withdrawing it, albeit discreetly, I again reduce his autonomy and maintain him in the position of a child who submits but who probably does not ignore.

Meek (1983) p.126

This teacher and her colleagues had worked together for many hours, supporting each other in the process of trying to understand their pupils' learning. They were becoming highly skilled in analysis, reflection and evaluation. They were aware of their pupils' rights to respectful teaching, and how those rights had been eroded by the practices that had allowed them to enter the secondary school as non-readers. They were aware of their massive responsibilities to these painfully fragile learners. And yet, watching this videotape, they suddenly seemed to see, for the first time, a new possibility. They realised how aspects of the physical interaction between teacher and pupil may 'transmit as powerful a message as anything spoken, and may critically impede or dramatically advance progress towards the goal of independent and meaningful reading'. This uncomfortable but revealing insight was not an outcome of their lack of interest or concentrated attention; just the reverse. It was brought about by their very willingness to look again, to look harder and more searchingly. However attentively, however intently we look at learning, there is always more to see, more to try to understand.

CHAPTER 3

Looking at Learning: What Is There to See?

I have suggested that the process of assessment can be thought of in three stages: the collection of evidence, the making of judgements, and the outcomes of those judgements. In the next two chapters I consider the range of evidence that teachers draw on in assessing children's learning. When we start to look at learning, what is there to see? How can we learn to see it more clearly?

The first of these two questions is uncomfortable to ask because teachers are only too aware of their professional responsibility to see everything. Teachers are expected to have eyes in the backs of their heads, to see accidents before they happen, fights before they break out and difficulties with learning before pupils begin to fail. For the purposes of classroom management and control, teachers have risen to the challenge of seeing everything, with only one pair of eyes, by developing a modified radar technique; the busy teacher scans the horizon of the classroom from time to time, watching for any blips of disturbance that might require intervention. If the radar sweep reveals nothing amiss, the teacher will probably refrain from looking any more closely. If classroom events seem to be progressing smoothly, or even according to plan, the teacher is temporarily released from the need to see everything, and can concentrate on a smaller segment of classroom life: work with an individual or a small group perhaps – until it is time for the next global classroom scan. But when teachers look at learning for the purposes of assessment, the radar technique is inadequate, because of the richness of what is to be seen. In a typical primary classroom, there is simply too much learning going on at any one moment for one pair of eyes to appreciate it all.

When an extra pair of adult eyes is added to the classroom, the possibility of seeing everything is instantly increased. With this purpose in mind, Michael Armstrong spent the school year 1976–77 in a primary classroom in Sherard School in Leicestershire, observing and teaching alongside the official class teacher, Stephen Rowland. His description of that year in *Closely Observed Children* is a completely convincing realisation of his tentative starting point:

> If two teachers were to assume joint, though not necessarily equal, responsibility for a single class of children it might be possible between the two of them to find sufficient time and space both for sustained observation and for sustained teaching.
>
> Armstrong (1980) p.5

It was indeed possible. Armstrong chose to concentrate on learning rather than teaching, and on intellectual growth rather than social development; his own list of what he wanted to study is formidably comprehensive:

> the character and quality of children's intellectual understanding: the insights which they display and the problems which they encounter, their inventiveness and originality, and their intellectual independence. (p.5)

By the end of his year of observation and teaching, Armstrong had written ten volumes of notes amounting to some 300,000 words; these notes form the basis for *Closely Observed Children*. Armstrong's practice of close observation, in place of the summary radar scan, reveals the intellectual and artistic richness of the lives of these nine- and ten-year-old children. Sometimes Armstrong's observations focus on an activity that has caught the attention of the whole class; pattern-making, for example, is the subject of an extended section of the book, from which Armstrong concludes that 'when children experiment and speculate with pattern, they are not only acquiring fundamental skills, they are also appropriating knowledge (p.129). For each of the children he describes in this section, Armstrong can specify both skills and knowledge acquired; in addition he discusses their expressive purposes in pattern-making. His factual, detailed descriptions show the excitement of children's growing understanding, as well as the exact dimensions of that understanding, which often surprises him and the class teacher by its speed and inventiveness. Paul, for example, was one of a group who spent several days working with strips of card, experimenting with problems of shape, pattern and rigidity. At the end of the week Stephen Rowland, the class teacher, noted:

Paul has now finally solved the problem of how to keep a square shape rigid, having failed to solve it by weaving. He ingeniously placed two pins in each joint, thus effectively preventing the struts from rotating around the joint. What a brilliant idea! In terms of technology it was both simpler and more economical on materials than the method I had suggested. He had successfully transformed the nature of the problem and its solution. (p.128)

Sometimes Armstrong concentrates his attention on one pupil's sustained and concentrated activity. For example, during a week in June, he observed Paul, who had brought a moth in a jam jar into school on Monday and made two 'startling' sketches of it. On Tuesday he decided to paint the moth: the painting began towards the end of the morning, and carried on throughout the afternoon. It was not finished till Wednesday (by which time the moth had been released) with Paul working intently and painstakingly, first on completing the moth painting, and later, on the background of the painting. When the whole enterprise was complete, Armstrong reflected on what he had seen:

The portrait of the moth, and the two sketches that preceded it, appeared to signify a further development in Paul's conception of art. The impressionism of the two sketches represented, I think, Paul's immediate response to the object and to the task of drawing it. Their success depended in part, I think, on the careful precision of previous drawings; in the freedom and roughness with which he now sketched a moth, Paul recalled and absorbed the lessons he had learnt in several weeks of close study of water insects and how to draw them. But Paul went further. He seemed to regard the sketches, retrospectively at least, as no more than preliminary drawings in the furtherance of a grander design. It was the painting of the moth that was to be his definitive statement, requiring a degree of calculation that would have been inappropriate in the sketches. In the end the painting achieved perhaps only a part, though a major part, of Paul's intentions. His technique was not yet wholly adequate for the task he had set himself and in viewing the process by which he painted his picture we can see him attempting to extend the technical boundaries of his skill. The sketches may therefore have seemed more remarkable than the painting. Yet I think it is most particularly in the inter-relationship of sketches and painting, though Paul himself may have been no more than half conscious of it, that we may perceive the growth of his understanding and the direction in which the sustained practice of his art was leading him...Paul's summer studies were, for me, the most appealing of all the examples, within Stephen Rowland's class, of knowledge as appropriation and the growth of intellect as a consequence of a child's successive attempts to appropriate knowledge through sustained practice, whether in art, science, literature, mathematics or any particular form of thought. (pp. 169–70)

These conclusions are not vague, optimistic generalisations about learning. They are the direct result of Armstrong's detailed observations. He has watched the pupils intently, and talked with them about their activities. He has discussed with them what he thinks he has seen and what he is trying to understand. It is these processes, of looking, of seeing, of understanding, that have given him such revealing insights into the pupils' learning.

Armstrong's work is widely used on initial training and in-service courses for teachers; in my own work as an in-service educator, I have often encouraged teachers studying for an Advanced Diploma in Educational Studies to undertake child-studies, or children-studies, modelled on Armstrong's example, as a way of exploring the question with which this chapter began: when we start to look at children's learning, what is there to see?

Ann Lawson, a teacher in a Suffolk primary school, carried out a child-study of Alison, aged six. Her completed study includes examples of Alison's mathematical problem-solving, her imaginative play, and her writing. Ann Lawson was puzzled by the apparent contrast between Alison's rich imaginative play in the playground and her story writing. She wrote:

> When I first read Alison's writing, I confess I was disappointed by her limited output and felt it did not really tie in with her skills in reading and talking. Each sentence was a struggle, and I observed lots of delaying tactics, finding rubbers, sharpening pencils and coming to me for words... About this time I had been influenced by reading John Holt and Margaret Donaldson and I began to realise the fault may lie with me. She was possibly re-acting against too many imposed tasks. To overcome this I encouraged her and the rest of the class to write their own story books. These books were for us all to read and keep in the book box. Immediately the children's attitudes to writing changed. Children were staying in at playtimes, writing, working on books for long periods of time and even taking books home to finish. They were writing for a real purpose, reading and enjoying each other's books, showing them to any adults who happened to pass through the classroom. It was in this atmosphere that I first really observed Alison writing.

Ann Lawson collected the books that Alison wrote over the next few weeks, and noted that her dictated stories were not only longer, but more imaginative, more unpredictable, more adventurous, than the stories she wrote down for herself. In a tape-recorded interview, Ann Lawson tried to investigate this discrepancy.

I asked 'Why don't you like writing?'
She replied 'I don't know really' shrugging her shoulders and pulling a face.
AL: 'What don't you like about it?'
Alison: 'I don't know.'
AL: 'Do you worry about spellings?'
Alison in a sudden rush said, 'the only kind of writing I do like is writing books – I'm going to start a new one tomorrow.'
In fact she started there and then. I wrote the title for her: *Sam the Spider's Christmas.*

Some days later, the teacher recorded another interview.

I taped Alison and Catherine talking about writing books and I was impressed by how seriously they took their work, referring to it as they talked and pointing out features on particular pages of their current books. But they were also able to stand back from it and look at their thought processes.

The conclusion to this case-study 'What I have learned from observing Alison' includes some fascinating insights into Alison's learning and development. But Ann Lawson also comments:

Observing Alison in such detail has helped to heighten my perceptions of the talk and actions of the other children in my class. I have learned to stand back and look and listen. As a result of this, I feel I am really beginning to know the children in a completely different way.

This teacher is very clear that her study of one child's learning, closely observed, and recorded in detail, has much to tell her about all children's learning, about their motivation, the challenges they set themselves, about their attitudes, and most importantly for her, about their own understanding of their learning. She knows that her own professional learning has been immensely worthwhile, but even at the end of this case-study, the question: 'What is there to see?' is for her, only a beginning.

Finally, having catalogued pages and pages of notes and observations I would have imagined I knew almost everything about Alison. On the contrary, I feel in some ways I know very little, and I wish I was able to do my observations all over again, as I would be looking for even more detail.

Another teacher, Michael Tennant, working for a full-time Advanced Diploma at the Cambridge Institute of Education, wrote a child-study of Margaret, an eleven-year-old girl in a junior school. Because of his full-time secondment, he was able to spend eight days in Margaret's classroom (every Tuesday throughout the Institute term). He recorded a wide variety of observations, including Margaret's work with a maximum-minimum thermometer. He chose this topic because during the class investigation of 'weather' Margaret's responsibility was to record the daily temperatures, maximum and minimum, for the class 'weather station'. Michael Tennant began his one-to-one session with Margaret by asking her to draw the thermometer from memory (figure 3.1).

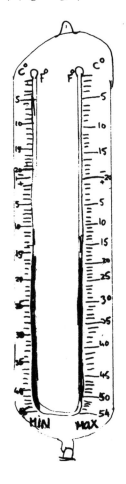

Figure 3.1

Michael Tennant analyses this drawing in detail:

I have to say that this was perhaps the most detailed and careful of the drawings that I saw from Margaret. Could it be that she recognised that she had an audience who was interested and hanging on her every pencil stroke?

This picture, drawn simply from memory in the peace and quiet of the library, and the subsequent discussion, reveal how little Margaret understood about the instrument and yet how much she had within her, given the opportunity, to tease out the essentials of the instrument and its relation to those areas of her own 'real existence' like hot and cold that were really important.

Centigrade and Fahrenheit caused some difficulty. They do for many of us. It is a pity that the instrument had both. But her ability to set them out on the picture and then merely concentrate on the Centigrade scale showed a capacity for rejecting irrelevance.

She was aware of the function of the floats, and knew that the bottom of the one on the left hand side marked a 'minimum' temperature, whilst that on the right marked a 'maximum' temperature.

She was confused about the materials inside the thermometer. The floats might 'be a little bit of mercury'. Mercury was 'a rubber liquid stuff inside the tube' (Margaret's own words). These are not bad attempts at explaining materials, and it is surely possible to use many a piece of equipment without understanding its internal construction.

Margaret drew the magnet under the thermometer, and explained in detail how this was used to reset the thermometer each day.

The scale itself caused great difficulty. She was being asked to think of a scale with negative numbers when she had clearly not explored this notion. Her attempt at a +/– scale in five degrees was it seems to me, a great feat of perception, albeit revealing her failure to understand the basic way in which the instrument operated. Nevertheless, when I asked her to talk to me about her drawing, she began to see for herself the inadequacies of her model. She totally failed to see the problem of 0° C being the same as 20° C. But then we were in November and not yet into temperatures below 0° C. When she came to read off the temperatures she read them off as 17° C max, and 13$\frac{1}{2}$° C min. She began to see the problem. But the solution was beyond her. In fact if one examines her drawing one can see that the two sides of her thermometer are really independent. The mercury does not go round the tube at the bottom. She seemed to see the instrument as two separate pieces of equipment in one. It had two different functions, maximum and minimum, and she had failed to make the link between them. She had not yet explored the fact that the mercury effectively moved around the tube from right to left and from left to right so that when it went down on the left it appeared to go up on the right. This of course meant that the scale on the left had to be the reverse to the scale on the right. Nor was Margaret able to see that the instrument could give us a reading of the present temperature.

This honest description of Margaret's thinking includes an appreciation of her difficulties, and makes an illuminating connection between the gap in the drawing (where the mercury is missing from the bottom of the tube) and a gap in her understanding. The drawing stands as an eloquent and accurate map of her present understanding.

But Michael Tennant was not content to let his observation stop at this point, where he had elicited all that Margaret knew and did not know, understood and did not understand about her drawing of the thermometer.

> Having gone as far as we could with her drawing, we went outside and began to handle and talk about the actual thermometer. She began to work on ideas. 'If we take it inside the temperature will go up too high' (her words). We began to explore together, going inside and outside, looking at the mercury and observing the floats. She wanted to cool it down quickly to get a minimum temperature, so she suggested putting it into the fridge.
>
> After some time playing with and discussing the instrument we came back to the library, to see more sheets that I had prepared. I asked her to look at the pictures. I explained how I had done simple drawings of the thermometer as I remembered it the day before when I had been at home. It was based on a simple plan. It was my plan. Could she understand it and relate it to her knowledge of the instrument? I showed her my first drawing (figure 3.2) and asked her to write down the temperature shown on the instrument. She wrote 1° C and it was only at the very end of this session, after all the other activities, that she was able to arrive at 5° C and record that response.

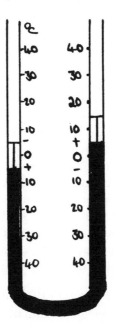

Figure 3.2

Given another drawing, Margaret correctly read off both the present temperature, and the minimum temperature recorded. On blank drawings of the thermometer, Margaret coloured in the mercury to show temperatures of –10° C and 25° C, and triumphantly, in one drawing, a present temperature of 10° C, a minimum of 5° C and a maximum of 15° C. One diagram continued to baffle her: a diagram of the thermometer with the right-hand side calibration omitted (figure 3.3). It is as if she has grasped that she is dealing with, in a sense, four different scales (plus and minus for both maximum and minimum temperatures) but has not seen how these four form a continuous series of numbers. There is still a gap in her understanding. But Michael Tennant is more excited by the thinking that has been going on, rather than concerned about the one missing piece from the jigsaw.

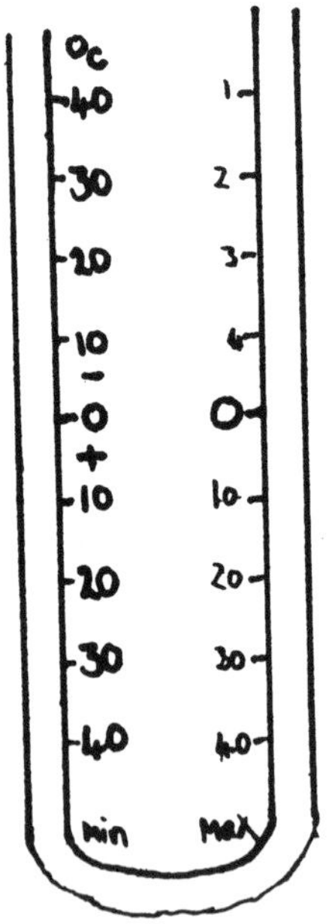

Figure 3.3

The most exciting aspect of that hour or so with Margaret was the level of our conversation. By talking about the instrument and drawings she came, I believe, to a definition of gaps in her own knowledge. Her excitement at wanting to control the instrument, to get it to move up and down at different temperatures, showed some awakening knowledge of what the instrument was doing and what it could tell us. She predicted that the maximum temperature should come at midday and the minimum temperature at midnight. This is not, of course, necessarily true, but it is a reasonable prediction given Margaret's present knowledge of meteorology.

But, for me, the telling phrases of our conversation were: 'It was freezing yesterday, and the ground was hard,' and 'It's quite a warm breeze really, isn't it?' The day before (4 November) had been a bitterly cold one. There had been a dramatic change. As we talked about the thermometer and drew pictures, there was a surprisingly strong wind – the proof of that remains on our taped interview. It was also a warm wind – coming straight up from the Azores. Margaret experienced and felt moved to comment on that wind. Its temperature and its force, and the contrast with the day before, were meaningful to her, but not in terms of expensive equipment supplied by Osmiroid. Her starting point was her own, and as a girl who spent a great deal of time outdoors, cycling, and who had spent her early childhood on a farm, she did show herself sensitive to her physical environment.

Here the teacher is recording his growing understanding of how a child's learning in the world outside school may remain detached and remote, unengaged, in activities undertaken in school.

These observations, and many more like them, constitute the bulk of Michael Tennant's child-study. At the end of the study he was able to move away from the specific details of what he had seen to raise some more general and much more troubling issues.

I believe that, through this study, I have begun to see a little further into an area of questioning which, if I was not aware of it last year, I cannot ignore next year. It is to do with the frequency with which we ask children to solve problems when a child may not be able to meet us on the terms we set. And how often do we set the most difficult problems for the children least able to cope? I have long been used, because of my background in multi-lingual and multi-cultural schools, to think in terms of a mismatch between what I ask and what the child perceives because of language and cultural differences. My experience with Margaret has shaken my composure, because what I diagnose as her underachievement cannot simply be located in linguistic or cultural differences. I have to talk in terms of underachievement. I have to conclude from my observations and discussions that here is a girl with the maturity and linguistic competence to identify and describe the important aspects of herself, her background, and her learning. In all the tasks that I perceived there was some measure of achievement (under the 'busyness' and activity) which could have been developed or maximized. But, left to her own devices, she was, so often, engaged in pursuit of the 'wrong' questions. There was a kind of astigmatism in her view of school, and herself, and her learning... She simply has not learned to listen and interact with her peers and her teachers in the way that school demands for success. When Margaret comes to school there is just too much which has to be left outside beyond the school gate. In this, Margaret is not alone.

What was there to see, when Michael Tennant looked at Margaret's learning? One child's achievements, struggles, joys and disappointments, certainly, but more, much more. The act of looking, and trying to understand, opened up, for this teacher, a range of much bigger questions about school, society, education, learning and personality. He did, in a sense, while working on this child-study, see everything.

In these two case-studies, both teachers adopted a qualitative approach, making no attempt to quantify their observations. Another teacher on the full-time Diploma, Geoff Fisher, used a technique of timed observations in a comparative study of two ten-year-old children in a small village primary school. He wrote:

> It was not possible to find two days with identical programmes, but I was able to observe on two Wednesdays which were reasonably similar. I timed the amount of time the child spent on one particular piece of work, moving from one place to another, preparing and clearing away, and the amount of teacher contact. The following table shows the results of the observations on the two days.

(See figure 3.4.)

	Times in hours and minutes for one school day	
	Kim	Michael
Breaks and movement	1,28	1,27
Musical activities and rehearsal	1,27	2,05
Listening to teacher and general discussion	0,35	0,19
Queuing	0,19	0,28
Preparing for work and packing away	0,30	0,17
Mathematics	0,16	0,25
Handwriting	0,10	0,03
Reading-workshop cards	0,22	0,06
Talking to the teacher	0,02	0,04

Figure 3.4 Timed observations of Kim and Michael (ten-year-olds)

Geoff Fisher expanded on these figures:

> One of the most striking features is the amount of one-to-one contact time on each occasion. It had appeared from my initial observations that Michael took a far greater share of this contact time than Kim, but the difference in total is only two minutes (even so, this is twice the amount of time). What the table does not show is the number of occasions that went to make up this contact time.
>
> The two minutes of direct contact which Kim had, came from two occasions when she went to the teacher's desk to have something explained...The four minutes which Michael spent in direct contact with the teacher were made up of 15 occasions when he went for help, five occasions when he was reprimanded, and two occasions when he was praised (i.e. 22 incidents in all). The longest of these lasted 40 seconds, and the shortest only 3 seconds...To speak to the teacher on those 15 occasions, meant Michael queuing for 28 minutes (over the day). For her two minutes of one-to-one contact, Kim had to queue for 19 minutes.

He goes on to comment that, if these days are typical, Kim would spend just over one and a half hours a week queuing to see her teacher, and Michael nearly two and a half hours!

What did this teacher learn about learning from this study?

> The whole study has made me much more aware of the importance of the learning which is taking place outside of the skills needed to produce 'accepted' work. These other aspects of learning include: How do I need to behave if I want to fit in? What do I need to do to gain recognition? How can I get by doing the least amount of work? What will please the teacher?

These disconcerting questions, opening up the whole troubled issue of children's unintended learning in schools and classrooms, are, however unwelcome, all part of the huge enterprise of looking at learning, of looking at everything.

These three case-studies were all carried out by teachers working on advanced, award-bearing courses. But the evidence of learning, which is the starting point for assessment, surrounds every teacher, whether or not she or he is registered for an Advanced Diploma. Clearing out an untidy cupboard some years ago I came across some old notebooks, preserved from my first full year of teaching (1967–68). I was working in a crowded reception class in a large multi-ethnic school in Hackney, in an area of extreme social disadvantage. My cursory initial training and some reading in the field of sociolinguistics had introduced me to the work of Basil Bernstein, and the concepts of elaborated and restricted codes. I did not, I think, consciously predict that all my pupils would speak in restricted code, by the book, as it were; but I was completely unprepared for the wealth of imaginative language that poured from the lips of the 42 children in my class. Dictating stories to the teacher, to accompany a drawing or painting, was a regular activity in that classroom, and the stories I have preserved are evidence of the extent of the children's language development and of my own excitement at being there to listen to these five-year-olds talking. I have selected examples of stories by three children, Phyllis, Sharon and Darren, to illustrate the range and variety of this spoken language.

Phyllis' stories meander through a vast territory: fairy tale, nursery rhyme, love story, cops and robbers, and classroom life:

> Here is a king. He has two crowns because he keeps breaking one of them.
> Here are a king and a queen. They are kissing each other because they want to get married.
> Humpty Dumpty says hello to the three moons.
> Sharon and Marie and Brenda went out shopping. They fell into the river and the frogs bit their legs.
> Here are five butterflies flying to the two moons.
> Here is a black black house. Miss Drum lives in it. Sharon and Diane and Phyllis and Jenny are helping her to sweep it.
> The thunderstorm is coming down on the sea and the river and the garden.

The different types of stories she has heard, from parents, peers, radio and television, in music, poetry and prose, are some of the past influences on her present story-telling. The content and characters are various and the themes divergent. Massive forces – kings and thunderstorms – cohabit with the intimate and particular – her friends, her teacher, butterflies and frogs.

Sharon's stories range less widely; they are variations on a single theme:

> The witch was hungry. She had nothing to eat.
> The witch went out. She saw a pencil. She was very hungry so she ate it.
> A little witch lady had nothing to eat, so she went to the hairdresser to put her hair on. Then she ate her hair.
> The shoes were so hungry they went to work and ate all the shoes.
> A little small boy was very hungry. So he bought some cake and ate it. Then he bought a book and ate the book too.
> A little lady was very hungry. So she went to work to make a lot of money and then she ate the money.

A little lady went out to work. She stole the governor's hair and ate it.
Here is a man with his wife. She couldn't eat the husband and the husband
couldn't eat his wife.

I did not then, and would not now, attempt to read lessons in Sharon's
personal psychology from these stories. What I did, and do, recognise is
a child working on a theme that is important to her; I found that it was
possible to respect Sharon's interests without demanding that she reveal
her private meanings. Whatever the words meant to her secret self, the
'eating' metaphor served, for the time, her expressive purposes well
enough; I am proud to recall that I never tried to encourage her away
from 'eating' stories ('Wouldn't it be a good idea to do a *different* kind of
story today?').

Darren's stories are eclectic in content, but structurally they have a
common element; they are all two-part inventions.

The monster broke out of his cage and ran away because he saw a leopard
coming after him.
A little old lady and a little old man are standing in the rain because they
want a bath and they haven't got a bath in their house.
A wolf ate an elephant because he was hungry and had no food.
The crocodile was going to eat the boat but Charlton jumped in the water
and killed the crocodile.
Captain Scarlet has gone to the pictures. He wanted to sleep in the cinema.
A man is on a boat which is sinking. Mighty Mouse is trying to save him.

Each of these six stories is like a necklace with just two beads; they are
stories composed of mini-stories. In the first, a monster story and a
leopard story are connected by 'because'; the same link is used for the
indoors story and the outdoors story in the second. In the fifth example,
the stories of Captain Scarlet awake and Captain Scarlet asleep are linked
by a connection of personal intention. Heroism and bravery are
celebrated in the fourth story (Charlton was a conspicuous member of
the class, soon to be excluded by the headteacher for anti-social
behaviour, but a hero to his peers); intrepid human effort stops the first
story in mid-flow and redirects the action: now the devouring crocodile
is itself destroyed. Given what Darren already knows about stories and
how to tell them, it will not be long before he learns to accommodate
three or more elements into his creations, and to widen still further the
range of connections that he uses. The necklaces he strings will be longer,
with beads and patterns of infinite variety.

When I wrote these five-year-old children's stories into my notebook, I was, in a sense, recording a tribute to their learning. The evidence was there for me to see, and I saw some of it; but the notebook is, in another sense, a record of missed opportunities. How much more I now want to know, how much there is to find out, about these children's play, about their developing concepts of story and story-writing, about their pressing intellectual and emotional concerns. I had not then seen the potential of looking at learning, except to admire it; I had not seen the possibility of using my observations of individuals to generate general principles. Many years later, reading Applebee's *The Child's Concept of Story* (1978), I recalled the story-telling activities of my first class, and was able to make connections between Applebee's constructions and my own first-hand experiences.

Just the same, for all their incompleteness, the records I made, as a beginning teacher, of what I saw of children's story-telling were an important step in my professional development. I had been led to expect, quite erroneously, that my pupils' language would, in some way, accurately represent their disadvantaged position in society. I was able to see with my own eyes, and hear with my own ears, evidence to the contrary. I proved to myself, by listening and looking, the richness and inventiveness of these children's spoken language. I was able to maintain stoutly to my colleagues that these children were not, as they often complained, 'language-deprived'. I was able to question the use of the *Happy Venture* basal readers (Dick and Dora, Nip and Fluff), which seemed to me to do wilful damage to these children's understanding of what stories were. I was able to use what I knew of these children's creativity, diversity and artistry, when I was required to complete the standard ILEA written records for each child – an admirably simple format asking for personal and subjective summaries of children's achievements, and their attitudes to themselves, to each other, and to their work.

If I did not see, then, all that I wish I could see now, as I look back over these children's stories, it was not because there was, then, less to see. It was because I had not then learned enough about the learning I was looking for; I had not yet understood how my own learning as a teacher could be fed and exercised by the close study of children's learning. I knew there was learning to be seen, and understood, and that I could put my understanding to good use; but I had not then grasped the enormity and complexity of the task of trying to see everything. In looking at children's learning, our urgent desire to see the whole picture need not, however, blind us to the possibility of looking at tiny fragments of learning, which may be like pearls of great price, immensely valuable in our search for understanding. Assessment in miniature may be a useful addition to our repertoire of professional strategies.

John Dowding, a Norfolk first school teacher, read in the letters of J. C. Powys to Nicholas Ross: 'I like the name (Klee) because it makes me think of KEY which to me is one of the six most exciting of all words: what would be your SIX PRECIOUS WORDS? Let me think if I can name MY six: Key, silver, grass, away, kite and wave. (I hesitate a little between grass and earth.)' He introduced his class of six- and seven-year-olds to the idea, who were fired with enthusiasm. Their lists of words were astonishing: not just for their diversity, but for the way in which they could be read as minute portraits of their authors' present understanding of the power and enchantment of words.

For example, Lindsay, who loves animals, who is as small as a mouse and influential as an elephant, wrote:

Cat, dog, mouse, bird, elephant, butterfly.

Giles, who reads *The Beano* in a literary way and has interesting hobbies wrote:

Hallowe'en, incandescent, rats, dogs, barn, Beano (and insisted on adding 'catapult').

Cara is quite unpredictable, full of ideas and little dramas:

May, Thursday, Book, impossible, magpie, if.

Alice is beautiful and precious, one of those children who seems to be full of light. She wrote:

china, crystal, drop, light, shine, blossom.

Tom is the class wit: his paper reads:

Friday May 34th
The cat sat on the mat.

As for Matthew! Whatever can one say about Matthew?

impact, impulse, interface, Shanghai, ice, cold.

His teacher challenged him to write a sentence containing these six words: undaunted Matthew wrote the sentence shown in figure 3.5.

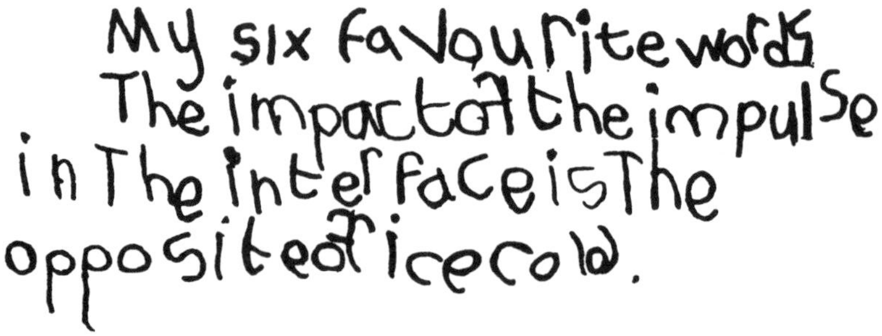

My six favourite words
The impact of the impulse
in The interface isThe
opposite of icecold.

Figure 3.5

The teacher treasured these pieces of writing and at the end of the summer term, included them in the portfolios of work that the children took with them into the next class. The receiving teacher was delighted with these miniatures, and the insights they offered into the children's thinking. The canvas was small, certainly, but the pictures of learning were glowing, intense, individual.

The studies of children's learning that have been presented so far have focused on children's intellectual abilities; but teachers in primary classrooms take a wider view. When we survey children's learning, when we attempt to establish the extent of the evidence at our disposal, we cannot afford to exclude the emotional domain. Without doing violence to our understanding of children as human beings, we cannot ignore either the emotional turbulence of their lives, or the emotional development that runs alongside the physical, social and cognitive changes that we see taking place in our schools and classrooms. Successive national initiatives and government policies may temporarily distract us from these aspects of children's learning, but we will be wise not to neglect them for very long. There are useful historical precedents; Susan Isaacs (1930), as we shall see in the next chapter, includes in her discussion of biological learning a consideration of the emotional states of cruelty and tenderness. Margaret Lowenfeld, a child psychiatrist, writing only a few years later, records in *Play in Childhood* (1935) the intensely emotional states to be observed in children's play.

Lowenfeld describes one form of play in which children give satisfaction to their feelings of hostility and resentment and she draws attention to the adult counterpart of this play: the satirical form in literature. When children create satirical forms, they are expressing emotions of resentment, anger, malice and rage, feelings that are normally checked by adults and repressed by children. In the freedom of Lowenfeld's playroom, in the Institute of Child Psychology:

> Children will work the drive of these moods out of their system by giving expression to them in fantastic versions of their home and school circumstances...The child, in working out such plays, is in part investing the adult actors of his drama with his own emotions and in this way minimising the pressure of them within himself; partly dramatising expressions of hatred and bitterness which he really believes to be present in himself; and partly incorporating into his play phantasy elements out of fairy-tales and myths he has heard. (p.146)

Lowenfeld's view of children's play as a 'valuable and indispensable vehicle of learning' (p.161) permeates the analysis of the observations recorded in *Play in Childhood*.

> Without adequate opportunity for play, normal and satisfactory emotional development is not possible. (p.232)

Her life's work was devoted to establishing this necessary, relationship between play, learning and the child's developing emotional life, and her conclusions must be taken seriously by teachers today who are trying to understand learning. The introduction of the National Curriculum in 1988 was swiftly followed by attempts to make children's play acceptable by matching descriptions of play and areas of play provision to specific targets in the core subjects (for example, Early Years Curriculum Group 1989). But there is more to children's learning in play than any number of predetermined attainments. Indeed H. Caldwell Cook, the author of the early and influential *The Play Way*, defines play largely in terms of the pupils' emotional involvement:

> When work and play are separated, the one becomes mere drudgery, the other mere pastime. Neither is then of any value in life. It is the core of my faith that the only work worth doing is really play; for by play I mean the doing anything with one's heart in it.
>
> Caldwell Cook (1917) p.4

When we look at learning, children's emotions are always there for us to see, if we choose.

Sometimes in ordinary classrooms we may be given the opportunity by the children themselves to make an assessment of their learning in the emotional domain. Here is an observation from my own experience.

James was in the beginning of his third year in the infant school, aged 6, when he made the drawing shown below (figure 3.6). James was an only child of a mother who was in her early forties when James started school, rather older than the majority of other mothers with children in that class. James' father was an officer in the Merchant Navy and away from home for up to six months at a time. James and his mother were particularly close to one another and both of them found the parting at the beginning of each school day very painful. During James' first year in school, his mother would stay beside him in the classroom for half an hour or so most mornings, but as James moved up the school, she tried to reduce the time spent in this way, though she was careful not to cause James any additional distress.

By the beginning of the third year in school James and his mother had worked out a ritual for parting from each other that seemed to satisfy them both. The route they took to school led down a narrow road through some trees to a spot where the school drive branched off to the right, leading uphill again to the school front door, about 50 yards away. James and his mother stopped at this spot and kissed each other goodbye. James bolted up the drive to the front door, while his mother waited on the same spot. From the doorstep of the school, James waved and blew kisses, which were warmly returned. His mother then started walking uphill, and as soon as she walked away, James came into school and flew down the corridor to his classroom. He stood on the classroom windowsill (luckily a low one) and waited until he could see his mother coming back into sight through the trees, as she walked homewards up the hill behind the school. When she saw him at the window, a second round of waves and kisses ensued, and then, satisfied, James was ready to join the class.

One misty November morning, James' class teacher was unexpectedly late, and I was standing in for her. I set out on one table some drawing materials – white chalk and charcoal and grey paper – with, frankly, no purpose except that of engaging the children more or less profitably until I had time to prepare myself properly for a morning session with them. James went straight to this table and settled to work. In about 20 minutes he produced this drawing, which is, I believe, extremely beautiful. It is certainly remarkably evocative of the damp moist mist that was curling around the trees outside the classroom window. Fragments of the same mist seemed to have crept into the school corridor, and the windows of the classroom were covered with chilly condensation. I asked James the title of his picture: 'Waving Goodbye to my Mother'. This should, of course, have been obvious, but James did not remark on my obtuseness.

When I had time to gather my wits, look more carefully at his drawing, and discuss it with colleagues (James' present and previous teachers and the non-teaching assistant who knew the family well), the importance of what he had done began to become clear. James had drawn himself from the outside, from the other side of the classroom window, looking in through the mist

Figure 3.6 'Waving Goodbye to my Mother'

and condensation. He had drawn what his mother saw, as she waved goodbye to him for the last time that morning. But he had also drawn an emotional portrait of himself – as a child who is both distressed and courageous, a child who hates parting but who has learned to say goodbye, a child who is near to tears but remains serene and composed – a very realistic self portrait. And the picture seems to represent not just this self, but James' awareness of the characteristics of this self, as something to be proud of.

For James' teachers, this was an enormously revealing incident. We had accepted the long drawn-out ritual of his leave-taking from his mother as a necessary, but not very desirable, compromise. We were none of us convinced that it was the best way to help James to learn to part more easily from his mother. But this picture seemed to offer us evidence that James' emotional development was proceeding apace. Before the age of seven, he had learned not only to understand his own – mixed – feelings he had also learned to represent those feelings. He had learned to represent them not only from his own point of view but from his mother's. This picture seems to say: 'When my mother looks at me, she sees her brave sad boy.' The picture records a profound understanding of the painful emotions that James experienced every morning on the way to school.

It is not very often that children present their teachers with such unsolicited testimony of their learning in the affective domain. This makes it all the more important for teachers not to overlook this aspect of life in schools and classrooms. When we ask what might constitute evidence of learning, we must be certain not to exclude the affective and the emotional. Whenever we ask ourselves: 'What is there to see?' or 'What am I looking for?' we must be certain to include children's emotional learning. When we reflect on our responsibility to try to see everything, we must not forget the children's right to respect for their emotional powers, as well as their intellectual ones.

CHAPTER 4

Looking at Learning: Learning to See

As a way of coming to understand children's learning, close observation has an honourable history. What we know today about Susan Isaacs' experimental school, the Malting House, is largely based on the detailed observation records she and her colleagues kept. In Chapter 2 I described how the working environment of the school contributed to the scope and variety of the teachers' observations. But these observations of daily life, the adventurous, imaginative, scientific and spontaneous life of the children in the school, were more than isolated anecdotes. They were also the starting point for an exploration of the processes of cognition. First Isaacs notes the nature of the children's thinking: 'active and prehensile...It moves continuously on, developing and growing, as their practical and social situations change and develop from moment to moment' (Isaacs 1930, p.49). Within this continuous activity, she goes on to distinguish different classes of behaviour, which she presents as a scheme by which we may understand children's cognitive growth. For example, she puts forward a scheme to describe the development of the basic concepts of biology: change, growth, life and death. The scheme is supported by a wealth of evidence, such as the following observation notes:

18.6.25: The children let the rabbit out to run about the garden for the first time, to their great delight. They followed him about, stroked him, and talked about his fur, his shape and his ways.

13.7.25: Some of the children called out that the rabbit was dying. They found it in the summerhouse, hardly able to move. They were very sorry and talked much about it. They shut it up in the hutch and gave it warm milk.

14.7.25: The rabbit had died in the night. Dan found it and said, 'It's dead – its tummy does not move up and down now.' Paul said, 'My daddy says that if we put it into water, it will get alive again.' Mrs I. said, 'Shall we do so and see?' They put it into a bath of water. Some of them said, 'It is alive.' Duncan said, 'If it floats, it's dead, and if it sinks it's alive.' It floated on the surface. One of them said, 'It's alive, because it's moving.' This was a circular movement, due to the currents in the water. Mrs I. therefore put in a small stick which also moved round and round, and they agreed that the stick was not alive. They then suggested that they should bury the rabbit, and all helped to dig a hole and bury it.

15.7.25: Frank and Duncan talked of digging the rabbit up but Frank said, 'It's not there – it's gone up to the sky.' They began to dig but tired of it and ran off to something else. Later they came back and dug again. Duncan, however, said, 'Don't bother – it's gone – it's up in the sky,' and gave up digging. Mrs I. therefore said, 'Shall we see if it's there?' and also dug. They found the rabbit, and were very interested to see it still there.

Isaacs (op. cit.) pp.182–3

These observations showed how children's biological interests are expressed and explored in a variety of ways – in curiosity and pleasure, in action and in feeling, in cruelty and in tenderness, in assertion and speculation, in careful observation and in the drama of a child's fantasy life. Under Isaacs' analytic eye, the raw material of her observations discloses a framework for understanding children's learning and, in addition, a set of conditions that will ensure positive educational outcomes from children's activity and enquiry.

Isaacs did not collect observations of particular individuals solely in order to build and substantiate generalised theories about all children's learning. The observations also served to establish differences between children, and to chart changes in individual children's behaviour. For example, a further set of observations of Phineas, the actively enquiring child we met in Chapter 2, is followed by an interpretation of their meaning.

14.2.27. Phineas (3;11) would not take off his hat and coat and gloves for a long time this morning. He sat, with them on, on the edge of the platform in a very quiet and subdued mood, and did not for a long time join in any of the other children's occupations, nor show any of his usual interests. This occurred every morning for about a week. Several times each morning he asked, 'Is it time to go home yet?', although in the ordinary way he is reluctant to go, and far too absorbed in his pursuits to think of the end of the morning. This week he has also been much more easily distracted by the others from any work he has been engaged on, leaving it every few minutes to take up theirs in a listless way, and then coming back to his own. After about a week, he returned to his usual self again. This has coincided with the birth of a baby brother (the third child in the family).

The misery of fear and jealousy aroused by the arrival of the new baby had thus awakened all Phineas' deep infantile phantasies, and grave anxiety connected with them. His general enterprise and active interest in the real world was quite inhibited and lost for the time being.

Isaacs (op. cit.) p.103

Observing children, Isaacs is showing us, can help us to understand them; we can learn from what we see, if we take the opportunity to do so. Isaacs uses this observation of Phineas' behaviour to make an interpretation of Phineas' internal state of mind. This interpretation then itself becomes part of the evidence for an important argument:

that anxiety is highly unfavourable to free inquiry and interest in the objective world...These negative examples support the view that mental alertness and an active interest in objects are very dependent upon freedom from anxiety and inner tension.

Isaacs (op. cit.) pp.103, 104

Isaacs' diaries show many other instances of 'negative' behaviours and the importance of children's feelings in their learning. Her search for evidence of children's learning, both emotional and intellectual, and her determination to learn herself from what she saw, obliged her to include in her study every variety of behaviour, however unwelcome it might be to her as an adult or as an educator. For example, in the long discussion of the development of biological interests and concepts, the observations are grouped under five headings: Active interest, Phantasy, Cruelty, Tenderness and Fear. Here is an example from the section on cruelty.

18.2.26: The children went into the garden. Priscilla wanted to pull a worm into halves, and said she would marry the boy who did. They all said they wanted to marry her. Dan eventually did pull the worm in halves. Frank then pulled the rest of it apart; they were very excited about this.

Isaacs (op. cit.) p.205

I have once, and only once, used this extract as a piece of discussion material in my in-service work with practising teachers. The ensuing uproar was so passionate that there was simply no possibility of the group of teachers learning anything about learning from the extract, or from discussion of the extract. Indeed, when teachers are invited to discuss a much less controversial (according to me!) extract – the description of Frank and Duncan attempting to dig up the dead rabbit (quoted on pp.54–6) – the temper of the discussion sometimes runs so high that the purpose of the discussion, an enquiry into learning, is completely lost. But Isaacs does not allow her feelings of approval and disapproval to come between her and her subject of study: children's learning.

The long section on Tenderness, which follows the (much shorter) section on Cruelty, includes a table showing some of the instances of cruelty and tenderness in the same children. This is clear evidence, Isaacs concludes, of the contradictory impulses of the children: 'the impulse to cherish alongside the desire to master and hurt.' By seeing and recording both impulses, Isaacs was able to show how, over the course of time, 'the impulse to master and destroy was taken up into the aim of understanding. The living animal became much less an object of power and possession, and much more an independent creature to be learnt about, watched and known for its own sake' (op. cit., p.166).

Isaacs' work on these themes carries an implicit warning for teachers in search of evidence for learning. If we choose to see only those aspects of learning of which we approve, we will lose the opportunity to see more of the picture, to learn more about learning... There is always more to learn, and more to see.

All the case material cited so far has been concerned with individuals and groups of children learning in schools; studies of individual children in experimental conditions, carried out by psychologists rather than by teachers, have also made enormous contributions to our understanding of children's learning. The strength of the experimental condition is that the problems offered to children can be minutely modified as the psychologists refine their hypotheses and come closer and closer to tracking the pathways of the children's thinking. Piaget's studies of young children wrestling with problems of conservation, inclusion, and perspective are too well known to need illustrating here. What we now know about these studies is that changes in the contexts in which the problems were presented can have dramatic effects on the children's thinking. For example, Piaget concluded from his 'three mountains' problem that children below the age of seven are unable to conceptualise or form a mental representation of what the model of the three mountains looks like from other than their own point of view. Children's performance on this task, for Piaget, illustrates their egocentrism, their inability to 'decentre' and to see the world as another might see it (Piaget & Inhelder 1956).

A group of psychologists working with Margaret Donaldson (1978) in Edinburgh transformed the three mountains problem into a story about a policeman and a little boy. Children are shown a model of two 'walls' intersecting to form a cross. Two small dolls represent the policeman and the little boy, and the children are asked to 'hide the boy so that the policeman can't see him'. The policeman is placed at different positions, and later a second policeman is added. Children are asked to hide the boy from both policemen, which involves considering and amalgamating two different (imaginary) points of view. The results are impressive: when 30 children between the ages of three and a half and five years were given this task, 90 per cent of their responses were correct. Donaldson's interpretation is that young children's thinking is crucially affected by the context in which that thinking is applied; where the problem makes sense to the child, where it refers to experiences and actions that are familiar, then the child does not respond egocentrically, but clearly shows the ability to see another person's point of view.

A similar conclusion has been reached by Paul Light (1986) in a cunning rearrangement of the conservation task. In Piaget's version of the task, two equal quantities of liquid are presented to a child, and one of them is then poured into a container of a different shape and size. Children below about seven can judge the initial equality of the two quantities, but wrongly describe the post-transformation quantities as unequal. In Light's 'chipped beaker' version of the same task, the transformation of the quantities was made to appear incidental to the activity presented to the children. Pairs of children were told they were going to play a game with pasta shells, which had to be matched one by one onto spaces on a grid; the first child to get all his or her shells onto the grid would be the winner. Two identical beakers were then filled with pasta shells and the children asked to agree that they were equally full, so that the game would be fair. But before the game could begin, the experimenter 'noticed' that the rim of one of the beakers was chipped to a razor sharp edge. The experimenter looked surprised, alarmed, perplexed and, finally, relieved at 'finding' another container, shorter and fatter than the first, and tipping the shells from the chipped beaker into it. The usual conservation questions followed, and 70 per cent of the five- and six-year-olds tested in this way claimed that the quantities were still the same. Light describes this as a 'massive' effect. Cognitive psychologists are still arguing over the precise interpretation of these and other similar experiments, but for teachers one conclusion is inescapable. When we look at children's learning, we are also looking at the context in which that learning is constructed and expressed.

In discussing the implications of his experimental work, Light argues powerfully that it is not enough to say that context acts as a performance variable, limiting or enhancing the child's apparent competence. He suggests that context plays a much 'more central and constitutive role' (p.185). The implications of this argument for teachers, rather than psychologists, looking at learning, are plain. Teachers assessing children's learning are assessing cognitive powers constructed within a complex culture of social conventions, a particular set of ways of talking and behaving.

This is the central theme of two studies, one by Mary Willes (1983), briefly mentioned in Chapter 1, and another by Gill Barrett (1986). Both these authors describe and analyse the learning that takes place during young children's first few weeks in school. The title of Willes' study, *Children into Pupils*, encapsulates the thrust of her argument: that a substantial part of what children learn in school is, in fact, *about* school. Their learning is essentially school-bound in that it is only brought about, demonstrated and assessed, within the context of being a pupil, in a classroom, in a school. The condition of being a pupil is, necessarily, rule-bound, and the pupils' prime task is to discover these rules, which will channel their behaviour into acceptable or unacceptable forms.

Willes' particular interest is in the spoken language of teachers and pupils, and the rules that govern classroom talk:

> Typically the teacher talks more than all the other participants. She takes the initiatives and the successful responses are those she anticipates. That she talks *more*, simply in terms of the number of words uttered, may be accidental or trivial, that she has more options and more and different responsibilities, certainly is not. The minimal inescapable requirement that a child must meet if he is to function as a participating pupil is not very extensive. It is necessary to accept adult direction, to know that you say nothing at all unless the teacher indicates that you may, to know that when your turn is indicated you must use whatever clues you can find, and make the best guess you can. (p.83)

Willes describes a story-telling episode from some pupils' first school day:

> ...they have already learned that the questions asked by the teacher require brief answers. They seem not yet to realise that answers that have to do with their own preoccupations, rather than with the facts of the story, or the facts

of the world of shared experience, just will not do. There is early opportunity to learn that it is the teacher, not the pupil, who makes the crucial decision about what is, and is not, relevant. (p.77)

Pupils who do not choose to abide by the unwritten rules of classroom and school behaviour, or pupils who do not even acknowledge their existence, are perceived as deviant by the teacher. Chatinder is one such pupil.

> One of the teachers had to cope with a persistently disobedient little boy... The child in question, Chatinder, understood and spoke English very imperfectly...(he) was isolated by his incomprehension of the language spoken everywhere about him. His teacher's warnings, however, were either deliberately disregarded or were simply not understood. Chatinder would not stay in one place, engaged in a single activity, for even a limited time. He rushed about the classroom, upsetting other children, damaging toys and endangering equipment...Chatinder seemed impervious to warnings, threats and coaxing, and quite unresponsive to the idea that most children seemed already to understand, namely that there was a competition in the classroom for approval and success into which everyone entered. Chatinder seemed by contrast uncomprehending of that part of the role of pupil, or unwilling to undertake it...Within a day or two of arrival he was identified as a problem. (pp.139–40)

Chatinder's perception of how to behave in classrooms, so clearly at odds with his teacher's, is likely to stand in the way of his learning in other domains. The context of his learning, the classroom culture into which he has not yet entered, will certainly play, in Paul Light's words, a 'central and constitutive role' in his response to the curriculum his teacher provides. It is unlikely to be a beneficial one. Willes' prognosis for learning in the classroom context is a gloomy one:

> It can of course be argued that children learn anyway that finding out what the teacher wants, and doing it, constitutes the primary duty of a pupil, and that considered as a learning strategy this is not a very good one, having no more than a slight and quickly exhausted usefulness. (p.138)

Barrett's study underlines Willes' emphasis on children's early learning about the cultural conventions of the classroom. A set of photographs of young children taken during their first few weeks of schooling was used to explore children's experiences of starting school. A photograph of two children, a girl sitting at a table using scissors, glue, cloth and paper with a boy standing watching her, stimulated these responses:

A boy is wondering what to do.

He's standing there not doing anything but he wants to do it.

He might be bored – or upset – I don't like playtimes – being pushed about.

The little boy would like a turn but he is too shy.

Matthew (a twin) was shy when he came to school. He wouldn't do anything.

Mark (his twin) was not shy, he did things.

T: Matthew why were you shy?

M: I am the shy one.

T: No – you do things now.

M: But I didn't know what to do when I came to school. There was too much of everything. (The twins had never been to nursery or playgroup.)

There's a boy standing watching.

He doesn't know how to do it. He's scared.

One's thinking what to do.

He's sucking his hand because he doesn't know what to do.

The little girl is showing the little boy what to do.

They are playing hairdressers.

That boy is thinking.

Barrett (1986) pp.76–7

The category, 'Not Knowing What To Do', that emerges from comments like this seems to be a powerful one for these children. Another form of inaction Barrett labelled 'not being involved', building on elements in children's responses such as 'I don't want to', 'I can't', 'They are not looking', 'They don't want to listen'. A third category 'worrying' arose from comments on a photograph of a child sitting at a table with an exercise book, sucking a pencil.

Girl can't do it. Perhaps she's drawing a ship.

One's putting her pencil in her mouth because she's thinking what to draw.

I like drawing mummy, daddy and me in a house with curtains.

A boy doesn't know what to do. He is sucking his pencil. He cannot do his work. He must tell his teacher.

I don't know how to do it. I don't know how to paint or mix the colours properly.

He's thinking about his mum and dad at home.

I didn't like to write when I came to school. I couldn't make a snail. I couldn't draw a picture. It was too hard. I was too little. I feel miserable when I can't do it.

I'm frightened I might get it wrong.

Barrett (op. cit.) p.82

These insights into children's perceptions of their first experiences in school are further evidence of the importance of context. The conditions of classroom life, and the ways in which children respond to the demands of the classroom, are an inescapable presence in the complex of factors that bear on children's learning, and teachers' assessments of that learning.

Michael Tennant's study of Margaret, described in Chapter 3, includes a description of her response to the classroom rules that governed participation in question and answer sessions with the teacher. Of one lesson he observed he writes:

> Margaret spent much of that lesson hunched up in a pose I came to recognise. Sitting at a table on a stool, rather than on a chair, she would rest her head seemingly vacantly upon her hands. The only sign of life was the occasional caressing of her cheeks with her fingers. Under pressure, either because I was looking at her, or, because hers was the only hand not up, she would half-heartedly raise her arm so that her upper arm never got higher than level with her shoulder, and her hand rarely moved away from the top of her head. This was a good strategy, because I rarely saw Margaret asked for a contribution, even on this occasion, when it was clear that Margaret could contribute. This diffident behaviour has to be contrasted with the energy which Margaret displays when not under pressure.

Margaret's diffident appearance may be effective camouflage for a pupil who does not want to be seen; but as a piece of learning, it is likely to be, in the long term, dysfunctional. The responsibility to behave like a pupil, imposed by the teacher, may conflict with the child's right to an active and personal involvement in the curriculum. Just as Jason's learned behaviour as a pupil was at odds with other aspects of his learning, so Margaret's attention to classroom codes of conduct may forestall a closer engagement with thinking, doing and learning.

Not all researchers who have studied the effects of context on children's learning have reached such worrying conclusions as Willes and Barrett. Sometimes such studies can reveal unexpectedly good news. For example, Sheila Gapp, an experienced deputy head in a Norfolk middle school, carried out a child-study of a ten-and-a-half-year-old girl, Linda. A phrase from Philip Jackson's *Life in Classrooms* (1968) had stuck in her mind: 'learning to live in a classroom...involves, among other things, learning to live in a crowd.' Sheila Gapp's starting point was that Linda was finding this process difficult: 'My early feelings about Linda suggested that she was quiet, passive and unsure of herself, as a result of coming from a rather insular home situation to the crowd of a large school.' (Linda lived in a village outside the town and travelled in each day by taxi, one of only three children out of a school population of 215 who attended the school from this small community.) Sheila Gapp, who was Linda's class teacher, carried out timed observations of Linda in a variety of contexts – in small self-chosen groups, in larger teacher-directed groups, in the whole class group, in the playground, working individually, and during extra-curricular activities. She investigated Linda's perception of herself, as a person and as a learner, and collated Linda's chosen friends' perceptions of her.

Her observations added up to a very agreeable surprise: 'My observations have led me to rethink my judgements. I have seen Linda regularly participating in group work, being actively involved in seeking outcomes and sharing experiences. Her contributions are highly valued by the other group members, who turn to her frequently for assistance and support.' This teacher discovered that her first impressions of Linda's difficulty in 'learning to live in a crowd' were not supported by the evidence she collected in other contexts. When each of Linda's regular working environments was closely observed, a fuller picture could be seen. This teacher concluded: 'It is not until you observe intently that you find patterns of events and behaviour which might have remained unnoticed.'

I have suggested that, as part of their daily life in classrooms, teachers set themselves the grossly unrealistic task of trying to see and understand everything. Inevitably we fall short. Inevitably we see more of some sorts of learning than of others, more of some children and less of others, more of one aspect of the curriculum and less of others that are not, currently, at the front of our minds. Inevitably, we see more of what we expect to see, of what we know is there, than of the unexpected and unintended. Occasionally we do get a glimpse of children's unintended learning, and although the experience may be uncomfortable, it may also be salutory in forcing us to remember that teachers' good intentions do not always translate directly into desirable learning outcomes. An observation I recorded of a four-year-old boy, Luigi, is a useful example of how teachers can learn from the unexpected.

Figure 4.1 shows a page of writing produced by Luigi on his fourth afternoon in the four year old unit of a primary school. He chose to work at the table where the writing materials were provided, selected paper, a pencil and a ruler, and drew a line across the page, about two-thirds down. He began to write on the left hand side of the page and completed his writing on the right hand side with a full stop. He added the two crosses at the top

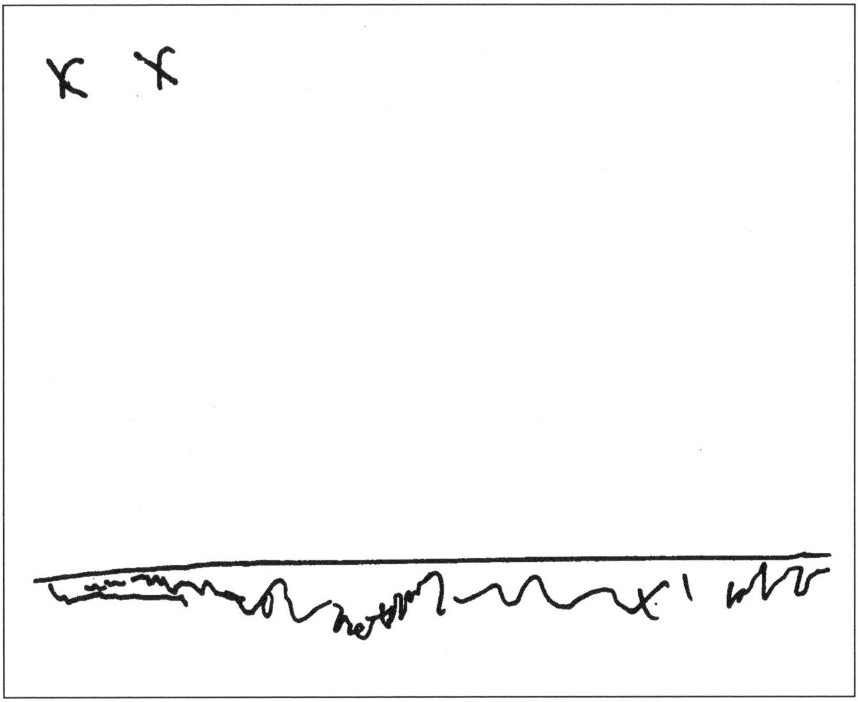

Figure 4.1 Luigi – 4 years 5 months – his fourth afternoon in school

left hand corner and prepared to leave the table. I asked him to explain what he had done: he identified his name pointing to the two crosses ('Luigi Giardini'), and his writing (pointing to the marks across the lower half of the page). He did not respond to my question about what the writing said. I asked him about the blank expanse of paper: 'That's for my drawing.' 'And are you going to do a drawing?' 'Oh, I can't draw.'

In four afternoons, Luigi has learned a good deal about school routines and expectations. He has also learned (though not necessarily at school) some of the important things he needs to know about writing. But he has also learned something much less worthwhile: that there are classroom expectations that he believes he cannot meet ('I can't draw'). It goes without saying that his teachers had not set out to teach him this; and it was fortunate for all concerned that the observer's question revealed Luigi's estimate of his own capabilities. His teachers were, as a result, made aware of their responsibility for preventing Luigi's perception of himself as a child who 'can't draw' from taking deeper root. Unintended learning is not often so easily discerned, and so our central responsibility as teachers becomes even more pressing – we must keep trying to see everything, even the unforeseen, and sometimes, the unwelcome.

Looking at learning is a massive undertaking. The examples I have given so far include specific activities, such as Paul's painting and Luigi's writing, well-defined curriculum areas, such as children's writing, Jason's mathematics and Margaret's science, and, in the case-study of James, children's emotional development. In any one part of this great commitment, there is a further responsibility: to listen, as well as to see. Children's involvement in classroom activities is surrounded by talk; to assess children's learning without considering the part that spoken language plays in it is, quite simply, impossible. Our attempts as teachers to get inside children's heads, and understand their understandings, are enriched to the extent that children themselves are prepared to give us, through their talk, access to their thinking.

Once again, our responsibilities are colossal. Children's thinking, and the language in which they express that thinking, roams far beyond the classroom walls and the fixtures and fittings of their primary schools. Margaret Meek (1985) argues that studies of language development have in the past tended to neglect imaginative aspects of language; this is to be deplored, since, she suggests, children's language is most powerful within imaginative structures. In imaginative play, children 'can say all they know, in any way they like…they attempt in play what they might not risk in everyday activity' (p.49).

Jennifer Pozzani, a primary school teacher in Suffolk, was seconded for a year to investigate the quality of the educational experiences being offered to four-year-old children in primary schools in Suffolk. Her unpublished report, *Significant People, Significant Time* is a powerful document, advocating an educational environment for these young children that matches their remarkable powers: their powers to do, to see, to listen, to think, to talk and to learn. One of her central concerns is that the crude distinction made by some educators between 'work' and 'play' should not be used as an excuse to water down, for four-year-olds in primary schools, the play-centred curriculum of four-year-olds in nurseries and playgroups. Her observations of children's imaginative play are used as evidence for her claims about the importance of play. For example, in a very small reception classroom, she observed play in the 'home corner', an area contrived from a cupboard, a set of drawers, some dressing up clothes and domestic equipment.

This week the area is being used as a shop, or rather a variety of shops.

John appears to 'own' the game. He has set up the ironing board as a shop window and is trying to stand two dolls up as he says they are 'shop dummies'. Three other children are also in the corner, stacking and sweeping. No-one wants to be a customer so I join and nearly ruin the game by asking for baked beans in a shop that clearly does not stock such items. However, the children are committed to the game and baked beans are sold in a shop which has dummies in the window.

J: Phone your dad to get home (gives me one of the telephones).

Andrew becomes the voice of 'my dad' using the other telephone and during a long conversation tells me:

A: I'll come at eight-thirty.

JP: He says he'll come at eight-thirty.

J: Well the shop shuts at two-thirty.

(There was then a lot of conversation between Karen, Andrew and John and the children set up a line of chairs as either a taxi or a bus. At this point it seemed my presence was no longer necessary but I stayed to watch and the children treated me as an equal.)

Everyone wants to be the driver and after negotiations the four children take it in turns every time Karen says, 'We've got to a stop'. The rest of us sit behind. Other children join in too but soon Karen decides we've arrived and moves out of the 'home corner' and spreads a tablecloth on the floor and organises plates, plasticine, conkers, etc. for a picnic. John and Andrew come and it appears we are in the woods in the middle of the night. A collection of small sticks usually used for counting are put on a piece of paper to represent the fire. There is a lot of discussion about where this should go. The children share the picnic and there is discussion about sharing and eating properly. It seems good manners are still important in the middle of the forest. Soon the children huddle under the table to sleep for the night.

Other children have joined and Sally whispers to me that she will be a wolf so she goes off to hide. Just then morning breaks and Karen and another child go off exploring. They find the wolf but it's all right because it turns out she's a friendly wolf! It is now time for another meal and the children build up the fire and 'eat' breakfast. Sally keeps in character as the children 'feed' her, by baring her teeth and sticking out her tongue. This is a very short day as suddenly it's bedtime and as the children snuggle under the table stroking the wolf, John tells us the story of 'The Three Bears'. This game continues for some considerable time with new children dropping in.

There are two more bedtimes and John is the storyteller each time. His last story, which his teacher writes out for him is:

Once upon a time there was Humpty Dumpty, and a wolf came along and ate Humpty Dumpty up and Humpty Dumpty shouted in the wolf's tummy, 'Help! Help!' And along came the woodcutter man. He chopped the wolf's tummy open and out came Humpty Dumpty.

The game finishes only when the children go outside.

Even this short observation offers a wealth of insight into these children's powerful use of language. They use their talk to establish the rules of their play, the regularities of life in the imaginary shop, bus, and forest encampment. They use their talk to move in and out of the real and imaginary; through their talk they cross the boundaries of the classroom world, where the teacher and the observer are still sitting and standing, talking and watching; the children enter a new world, which contains firelight, darkness, danger and mystery. Their talk establishes acceptable ways of behaving – keeping the fire going, preserving proper table manners, retaining bedtime rituals. Above all, they use their talk to string together the narrative of their play, their own story, to which they appropriate the stories they have heard outside, in the adult world (the three bears, Humpty Dumpty). Their story is passionately involving, emotionally taxing; within it they both express and control their feelings. In Meek's words: 'In play, children create the imaginative terms of their knowing' (op. cit., p.53). The observer or teacher who notes down the language in which this happens thereby gains access to vital aspects of children's learning.

The importance of spoken language is widely recognised in practising teachers' case-studies of learning, which typically draw on tape recordings or jotted notes of children's talk in every corner of classroom life. Structured and semistructured interviews, in which teachers invite their pupils to reflect on their learning, evaluating their own progress, have become part of the professional repertoire of evaluation strategies. Teachers have been encouraged in these developments by authors such as Helen Arnold (1982) and Andrew Pollard and Sarah Tann (1987). Arnold's *Listening to Children Reading* draws on the work of the 'Extending Beginning Reading' project in recommending the regular diagnostic use of the 'reading interview', in which childen's concepts of reading and themselves as readers can be explored, as well as their understanding of their reading material. Pollard and Tann's *Reflective Teaching in the Primary School* encourages teachers to use a variety of techniques for monitoring learning, including 'conferencing' – a term used to describe an extended discussion between teacher and child. The technique is based on the premise that teachers have much to learn from children's verbal accounts of their own learning.

Children's spoken language when the teacher is not present has also been the subject of some teachers' studies. For example, Thea Prisk (1987) gives a fascinating account of infant children's unsupervised group talk, in which she admits to astonishment at the linguistic skills revealed, skills 'more usually attributed by language researchers to children more than twice the age of those I had recorded' (p.90).

My own close observations of young children working in small discussion groups, with a teacher (myself), suggest that there are unlimited opportunities, in such a setting, to see, if not everything, then many important and worthwhile aspects of learning: children listening, collaborating, agreeing and disagreeing; children thinking logically and imaginatively, connectedly and with sudden flashes of insight; children using simile and metaphor; children moving from the concrete example to the abstract formulation; children recognising casual and functional relationships, making generalisations and qualifications; children's humour and originality; children learning the purposes of the act of discussion itself, and their own powers to contribute to it.

The routine for these small group discussions, which took place in an infant school in Sheffield over a period of four years, was very simple, and quickly learned by the children who took part, who were between the ages of four and a half and seven and a half years old. First, I introduced the children to the idea of 'discussion' itself – a time when people come together to talk about their own and each other's ideas. Next I explained that their task in the discussion was fourfold; to think of their own ideas, to tell each other their ideas, to listen to each other's ideas, and to question and comment on them. My task was to record their ideas on large sheets of sugar paper, numbering the contributions for easy reference – an element of the ritual greatly appreciated by all the participants, especially those who were not yet reading independently. After a discussion session children were often to be seen pointing out their ideas on the discussion sheets – which were carefully preserved – to their friends, referring to them by number if they could not read back the sentences or phrases. Parents, too, were drawn in to appreciate and admire their children's contributions.

The listening part of the activity, which I had expected to cause difficulties for some, was, in fact, easily mastered by all the children. I suspect it was, at first, a competitive rather than a collaborative spirit that moved them to listen so intently, and to reject or qualify each other's contributions. An idea that had already been recorded was summarily dismissed, and an idea that lay outside the chosen topic was swiftly despatched, unless its author made a good case for its inclusion in the record. The topics for discussion were negotiated between the members of the group (of six or seven children) and myself; some groups had a list of prepared topics which we worked through together; others selected the topic for the next discussion, as they came to the end of each session; others made more spontaneous decisions, based on recent incidents or relevant topics of the moment. The discussion on 'saying goodbye', cited below, was triggered by a teacher's imminent retirement; 'chairs' by a school-wide topic on furniture; 'white' by an exhibition of work in the school lobby; other topics were part of a staff development project – a number of discussions about 'concerts', for example, supported a staff enquiry into the purpose and value of our annual summer concert. Some discussions preceded a class-based topic, acting as a flow-chart of ideas for later development ('brushes' and 'bags' for example) and others were used as a way of revisiting and reviewing a topic at the conclusion of the class's work.

The discussion groups met weekly, for up to 45 minutes at each session; the children were often keen to continue for longer, but I felt it would be more motivating to stop before every last drop of interest had been wrung from any one topic. One memorable discussion lasted for three sessions spread over three weeks; it was an investigation into the concept 'in and out' and the discussion sheets record that over one hundred contributions were made – a record still standing when I left the school. The participants in that discussion were the heroes and heroines of school-corridor gossip for a brief hour, when they reached their target of a hundred, and spread the noise of their achievement up and down the classrooms. But the real excitement of these children's thinking can only be experienced by studying the discussion sheets that capture their creativity, their seriousness and their gaiety.

A discussion on St Valentine's Day, for example, released a stream of imaginative associations, humorous partnerships and beautiful images. 'Who sends Valentines to whom?' we asked. Amongst dozens of other contributions I recorded:

- the cup to the saucer
- the spoon to the fork
- the toothpaste to the toothbrush
- the truncheon to the handcuffs
- the changing guard to the Queen
- the button to the buttonhole
- the doormat to the door
- the drum to the drumsticks

- the bow to the violin
- the arrow to the bow
- the stars to the night

This was an exercise in humour certainly, but also something more. It was an impressive effort, by these children of six and seven, to give concrete illustrations of the tender, mutually dependent and loving relationships celebrated on that day.

Younger children, working on topics that might seem simpler – a colour, for example, an animal or a piece of furniture – showed equally impressive powers. 'White...is quite a difficult discussion' records one sheet. There was an added constraint to this discussion – I stipulated that the children should discuss only those things that were always white, and exclude suggestions (such as paper or paint) that might be any colour, or were only sometimes white. 'Teeth' was rejected as an idea, until qualified as 'good teeth'. 'Fine weather clouds' were allowed, and so was 'falling snow', and each of these precise definitions was carefully scrutinised by the group. This kind of critical listening was one of the most impressive aspects of what I saw; another was the way in which children built on each other's ideas, not just by contributing a word closely associated with the last key idea, but in other ways as well. In the 'white' discussion, 'the inside of an apple' was quickly followed by 'the inside of a pear/banana/lychee...'. More interestingly, 'the white of your eye' was followed, after an interval, by 'penguins' tummies', 'part of the Union Jack', and unforgettably, 'half a zebra'. Here the children are building on the original idea that showed how, in this discussion, a part is as good as a whole.

Sometimes I divided the topic into two parts and invited the children to indicate where their contribution fitted. For example, a discussion on cars was divided thus:

Moving Parts	*Non-moving Parts*
wheels	the paint
windows/window winders	the wheel arch
pedals/boot-lid/keyhole	the mudguard
tyre in a puncture	the wires in the back window
gear stick/people in the car	(it's harder than it looks)
the button on the hand brake	
handle	
the mirror	
air	

Children from the reception class came to discuss tortoises one day; three tortoises had visited them that very morning and they could think of nothing else. In this discussion, they used a strategy I deliberately encouraged – that of describing by the use of negative concepts. For example, tortoises *can* run, but they *can't*:

> run fast
>> ride a bike
>>> drive a car
>>>> climb trees
>>>>> eat sweets
>>>>>> have a belly button
>>>>>> wear clothes

At this point a child contributed 'They can't come to school'. He was immediately corrected by a chorus of contradiction, but stood his ground, restructuring his thinking in a remarkable way, I believe, for a five-year-old: 'They do come to school, but they don't learn anything.'

A discussion on the topic of 'saying goodbye' is a good example of how these children were able to move from the specific details of their life in the here and now, to more general propositions, and, indeed to a metaphorical representation of the same idea. Contributions included:

saying goodbye...

- to Laura, because she's going on holiday
- to Mummies because they go home or to work
- When you've been on a holiday – to where you're staying (followed immediately by...)
- Lucy said goodbye to France
- Andrew said goodbye to Wales
- Lyndsey said goodbye to the ferry
- On the telephone – so they know you've finished
- Say goodbye to your dinner when you've eaten it
- Goodbye day – hello night – goodbye night – hello day
- Goodbye Friday, hello Saturday
- Goodbye sleep, when you wake up

Here are children working towards the real essence of 'goodbye' – a word that conveys not just a parting of persons, but an ending, a cessation of a particular relationship and, by extension, the beginning of a new relationship ('goodbye to the sun, hello to the moon').

Even very concrete and down-to-earth discussions revealed these children's astonishing ability to sort through their experience, and reclassify it in new and unexpected ways. In a discussion of 'chairs', for example, the comment that 'on a ferry boat, the chairs are fixed' provoked a torrent of further examples of fixed chairs – in a plane, a helicopter, a train, a hovercraft, an airship, a rocket, a cinema, a theatre…

Later in the discussion I recorded the contribution 'chairs in shops'. In the period of discussion that followed, the group described three different kinds of 'chairs in shops':

- chairs in chair shops
- chairs in junk shops
- chairs in shoe shops

The richness is not so much in the experience, as in the apparently illimitable ways in which these children were able to group and regroup their experiences.

Discussions of contrasting ideas were popular with older children, who liked to try and see both sides of an issue. A comparison of 'sewing with a needle' and 'sewing with a machine', produced two exactly complementary lists of benefits and disadvantages.

For example:

You can't lose a sewing machine	You can find a needle with a magnet
You can't buy a packet of sewing machines	You need lots of needles
Won't be much room in the car if you take it on holiday	On holiday, take a needle
You can store things inside a sewing machine	You don't need a cupboard for it

The last words of the discussion came down in favour of the needle – 'needles were invented first, they are smaller and much simpler'.

Once I began to appreciate the linguistic strengths revealed in these discussions, I encouraged the children to pick abstract topics – not just 'things they could see'. 'Silence' was a fruitful topic, as was 'movement'. 'Things that do not move' gave the children some difficulty. They had already listed, under moving things, cars, eyes, people, all the different animals, motorbikes, vehicles, all the different vehicles, wind, rain, clouds, the moon and the world but not the sun. The first suggestion for 'non-moving things' was 'the sunshine', and heated debate followed. When the sun 'goes in', where does it go? What is it that moves, or appears to move? Debbie was insistent that the sun did not move, and 'the sunshine' was allowed to stand at the top of the list. The next suggestion 'this school' was promptly ruled out by the consideration of an earthquake – it would move then!

The earthquake clause was applied to many suggestions, which were, after a while, recorded as 'the bricks of a house that isn't in an earthquake', 'a road that isn't in an earthquake', even 'a coffin in the earth that isn't in an earthquake'. To get us out of this difficulty I suggested 'Sheffield' – 'we don't have earthquakes here'. Debbie responded with 'Yugoslavia', which Nancy generalised to 'countries'. Harking back to the solar system, Bryony suggested 'outer space'. Controversy started in earnest with Nancy's suggestion of 'Tuesday'. We wrote down all seven days of the week while we tried to decide. The sheet ends on a note of genuine indecision. 'We think tomorrow but we're not sure,' and a scribbled note along the side of the page records Sarah's comment as we left the room, 'Time doesn't move . . .' Debbie challenged her to look at her watch, but Sarah stood her ground . . . I was silent – in admiration and respect.

Even after four years, with weekly sessions with each of seven classes, I was still constantly surprised by the quality of the children's ideas and their ability to express them. One last example: in a discussion on umbrellas (a current exhibition in the school hall) the talk had moved through types of umbrellas (anglers', photographers', cocktail sticks) to an extended consideration of the function of umbrellas, and umbrella substitutes:

- a mushroom is an umbrella to a mouse
- a bus shelter is an umbrella to the people in the queue
- the roof is an umbrella to the house
- the shell is an umbrella to the tortoise
- the fleece is an umbrella for the sheep
- a flower is an umbrella for the bee
- a greenhouse is an umbrella for plants

Into the midst of this burst Helen: 'Channel swimmers are covered in butter'. I gasped, but the group nodded approval, and agreed with interest. It took me some time to realise how far Helen had taken her understanding; we were really discussing forms of protection against water, and so, metaphorically speaking, the channel swimmer's grease *is* an umbrella. Helen's thinking was original, divergent, illuminating – and strictly logical.

In these small groups it was easy for the teacher, in spite of the excitement of the group discussion, to focus on individuals, especially on those who were causing their teachers concern, for whatever reason. Eve, for example, aged six, was very, very quiet, indeed almost totally silent in classroom settings; her class teacher was anxious to find a context in which she would feel disposed to enter into an exchange of thoughts and ideas through talk; she hoped that these small group discussion sessions might be an encouraging setting for Eve. But for nearly a year Eve attended weekly discussion sessions without speaking. She listened, certainly, and responded with laughter and other signs of appreciation to the contributions of her friends; but never a word did she utter.

Late one autumn afternoon however, after the close of our discussion period, the tide turned. We had been discussing 'stripes', the theme of a current exhibition of children's work displayed in the lobby outside the room where the sessions were held. Eve had been as silent as usual. But as we walked back to her mobile classroom, across the playground, we passed the window cleaners at work. Eve tugged at my hand and whispered in my ear 'ladders have stripes'. This achievement, which was celebrated throughout the school (with, we hope, appropriate tact as well as enthusiasm) was just the beginning of the apotheosis of Eve. She became, in her own way, one of the leaders of the group she worked with: other children listened attentively to her ideas, which varied from the accurate and penetrating to the wildest flights of fantasy. The range of her linguistic powers (in spoken language – she was not yet reading or writing independently) grew, quite visibly, week by week.

When I started the practice of small discussion groups, I had no idea what I was going to see; my interest in spoken language was one motivating factor; another was my desire to get to know really well at least some of the children in each of the classes of the school (where I was headteacher). The outcomes exceeded my wildest dreams. Even now, after many years have passed, I am still amazed at the richness of this learning, stored on those discussion sheets, now growing tattered and frayed. I started by listening, by trying to see what children could do with their spoken language; almost immediately I realised I was looking at learning. If I did not see everything, at least I learned to be ready for anything.

CHAPTER 5

Ways of Seeing:
Trying to Understand

In assessing learning, the act of seeing gives way to the act of understanding; the process of collecting evidence is followed by attempts to make the evidence meaningful. Description and narrative stimulate interpretations and judgements. In this part of the practice of assessment, the assessors strive to make sense of what they have seen and remembered. As they do so, however, they are always aware that the collection and selection of evidence is, in spite of every effort at completeness, inevitably partial and incomplete. The characteristics of the human mind limit the extent to which we can develop totally objective ways of looking. The conditions of classroom life set severe constraints on our ability to amass evidence of children's learning.

When we begin to analyse and reflect on our evidence, there is no reason even to aspire to absolute neutrality or objectivity; we are committed to our own perspective, which is partial and relative; it can be changed if we change. Mannheim (1936) defines the essence of 'perspectivity' in the following way:

> the false ideal of a detached impersonal point of view must be replaced by the ideal of an essentially human point of view, which is within the limits of a human perspective, constantly trying to enlarge itself. (pp.266–7)

Mannheim was writing 'an introduction to the Sociology of Knowledge', but his central argument 'knowledge is always from a position' is as true for classroom teachers as for his original audience. When we act on our collected evidence to forge meaning from it, to shape it into new understanding, we do so 'from a position'. We are human beings with biographies, with educational experiences of our own; we are teachers, trained in particular traditions and institutions; we are emotional beings, suffused with sympathies and antipathies. We are enriched by our own reading and study, so that we have come to understand the conceptual frameworks of others, as well as building and learning about our own.

Both the early observers of children's lives, Margaret Lowenfeld and Susan Isaacs, whose work I have already drawn on, introduce their accounts with severe warnings about the impossibility of accuracy and impartiality. Lowenfeld (1935) cites four distinct sources of error which arise from the essential structure of the observer's mind:

(1) The mind cannot grasp that which is wholly unfamiliar to it...

(2) The mind is more apt to see that which it has already noticed...

(3) The mind is unable to see that which it has not been trained to accept...

(4) The mind unconsciously distorts what it hears and sees, according to its own prejudices. (p.35)

As an instance of the last type of error, Lowenfeld describes how the personal feelings of the observer become active in the impersonal work of 'watching a roomful of children at play... An adult is apt to project on to children ideas he has already formed in childhood, and to see children not as they are, but as he wishes them to be' (p.36).

But Lowenfeld does not take fright at her own warnings of possible misunderstandings. She goes on to use her observations, scoured, as she hopes, from error and prejudice, to build frameworks of understanding. For example, Lowenfeld's description of the satirical form of children's play, quoted in Chapter 3, is part of a broader classification of play: play as social realism, play as romance, and play as satire (p.135). If we follow her example, and accept the provisional nature of the frameworks we construct, we will not be falling into irretrievable error, but cautiously and carefully working within the limits of our human capacity to understand.

The work of Vivian Gussin Paley (1981), an American kindergarten teacher, provides many instructive examples of the educator seeing children 'as (s)he wishes them to be'. Or rather, seeing them *at first* in this way; Paley records her detailed evidence and sets it against her wished-for interpretation. Time and again, the educator's perspective, the educator's intentions, do not match the evidence. Time and again, Paley is forced to reconsider, to reconstruct the framework within which she makes meaning. In the following incident, the five-year-old children in Paley's kindergarten class have planted lima beans in individual milk cartons, but after three weeks no green shoots have appeared. Wally discovers that his beans have disappeared.

'They're gone!' he yelled, bringing me his carton. 'Gone! I looked through the whole dirt!'

'Can I look in mine?' asked Rose.

'You might as well,' I answered. 'They don't seem to be coming up.'

There was a rush to the planting table. Everyone began digging into cartons or dumping their contents on the newspaper-covered table.

Andy: Where are the beans?

Wally: They're invisible.

Andy: Impossible. They came from a store. Someone took them out.

Teacher: Who?

Andy: A robber.

Eddie: When it was dark a criminal took them.

Teacher: Why would he do it?

Jill: Maybe someone came in and said, 'Oh, there's nothing growing. We must take some of them out.'

Eddie: I think a robber broke in and said, 'They don't need to plant those beans.'

Teacher: Why would a robber want them?

Wally: To sell them.

Andy: Or cook them.

Ellen: No, maybe to fool people with. See, he could plant them in his garden and when flowers came up people would think he's nice.

Teacher: If I were a robber I'd take the record player.

Eddie: Not if you wanted to plant seeds.

Paley (1981) pp.57–8

Here we see two ways of understanding the world at work. The children account for the missing beans with imaginary robbers; the teacher is intent on the logical connections, as she sees them, between a real robber and what he would be likely to steal. The children do not consider that the robber's imaginary theft needs any further explanation: stealing is what robbers do. If there are beans to steal, and a robber about, then the robber will certainly steal them. Trying to understand her pupils' thinking, Paley talks to another kindergarten class about the decaying Hallowe'en pumpkin that they are observing.

Teacher: Why does your pumpkin look like this?

Tim: It's full of mold.

Carter: It's moldy. Plants are growing inside.

Julia: Little vines.

William: They make the top fall in.

Kevin: Dead plants and animals get mold.

Tim: Old pumpkins get moldy.

Julia: It's going to become dust.

Teacher:	How does that happen?
Julia:	It'll get so dry you won't even see it.
Teacher:	By the way, we have a problem in class. We planted lima beans and after a long time nothing came up. We looked in the dirt to see if any roots had grown and we couldn't find the beans. They were gone.
Kevin:	Was the window open? The wind blew them away.
Teacher:	They were deep down in the dirt.
Candy:	A squirrel could have took them.
Teacher:	We didn't see a squirrel in the room.
Candy:	It could have hid somewhere.
Teacher:	Our windows are locked at night. How could the squirrel have gotten back out?
William:	He could scratch a hole in the window.
Kevin:	Or in the door.
Carter:	Maybe a robber stepped in. They can get in windows very easily.
Teacher:	Why would he want the beans?
Carter:	For his garden.
Julia:	Or to cook them. Somebody has a key to your window, I think.

There was no further talk of squirrels once the robber theory was suggested. I was so surprised by this change of opinion after talking about a rotting pumpkin that I presented my question to the third kindergarten. One child said a bird might be the culprit, another suspected worms. However, when a third mentioned robbers, everyone immediately agreed that the beans had been removed by a human intruder to plant, eat, or sell.

Paley (op. cit.) pp.59–60

The children use 'robbers', Paley comes to see, as a powerful explanatory theory for all missing items. Mislaid coats, beans, rugs and sweaters are all attributed to robbers. These children's theory satisfies their need to account for missing objects, by drawing on one single attribute of robbers – their propensity to rob. All other aspects of a robber's behaviour are left out of the account; the teacher's attempts to make the supposed robber's behaviour consistent in adult terms are rejected out of hand, not because they threaten the children's explanation but because they are simply irrelevant. The children's implicit syllogism is too pure and simple to be contaminated with the teacher's irrelevancies. Their argument seems to go:

Robbers steal things.
The beans have disappeared.
Therefore robbers stole the beans.

Unlike the adults from whom they learned what robbers do, the children see no reason to be frightened of robbers:

> The robber feared by adults bears no relationship to the one created by the children. Their robber is so busy stealing lima beans he has no time to cause harm. (p.62)

Paley's account of her pupils' thinking is deeply rewarding, since it enables the reader to follow in her footsteps as she comes, little by little, to understand and respect the role that illusion and fantasy play in the minds of five- and six-year-olds. They have, she concludes, 'become aware of the thinking required by the adult world,' but are not yet 'committed to its burden of rigid consistency' (p.81).

Paley is not dismayed or destroyed by the necessity of reshaping her interpretations of children's thinking; she is, rather, humbled by what the children have taught her to see, and grateful for the opportunity to learn from them. For Paley, as for all of us, 'knowledge is always from a position'. The new 'position', from which she applies her knowledge of children's minds, may in turn be reformed and renewed; in the meantime, there is no weakness in her understanding, but a strength, in that as she strives, in her daily work, to understand what she has seen, she also constantly and critically reviews this very process of coming to understand.

It is this willingness to review one's position, one's attempts to make meaning, that is absent from so-called objective tests and measures of learning. It is absent too from judgements that are made on the basis of taken-for-granted expectations of what children should know and understand. A seven-year-old child in this country who has not learned to read may, and very probably will, be a cause of concern to his or her teachers and parents. But a child of seven in those American states where seven is the statutory age for starting school will excite no alarm if he or she is not a fluent reader. From the position of US educators, knowledge of seven-year-olds does not include an expectation that they should already have learned to read.

'Positions', in Mannheim's sense, shift in historical time and geographical space. In *Mansfield Park* Maria and Julia Bertram, aged 12 and 13, are horrified to discover that their ten-year-old cousin, Fanny Price, was 'ignorant of many things with which they had been long familiar', but delighted to be obliged to recognise their own superiority. Indeed, they thought her prodigiously stupid and for the first two or three weeks were continually bringing some fresh report of it into the drawing room. 'Dear mamma, only think, my cousin cannot put the map of Europe together – or my cousin cannot tell the principal rivers in Russia – or she never heard of Asia Minor or she does not know the differences between water-colours and crayons! – How strange! – Did you ever hear anything so stupid?'

'My dear,' their considerate aunt would reply; 'it is very bad, but you must not expect every body to be as forward and quick at learning as yourself.'

'But, aunt, she is really so very ignorant! – Do you know, we asked her last night, which way she would go to get to Ireland; and she said, should cross to the Isle of Wight, She thinks of nothing but the Isle of Wight, and she calls it *the Island*, as if there were no other island in the world. I am sure I should have been ashamed of myself, if I had not known better long before I was so old as she is. I cannot remember the time when I did not know a great deal that she has not the least notion of yet. How long ago it is, aunt, since we used to repeat the chronological order of the kings of England, with the dates of their accession, and most of the principal events of their reigns!'

'Yes,' added the other; 'and of the Roman emperors as low as Severus; besides a great deal of the Heathen Mythology, and all the Metals, Semi-Metals, Planets, and distinguished philosophers.'

Jane Austen is certainly not suggesting that Mansfield Park was an educational centre of excellence, compared with Fanny's impoverished schooling in her house in Portsmouth. Rather, she is satirising the complacency and the ignorance of the Bertram girls, and mocking their superficial judgements of the worth of the inestimable Fanny. It is entertaining to imagine how Austen might treat our present obsession with specific attainment targets, no less arbitrarily conceived than the Heathen Mythology.

By contrast, the work of Chris Athey and the Froebel Early Education Project is a fascinating example of how a desire to understand can enrich our powers of seeing. Athey began her study of repeated patterns in children's play without preconceived ideas of what children of two or three should have learned to do or to understand. Her 'position', her starting point, was the point at which Piaget's observational studies of his own children had left off. Piaget's work with two- to five-year-olds did not disclose invariant patterns of thought over those years, because he used test situations, rather than open-ended observations. The concrete operational test questions that Piaget put to two- to five-year-olds produced evidence that they could not conserve or categorise correctly: the judgement followed that these young children are cognitively incompetent. Athey set out to imitate Isaacs' 'bottom-up' perspective;

instead of seeing younger children as less competent than older children, she based her analysis on her observations of cognitive competence in young children, with the result that: 'when the more advanced thinking of older children is analysed, cognitive advances are apparent but do not detract from earlier competence' (Athey 1990, p.17). Athey describes her own work in this tradition as 'illuminative research', using a 'natural history' approach of observational interpretation. She uses the term 'schema' to describe the concept that is at the core of the child's developing mind, the central element of intellectual growth.

Athey's observations, by focusing on invariant patterns of activity, and use of language, revealed the 'cognitive forms', the schemas, of children's thinking, which remain constant across a variety of different activities or curriculum areas. For example, as young children work on the schemas of *horizontal* and *vertical* lines, which sometimes intersect to form *grids*, they pay close attention to these patterns in their immediate environment, as well as representing them in their language and in their mark-making with paint and pencil. The following observations illustrate Athey's findings.

(The children's ages are given in years, months and days.)

Jock began to draw *circular scribbles* at 1:2:0. At 1:8:28 he watched, at short range, people playing golf. Suddenly he shouted exuberantly, 'football'. A few days later, on a visit to Teddington Lock, he gazed at a buoy for some time, pointed and shouted, 'football'. Mrs B explained 'that's a buoy' – a reaction of disbelief. Two weeks later on a visit to Kew Gardens, he was absorbed by a *circular pattern* on the floor.

When he was 1:9:6 he spent almost the whole morning with his father selecting *spheres* from a range of other shapes. At 1:9:10 he named a *circular scribble* for the first time. He called it 'football'. On a subsequent visit he spent a lot of time examining *spherical* door-handles. After seven months of absorption with *circles* and *spheres*, Jock had begun naming objects that had a perceptual correspondence with the visual effects of his *circular scribble*.

This sequence can be compared with another sequence from the same child, which suggests that the relationship between mark-making, perception and representation is not random. Jock (2:5:22) drew a *vertical line* and named it 'crocodile...a tail that's burning'. One month later he painted a strong *vertical line* he named 'animal, one leg'. He repeated the *vertical line* the next day and called it 'leg'.

Jock (2:7:8) painted a thick *horizontal line* with a *vertical line* next to it. He named this 'aeroplane'. He was dissatisfied with this and struggled through 30 paintings trying to *intersect a vertical* with a *horizontal line*. He finally succeeded in producing a perfect *grid*. He became as absorbed with *grid-like* configurations as he had been with *spheres*. At 2:7:9, while on the project bus, Jock shouted to his mother twice on the journey, 'look'. Once it was 'scaffolding' and once it was 'a fence'. On that same day he rolled out some long pieces of clay and called them 'spider's legs' and, later, 'stripes'. This is an example of 'fitting' form (*parallel lines*) onto suitable content.

Jock (2:7:14) would not be parted from a tennis racquet. He hugged it and gazed at it alternatively. Two days later he pointed to a *grid* configuration and said, 'Windmill'. He followed this with a painting of *four vertical lines* named 'Horsey, Man, Sheep and Tree'. Jock (2:7:28) carefully inspected a hammock. Jock (2:8:0) made a model. He called it 'tiger', pointed to the nails and called them 'stripes'.

Athey (1990) p.93

Teachers and other educators who have attended in-service meetings or workshops led by Chris Athey, and who have seen some of her vast collection of representations of 'schemas', return to their nurseries and classrooms in search of 'schemas'. Sceptical at first, they quickly discover patterns of activity they had never noticed before. A group of teachers in Cleveland became involved in a collaborative investigation of schemas (Nicholls 1986). Cathy Nutbrown (1987) used observations of children's play as the basis for an assessment of their learning.

Adam (3:2) used stones and a thin strip of tree bark collected in the nursery garden to construct two pillars with tree bark balanced between. He spent time testing which things could go under and which had to go over because they would not fit underneath. He said, 'This is a bridge, some can go over it and the little bits go under'.

What understanding of Adam's thinking can we achieve through reflecting on this observation of a child's play? If we consider the processes and not just the end-product, we see Adam describing, explaining, organizing, constructing, selecting materials, forming hypotheses, testing and categorizing. Adam used the natural materials he could find in the garden to develop his own forms of thought. It would seem that at the present, the schema that absorbs him is related to things that 'go over and under', simple spatial concepts, which will develop further in time. His surroundings enabled him to explore his schema and the observant and listening adult could identify and support his actions and thinking. Much more is learned by reflecting in this way than by simply looking at the content of his work; so much would have been lost here, were the observation simply to record 'Adam made a bridge of stones and tree bark'.

Kate (4:1) was partially sighted. She was familiar with the environment of the nursery and used it to extend her own 'enveloping' schema. The following observations of her took place over two days on four separate occasions.

(1) Kate was dressing up and wrapped first a sari and then a large shawl around her.

(2) She went into the home corner and pulled the ironing board across the gap, 'I'm here now – it's private'.

(3) She took a wicker basket and went around the nursery collecting objects such as shells, nails, screws, small boxes and paper bags. She felt each object, apparently exploring texture and shape. On reflection, the adult who made this observation realized that each object that Kate selected was either a form of container or, in the case of nails and screws, 'went into' something else.

(4) Kate was talking on the telephone, the line went dead. 'It's the inside that's broken I think,' she said.

These notes show a consistent thread of thinking over the two days, a thread running through four separate activities. Kate was exploring 'enveloping and containing' with all the experiences available to her. In the process she was collecting according to clear criteria and categorizing objects, using her senses. She was defining space, hypothesizing and using language to express her thinking.

Drummond and Nutbrown (1992) pp.94–5

Nutbrown's work is just one illustration of the impact of Athey's work on early years practitioners. Athey's detailed observations within the four walls of the Froebel Project nursery class have enriched the seeing and the understanding of thousands of teachers and educators who have never set foot there, but who have learned from Athey to see from a new 'position', and to forge new forms of understanding.

Jane Abercrombie's influential work *The Anatomy of Judgement* also draws on the concept of the schema, as an internal pattern of thought, but she applies this concept in a very different way. In her work with medical students at University College London just after the second world war, Abercrombie became interested in ways of helping these students to make more effective judgements, by becoming mentally more flexible in considering alternative interpretations of the evidence in front of them. She offered students the experience of working in small discussion groups, looking, for example, at radiographs, and comparing their observations. At the time, this was a highly unconventional approach to teaching medical students. Abercrombie spells out the importance of the discussion technique:

The main difference between this and traditional methods of teaching is the amount of attention that is paid to the *processes* of observing or thinking, as distinct from the results. In traditional teaching the student makes an observation, and finds it to be correct or incorrect by comparison with the teacher's (or the currently accepted) version. He learns by discovering disparities between his result and that obtained by more experienced and skilful persons. In the discussion technique of teaching, the student learns by comparing his observation with those of ten or so of his peers. He compares not only the results, but how the results were arrived at and in doing this the range of factors taken into consideration is much wider than is usual in didactic teaching. What the student learns, it is hoped, is not only how to make a more correct response when he is confronted with a similar problem, but more generally to gain firmer control of his behaviour by understanding better his own ways of working.

Abercrombie (1969) p.19

This approach, which seems much less controversial to us today than it did at the time, was based on Abercrombie's understanding of the relationship between the external world and the inner world with which we perceive it. She argues that internal schemata 'persistent, deep-rooted and well-organised classifications of ways of perceiving, thinking and behaving' (Vernon 1955 cited in Abercrombie 1969) are always at work when we try to interpret a new situation or set of sensory data. Sometimes our schemata help us to see more accurately: 'waiting in a bus queue we can distinguish the numbers of an approaching bus at a much greater distance if we know which numbers are likely to come along the road'. But sometimes our schemata lead us astray, especially when what we expect to see is not there, or when our schemata affect our choice of an explanation for what we see, as in this example:

A child with a persistent cough had its throat X-rayed for diagnosis. The radiologist reported that there was nothing in the radiograph to show why the child was coughing. The cough persisted, and the child returned to have another radiograph taken. This time the shadow of a button was seen in the throat region, the button was removed and the child stopped coughing.

When the first radiograph was re-examined the shadow of the button was seen there too, but the radiologist had explained it away to himself, supposing that the child had been X-rayed with its vest on. He had failed to see the significance of the button for the problem in hand – diagnosis of the cause of the cough – because another explanation for its presence seemed more probable.

Abercrombie (1969) pp.60-61

This radiologist relied on a schema (buttons are worn outside, not inside the body) that misled him for a while. Only when he was forced to reconsider could his perception become more open and reflective.

Abercrombie is not suggesting that we try to escape from our schemata for understanding the world. She is emphasising that there is no possibility of escape. She argues instead that we should learn to live with our schemata; she encourages us to try and understand more about how we mentally construct the perceived world, so that we can come, in time, to a fuller understanding of it.

Because children's behaviour and children's learning are so various and complex, it is highly unlikely that any one simple framework of understanding, any single model of learning, will give us the 'position' from which we will be able to understand everything we see. It is more likely that we will choose to draw on a variety of models, linked within an over-arching hypothesis about the nature of human experience. Our best attempts to make meaning of what we see when we look at children's learning, are, I believe, inseparably linked to a view of human existence as in itself an attempt to make meaning. This view (whether we choose to use its formal label of 'social-constructivism' or not) is the uniting factor that brings together a range of different interpretations of learning, such as those of Athey and Paley, which I have illustrated in this chapter, and those of Armstrong, Isaacs and Lowenfeld in others.

Another illuminating framework is to be found in the work of Kieran Egan (1988), and I will describe his position by using it to reflect on an observation of my own of the imaginative play of a group of four-year-olds.

Egan's starting point is the traditional opposition between rationality and fantasy, the way in which fantasy is represented as at odds with constructive rational thought. Egan describes this opposition:

> Rationality and reality are closely entwined in our mental lexicon: rationality is the tool we use to discover reality. Education is the process in which we use rationality to show and discover what is real and true, and so fantasy, which ignores the boundaries of reality, is seen as the enemy which slips out of the constructive constraints of reason and runs mentally amok in unreal and impossible worlds. Fantasy asserts the impossible, the unverifiable, the unfalsifiable; it is casually hospitable to contradiction, irrelevance, and inconsistency. In rational activity the mind is awake, about constructive work, in accord with reality, attuned to the logics whereby things operate; in fantasy there is mind-wandering illogic, dream-like indulgence of the flittering shapes of the idle mind, disregard of hard empirical reality.
>
> Egan (1988) p.11

The consequence of this opposition, which Egan rejects, is that children's fantasy has been neglected and depreciated throughout educational literature, from Plato, through Rousseau, to Dewey, and especially in Dewey. However, Egan argues that some of Dewey's propositions have been debased and misinterpreted. For example, when Dewey writes 'it is a cardinal precept of the newer school of education that the beginning of instruction shall be made with the experience learners already have', the term 'experience' has come to be seen 'largely in terms of the everyday practical world of children's lives' (Egan op. cit., p.190). The focus of educators' attention has been 'the mundane and practical world in which children live. What has been lost is the ability to see that world as the child sees it, transfigured by fantasy' (p.20).

Egan maintains that this is a serious loss; a prominent part of children's mental lives is fantasy, a wholesome and important activity, and yet research programmes into children's cognition and development have tended to ignore this element of fantasy. Egan suggests that Piaget, too, is partly to blame, in that his interest in the rational and logico-mathematical operations of young children blocked from view what Egan calls 'the wild energy' of their thinking.

> This early focus of Piaget's work discouraged other energetic and evident features of young children's thinking. Their romance and fantasy were considered merely contaminants to his attempt to chart the growth of what he calls intelligence. The child who cannot, on the one side, conserve liquid quantity may, on the other, lead a vivid intellectual life brimming with knights, dragons, witches and star warriors. It would be needlessly bold to prejudge which is more important to future intellectual growth. (p.23)

Egan goes on to recognise that many teachers do encourage fantasy, in spite of what major educational theorists say, but even these teachers have not, he believes, fully worked out the implications of children's fantasy for their curriculum and their teaching methods. Egan's *Primary Understanding* is an attempt to devise a whole primary curriculum and a range of teaching methods that would enable teachers to get closer to children's robust and dramatic imaginative lives. We might also choose to draw on Egan's position in our assessment practice, taking account of children's fantasy as we describe their thinking and their learning. The following observation is an illustration of this possibility.

> In a class of 35 four-year-olds, staffed by one teacher and two nursery nurses, a group of four children burst into the classroom from the outside area. They rushed up to the teacher: one of them, Shazia, had apparently fainted, and was being supported, pale and still, by the other three. A dramatic explanation was given: 'Shazia has been shot by a wolf!' The teacher reacted

calmly, asking only a few questions – 'What does she need? Did anyone see it happen?' Intense activity and discussion ensued; within moments four children arrived as an ambulance team, riding in an imaginary ambulance, in response to a phone call from one of the original group. Two other children, transformed into a doctor and a police officer, appeared in response to further phone calls. The doctor palpated Shazia's belly (as she lay on an improvised bed): 'I can feel the bullet wound. It's very serious.' Witnesses joined the play, pressing close to the police officer to give their version of the incident: 'I saw his bushy tail.' 'I saw his face.' The police officer wrote each contribution down on a sheet of paper on a clipboard (in 'imaginary' writing). One of the ambulance team was pessimistic: 'I tried that medicine and all the tablets Emily gave me and she still won't wake up. She's dead. For ever.' Another child agreed: 'Her heart's broken and she'll never wake up.' And a third: 'I felt her heart and it's broken.' Fortunately, at this point, Shazia revived and rejoined the play, which by now involved ten or twelve children, improvising and embellishing the continuing drama. Half an hour later, at the end of the session, the whole class came together to sit on the carpet and recall the main events of the morning. Shazia's narrow escape was heatedly discussed, and thought taken for the future. One child remarked: 'If the wolf comes this afternoon I think I'd better call the woodcutter.' Another child responded to this contribution by leaving the group to fetch the Yellow Pages. After a few minutes she told the class, 'His number's 202'. Further suggestions included 'We could call Robin Hood, because he's got arrows.' In the afternoon session I observed Shazia designing a 'Wanted' poster, which incorporated a vivid portrait of the wolf – 'His ears went like this...he was standing behind the tree...He was *really really* thin.'

What are we to make of this episode? Were these children simply 'playing', trying to avoid 'work' set them by the teacher? Is it that their fantasies are more important to them than the everyday world of the classroom? Egan sets himself just this problem, and puzzles over why children playing with smurfs, witches and dragons – and we may add, wolves carrying firearms – apparently find them more intellectually engaging and meaningful than the real world of the everyday. His conclusion is that this way of framing the question is based on an improper distinction. Smurfs and wolves may not be part of everyday reality, but what they represent *is* intensely real, since, in children's play, wolves and smurfs and dragons stand for

the unrelenting conflicts between the good and the bad, the big and the little, the brave and the cowardly, the oppressors and the oppressed...the embodiment of struggles between security and fear, love and hate. (p.25)

In Egan's view, Shazia and her friends were not, in their play, running away from the proper business of schooling, the acquisition of the basic skills. On the contrary, the curriculum they were forging for themselves in their fantasy play is close to the curriculum he advocates for all young children:

> Our early curriculum then, is to be made up of *important* content that is rich in meaning for children. Its meaning will derive from its being articulated on concepts they know from their experience – love/hate, fear/security, good/bad, courage/cowardice and so on – and our curriculum concern will be to get at what is of human importance to our social and cultural lives. (p.199)

What Egan writes about curriculum, we may extend to learning. Shazia's learning is distinguished by its intellectual excitement and emotional engagement. It is both playful and intensely serious. Learning in young children begins with the serious, the important, not the trivial (the names of the colours, or the properties of a rectangle). Learning to be literate is only serious and important to children when they themselves perceive its relevance and worthwhileness. Egan's curriculum of the imagination will, he argues, 'show children why literacy is worthwhile' in giving them access to a 'world of wonder, brutality, hope and fear that *really* can mirror and *really* expand their experience' (p.201).

So in the encounter between Shazia and the wolf, we can see how the curriculum of the imagination bears fruit in learning. These children have learned about different functions and different relationships within the social complex. Adult roles, they understand, are differentiated and specialised – doctor, police officer, ambulance driver. Adults group together to work in teams, supporting each other's functions. The spoken word, they have learned, can be translated into the written word (and used in evidence against the wolf). The written word can be translated back into speech (from the poster caption 'Beware! wolf in playground') and put to good use. These children have seen adults using their literacy in these ways, and have appropriated those acts for their own imaginative purposes. They have learned that reference books and specialist services are available to the literate; they have learned to represent the world of experience in a variety of ways – on paper, in speech, in role play. Perhaps more important is their learning in the moral and emotional domain: they have learned that dangers can be survived, that help and succour can be given to the wounded and distressed. They have learned to take thought for the vulnerable and to sustain and care for one another. Their fantasy play is both a rehearsal and a celebration of this learning.

When Egan watches children playing with smurfs, he sees them engaged by the unrelenting conflict between binary opposites; when Athey looks at children's mark-making, she sees patterns of vertical and circular schemas. When Lowenfeld observes children's play, using the 'world cabinet', she distinguishes three different emotional functions served by miniature world play. These three authors, who see the world so differently, are powerful illustrations of the human desire to make sense of our experiences, by creating patterns and structures of meaning. When teachers assess children's learning in schools and classrooms, we too draw on internalised patterns of understanding, seeing perhaps, as confirmed Piagetians, signs of specific cognitive stages, or, like Michael Armstrong 'knowledge as appropriation'. We make sense of children's learning by setting what we see and hear up against our working models of children's learning, and noting the areas of congruence and disparity.

But not all forms of assessment are based on clear and coherent models of children's learning; and where there is no underlying understanding of the process of learning the outcomes of the assessment will be relatively trivial, telling us little of any purpose. Ted Hughes calls stories 'little factories of understanding'; if we are to understand children's learning, we must tell ourselves stories about that learning, stories that build on what we already know and that explore what we are coming to realise. On the other hand, if we have no narrative or explanatory framework for observations of children's learning, there will be no stories to tell, and no 'factories of understanding'. We will be left with the unvarnished facts, or a string of numbers, from which we will learn nothing.

Until 1997, when baseline assessment on entry to the reception class became a statutory requirement, teachers were free to design their own entry assessment schedules. Throughout the 1990s, until new requirements came into force, I set myself the curious task of collecting examples of these, some of which are, as we shall see, grossly inappropriate in a whole variety of ways. I was shown one such schedule in its trialling version, which was to be used during the children's first term in the reception class. It comprised a list of attributes and areas of development, ranging from toilet-training to creativity and cooperation, with a six-point rating scale for each attribute (for example: Interest 1 2 3 4 5 6; Enthusiasm 1 2 3 4 5 6; Concentration 1 2 3 4 5 6). Teachers were expected to assign a number between one and six to each child for each item on the schedule: no written criteria or descriptions were given. Teachers are here being invited to reduce the complexity of each pupil's individuality, and the richness of each child's learning, to a meaningless numerical scale. There is no underpinning representation of the process of learning; as a result there is no possibility of using the schedule to understand a child's learning.

I would like to think that, by the end of the trialling period, the reception class teachers using this schedule realised that it would do little to enhance their understanding, or their pupils' learning. However a paper by Barry Bensley and Stuart Kilby (1992) reports the trialling and subsequent adoption of a similar procedure in two Lincolnshire primary schools. The baseline profile described in their paper was designed and developed by the staff of these two schools, with perfectly honourable intentions. But the end-products, particularly in the three-point scale format preferred by one school, give me grave cause for concern. Children are to be rated, for example, on

Sociability	(a) loner/avoids others	(1)
	(b) normal	(2)
	(c) friendly/enjoys/seeks company	(3)
Leadership	(a) seldom leads	(1)
	(b) sometimes leads	(2)
	(c) usually leads	(3)
Temperament	(a) irritable/moody	(1)
	(b) balanced	(2)
	(c) happy/calm, even-tempered	(3)

Bensley and Kilby (1992) pp.42-3

What can such categories, and judgements in these categories, possibly tell us about children's learning? They tell us a good deal about teachers, certainly; we can see that these teachers clearly, if implicitly, value gregarious, even-tempered four-year-olds, who show leadership qualities. But the schedule certainly cannot support teachers who would like to understand how their pupils are learning to behave in the ways that are seen as more or less appropriate. The categories are not rooted in a principled understanding of children's learning, and show no evidence of a desire to understand the processes by which children learn.

The categories in the cognitive domain are equally unlikely to help teachers understand children's learning. For example:

Number	(a) no knowledge	(1)
	(b) numbers 'parrot fashion'	(2)
	(c) counts objects to 10	(3)
	(d) knowledge of ordinal number	(4)
	(e) competent handling of numbers more than 10	(5)
Colour	(a) no knowledge	(1)
	(b) limited knowledge	(2)
	(c) knowledge of primary colours	(3)
	(d) knowledge of a range of colours	(4)
	(e) knowledge of colour mixing/ rainbow/spectrum	(5)

Alphabet/reading skills

	(a) no knowledge	(1)
	(b) knowledge of letters out of sequence	(2)
	(c) phonetic alphabet 'parrot fashion'	(3)
	(d) recognises isolated letters	(4)
	(e) reads simple words	(5)

These categories fly in the face of everything we know about the learning of young children in the four or five years before they start school. It is simply impossible to imagine a child without very severe disabilities who has 'no knowledge' of number or colour. The only conception of learning that can be discerned here is one of the child as 'empty vessel', taken to such an extreme that it assumes some children arrive at school still 'empty', and waiting to be filled (with colour names and numbers to 10). Children have the right to be taken more seriously and respectfully as learners; an assessment process such as this will do little, if anything, to advance and support their learning.

It remains to be seen what the effects will be of the new statutory requirement, introduced in the academic year 2002–3, to use the Foundation Stage Profile, an instrument composed of 13 scales, each of nine levels, to assess the learning of four- and five-year-olds at the end of the Foundation Stage.

Richer and more rewarding assessments than those described above can only be made when the process is driven by a desire to make sense of learning in action. For example, the educators in a High/Scope nursery or kindergarten keep detailed record sheets for each child collected under the headings of the nine 'Key Experiences' that are at the heart of the 'cognitively-oriented curriculum', the hallmark of the High/Scope programme. This curriculum has been developed on Piagetian principles with the concept of 'active learning' at its core (Hohmann *et al.* 1979). The curriculum is conceptualised not in terms of future events, aims and objectives that might be realised, or targets that might be achieved, but in the present tense, the here and now of each child's experience. The key experiences shown on the record sheet represent nine areas of learning that together constitute the young child's developing cognitive and affective powers. Every child's learning can, it is claimed, be fostered by the provision of resources and activities in each of these nine areas of experience.

The High/Scope classroom or nursery is laid out in clearly defined areas, each of which is well provided with materials selected with 'key experiences' in mind. The educators' role during the 'work time' period of each High/Scope session is to observe and support children's free and unconstrained involvement in these activities, using the key experiences as a framework for recognising significant evidence of each child's learning. They are not concerned with monitoring a child's progress along a preordained line from one to six, or from one to three; they are alert to richer possibilities.

On this particular example of the High/Scope record keeping system (figure 5.1), we can see how the educators have contributed anecdotal evidence of Jinnie's learning under the headings of the key experiences. They are not constrained in their observations by the subject areas of the National Curriculum, nor by the six areas of learning set out in the *Curriculum Guidance for the Foundation Stage* (QCA 2000), but are free to see the whole variety of ways in which Jinnie is learning to represent her experiences to herself, to make sense of the world, its patterns and its generalities, and to communicate her understanding to others. These educators are recording learning in action, rather than performance on a teacher-designed task, or achievement against a preconceived standard. They are interested in seeing, and recording, how Jinnie puts her learning to use, in her play, and in her relations with others. She has learned, for example, to distinguish construction and mosaic blocks by shape and colour; but her educators do not simply record her knowledge of these attributes. They note that she uses the knowledge in a variety of ways: to make comparisons, connections and patterns.

These detailed anecdotal records of children's active learning are used in a number of different ways. First and foremost, they constitute a framework for coming to understand each child's learning; but they serve

Pam Lafferty 1992
High/Scope Endorsed Trainer
Child's Name: Jinnie

HIGH/SCOPE EDUCATIONAL RESEARCH FOUNDATION
Child Anecdotal Record (C.A.R.) (Condensed Sheet)
Birth Date: 16/9/86

(Remember to date all entries)

LANGUAGE	REPRESENTATION	CLASSIFICATION	SERIATION	NUMBER
3/9/91:- Said "Go Jo Flo Blow – they sound the same"	2/9/91:- Playing with the plastic animals and making the appropriate sounds for horse, cow and pig	7/10/91:- Stacked up the brick piles into separate colours – red, blue, green and yellow	11/9/91:- Remarked that the new fruit bowl was heavier than the old one	18/9/91:- Said "a few means not a lot"
5/9/91:- J was sitting looking at a story book and telling a story from the pictures	24/9/91:- Nailed two pieces of wood together in a cross shape and said it was an aeroplane	12/11/91:- Said "My boots are red and yours are blue"	27/9/1 :- Comparing brushes said "Mine's larger and fatter than yours"	18/11/91:- Cut dough into four pieces and said "I've made four cakes"
3/12/91:- Whilst sitting on a toilet seat said that she was sitting on an "O"	8/11/91:- Drew a robin with minute details and coloured it in accurately with red	6/12/91:- Looking at the words "Jack" and "Jake" said that the two names were nearly the same, just a little bit different	17/12/91:- Chose a number of triangle shapes from the box and arranged them in order of increasing size	6/12/91:- Counted 7 penguins accurately on a friend's jumper

SPACE	TIME	MOVEMENT	SOCIAL/EMOTIONAL
23/9/91:- Talking to another child about a hat said "You need the ribbons at the back, not the side"	8/10/91:- When the tidy-up sound was made, J began to put things from the floor into their correct baskets	12/9/91:- Was walking around the nursery on all fours swaying from side to side being an elephant	4/10/91:- On coming from the garden to the inside, stopped in the doorway to leave muddy wellingtons outside
30/10/91:- Folded a piece of card in half to form a tunnel and then walked plastic animals through it and used the word "through"	28/11/91:- Said "If you want to find me later, I'll be in the Book Area"	21/10/91:- For the first time managed to use her legs to make the swing go	29/10/91:- Took a friend into the bathroom and used a cotton wool ball to wipe mud from his knee
9/12/91:- Noticed a triangular patch of light on the carpet and found a triangle shape to fit exactly on top of it	29/11/91:- Looked at a list of names on the board and said "It will be Matthew's turn to open the door tomorrow"	13/12/91:- Used scissors to cut a "fringe" along the side of a piece of paper	12/12/91:- At snack time said "G only likes bananas – please save one for him"

Figure 5.1 High/Scope Child Anecdotal Record

other purposes too. They are used for planning provision that supports and extends that learning, as the basis for staff discussion about each child, and as the starting point for talking to parents about their children's learning.

In this chapter I have described a number of different approaches to that part of the assessment process in which educators try to understand children's learning. What these approaches have in common is a focus on learning as it happens, on the process, rather than on the performance, or the products of the learner. Athey, Paley, Egan, and the High-Scope educators are all concerned with the internal, dynamic thinking processes that they discern as they look at children and try to understand them. The products of children's learning – their dramas, or block constructions, or dictated stories – contribute to the process of assessment only in so far as they provide concrete evidence of the abstract, mental processes that are these authors' main concern.

The daily assessment practice of primary teachers in crowded classrooms is much less likely to sustain this emphasis on process rather than on product. In classrooms, children's thinking is tantalisingly transient, fast-moving, elusive; busy teachers understandably turn to products as evidence of teaching and learning. Inevitably, once children have learned to write independently, and to complete written mathematical tasks on their own, there is a tendency to regard written work as good enough evidence of what children are learning. However the judgements that can be made on the basis of this kind of evidence are unlikely to be as worthwhile – for teacher or for pupil – as judgements that draw on other sources of evidence as well. Teachers who investigate, for example, children's mathematical thinking, by listening to their pupils' thinking aloud, explaining their calculations, very quickly discover that apparent errors in the written record of those calculations are often the result of systematic mathematical reasoning, which has been mistakenly applied. Patrick Easen describes a number of children who appear to be experiencing difficulty in learning mathematics. Dean, for example, aged 12, writes on his paper:

$$\begin{array}{r} 6591 \\ -\ 2697 \\ \hline 4106 \end{array}$$

'Wrong yes, but a freak answer no … Dean always subtracts the smaller number from the larger number. He has an intuitive sense that this is what subtraction is all about.' (Easen 1987, p.28.)

Developing this point, Easen describes Paul (aged nine) who had trouble with multiplication. Asked to multiply 148 by six he gave the answer as 632. In asking him to talk through the calculation his teacher learned, first, that he worked from left to right, and secondly that he could multiply (he knew the products of 6 x 4 and 6 x 8), but thirdly that his system for representing intermediate calculations sometimes led him astray. In his final calculation he adds 8 (from the 48 derived from 6 x 8) to 24 (from 6 x 4) to achieve the 32 of his written answer. With spoken numbers Paul is operating well; with written numbers his invented, systematic procedures let him down. But his errors are not random. No more are the errors of Andrew, a seven-year-old boy who was the subject of a case-study by Maggie Ellis, an Advanced Diploma student at the Cambridge Institute of Education. In a tape recorded session, she asked him to complete the written sum:

$$11+$$
$$7$$

He wrote 29 as the answer. She asked: 'Would you tell me how you did it?'

A: I just mm – well I got to 1 or 1 um, 1 um, add them two together and that makes 2. I put 2 down there, counted another 7, then, then add it to 2 – 9.

His difficulties with subtraction (on the same sheet he has written:

$$46 -$$
$$21$$
$$\overline{}$$
$$10)$$

are much harder to explain. But after some time using Lego bricks, one possible explanation emerged.

To work out 13 – 5 he set out his Lego bricks in two rows like this:

□ □ □ □ □ □ □ □ □
□ □ □ □

A: Then which one shall I take away, that one or that one? (points to each row in turn).
M: What do you mean, Andrew?
A: Take away, take away 5.
M: Yes, take away 5.
A: Well, this one 'cos this is the longest (points to top row of bricks).
M: How many are left?

A: (He writes 8 as the answer.)

It seems as though the concept of subtraction, for him, involves the concept of comparative length, and that the longest item in a display is the one that must be operated on. This reasoning may possibly explain his difficulty with 8 – 8.

M: Can you tell me what you're doing please?
A: Um, I'm just counting to 8 (sighs) then I got add.
M: Take away, haven't you?
A: Cor!
M: 8 – 8 isn't it?
M: Can you reach it? (points to a Lego brick).
A: Cor!
M: 8 – 8 isn't it?
A: 8–8, Yeah, 1, 2, 3. Right I got another 8.
M: It's take away though isn't it? Take away 8.
A: Oh! You can't take away 8!
M: Can't you?
A: No. 1, 2, 3, 4, 5, 6, 7, 8.
M: But there are 8 there.
A: Take away 8.
M: Take away 8. Take them away. (He writes 0.) That's right!
A: Oh no! Look at the time!

Further observations, careful listening, and respect for the child's thinking, would tell us more about Andrew and the thousands of other children who willingly embark on the trivial mathematical tasks they are set in school with a systematic determination that, unfortunately, so often serves them false.

'Knowledge is always from a position' – if, in assessing, we position ourselves alongside the learner in the act of learning, we will certainly understand what is happening better than if we concentrate our attention on the end-point of the learning process – the written page, the completed task, the problem solved, the right answer slotted into the space provided.

In the summer term of 1991, teachers of six- and seven-year-olds in England and Wales carried out the first national trial of the new statutory Standard Assessment Tasks, designed to measure children's attainments at the end of Key Stage One. One of these tasks was designed to assess children's learning in the area of 'exploration of science'. The instructions given to teachers for the presentation of this task were very precise and detailed, and included examples of the questions to be asked of the pupils. Pupils were required to predict which of four selected objects would sink or float when placed in water, to test their predictions and then to generalise from their findings.

My own observations of this task, carried out in five different classrooms, showed that when the teachers' questions focused on the children's recorded predictions, and the outcome of their testing of the four objects, the evidence of attainment was unambiguous. Questions such as 'What happened?' 'How many objects floated?' and 'What have you found out?' stimulated responses that satisfied the criteria listed in the Teachers' Handbook. But questions that opened up the children's thinking were very much more revealing, and more challenging, for the teacher. When the children were asked, before they tested their objects, why they thought they would float or sink, their answers revealed great disparities in their understanding. I did not hear any child reply that floating or sinking was linked with the colour or texture of the object, as the Teachers' Handbook suggested they might, but the responses I heard included numerous references to the weight of the objects: 'This'll float because it's light,' 'Sink, because it's heavy.' Some of these predictions were not in fact 'correct', but scored at level 3 because they 'involved reasoning'.

Far more interesting were the responses of the children who seemed to be on the verge of expressing an understanding of the concept of density. For example: 'It's the stuff,' said one child, 'the stuff it's made of.' The teacher asked, gently, 'What do you mean by "stuff"?' but the child did not reply. The teacher did not continue this part of the conversation, because the child had already, in her judgement, achieved level 3 on this part of the task. The performance was already over, the level of attainment already logged in the Teacher Record Book. But the quality of the child's thinking and the extent of her learning remained unexplored.

I have discussed elsewhere (Drummond 1991) the crudity of this particular task for examining scientific thinking; here I am making a different point. If we want to assess children's learning, it is their learning we must attend to, and not their ability to answer a question 'correctly', according to tight, pre-defined criteria. Children in their third year of schooling, like the six- and seven-year-olds whom I observed completing the floating and sinking task, have had the opportunity to learn a good deal about how to answer a teacher's questions. They are skilled at using all the clues available from the teacher's face, body and tone of voice, and they are amazingly quick to change their minds if the teacher indicates, however unwittingly, that their first response was incorrect. We have no chance of learning about children's learning if our questions focus on their performance in a highly predictable question and answer routine. We must not underestimate children's ability to divine the required answer without any mental activity corresponding to the learning we believe we are assessing.

Equally, we must not pretend to ourselves that all children are prepared to play the question and answer game according to the teacher's rules. There are plenty of free-thinking young children willing and able to sabotage our careful interrogations with fantastic interruptions of their own. My observation of another Science Standard Assessment Task in the trialling period in 1991, which was designed to assess knowledge and understanding of life processes, provides an illustration. A group of children had been asked to record, by drawing, 'the main stages of their life-cycle,' showing themselves at the present time, at babyhood, as they grow up, and having grown old.

> Sheila is seven years and two months and has drawn three very schematic human figures, and has labelled them one, four and seven. As she draws and colours, she keeps up a cheerful running commentary. 'Now I've got to do my eyes. My eyes are brown. Very delicate to colour isn't it?' (writes) 'Look that makes a hundred and forty-seven doesn't it? I'm four there. Now I'm colouring this one. When I was at playgroup, I used not to let the kids go down the slide. Now I'm going to do when I'm big...' (draws figure with a much larger head) '...*That's* how big I'm going to be...I'm *bald* there! How old will I be when I grow up? I'm going to be 30.' I asked Sheila if she knew anyone bald. 'Yes, my Donny, he's got a little bald hair...Now I'm going to be 80!' (starts a new figure). 'My Donny is 82, nearly 83.' So far, so normal. But at this point, as far as the teacher was concerned, the assessment process went off the rails. Sheila began to embellish her drawing: 'Here's my ears! I'm going to be a rabbit when I grow up!!' (excited giggling to herself). 'There's my big legs and my shorter arms. I've been to Disneyland...Look when I'm 80...This is my big tummy. My brother's ten. He's at a middle school. I'm going to be eight on Feb 7th.' (Adds feet, prompted by the teacher, to the matchstick legs. Pauses, and draws four feet on each leg.)

What can we say about this child's learning? We might remember Vivian Paley's class, discussing the robber and the beans, and note that while Sheila has learned a good deal about youth and age, growth and maturity, in the context of her own immediate social world, she has not yet learned to treat these topics in an entirely adult way, excluding play and fantasy. She has, in Paley's words, 'become aware of the thinking required by the adult world' but is not yet 'committed to its burden of rigid consistency' (Paley 1981, p.81). We might also consider the possibility that Sheila is using the words 'going to be' in two different senses at one and the same time. Like any good surrealist, she is not alarmed by ambiguity and contradiction, and so is quite prepared to use the same form of words to refer to biological ageing ('I'm going to be eight on Feb 7th') and to her own imaginative inner world ('I'm going to be a rabbit'). What a child is 'going to be' is not, in the eyes of the child, simply a matter of physical maturation, but also a question for the imaginative will. (Today, perhaps, or tomorrow, I'm going to be a rabbit, a pirate, a robber, a princess. Or perhaps I'm going to be shot by a wolf.)

But Sheila's teacher had been instructed to attend to her scientific, not her fantastic, thinking, and she was, understandably, uncertain how to record this child's level of achievement. The Teacher's Handbook she was following did not allow for rabbit's ears or four pairs of feet. The Handbook assumed that children's responses would either meet the specified criteria or not. There is no place, in this assessment task, for the flight of fantasy with which Sheila enlivened an unpromising exercise, a task which was, as we have seen, well within her understanding. Sheila's non-conformity illustrates the folly of setting our sights too narrowly. We cannot control the openness with which children may respond to the deliberately closed questions we set them.

These examples from the trialling period of the first statutory assessments of six- and seven-year-olds demonstrate the difficulties, and the dangers, of product-focused assessment. The dangers of the whole range of statutory assessment procedures, as defined in the 1988 Education Reform Act, were promptly and meticulously defined by Blenkin and Kelly (1992). Time has passed, and many primary teachers have come to see Key Stage One and Key Stage Two SATs as taken-for-granted events in the school year: stressful, often and sometimes superfluous, but an inescapable fact of life. This familiarity, however, should not blind us to the weaknesses of the whole SATs approach. We can, if we choose, hold on to our earlier conviction that assessment that focuses on the learner, and the process of learning, rather than on the product or the performance, while it may not satisfy the demands of the QCA for precision and accountability, will pay other dividends. The judgements that teachers make in assessing learning are a vital expression of their responsibilities to the learners in their care. To restrict the scope of such judgements is to restrict the possibility of acting with full responsibility. Teachers have the right to make informed judgements about learning and about learners. They therefore have a responsibility to construct and develop frameworks of understanding within which to make these judgements. Pupils have the right to expect their teachers to act wisely, in the pupils' interests, as a result of the judgements they make. Assessment practices that do not recognise these rights and responsibilities are not in the interests of pupils. In effective assessment, the teacher's ability to see and understand, the teacher's acts of making meaning, are all at the service of the pupils, not of the national bodies to whom primary teachers are now held accountable.

CHAPTER 6

Understanding Ourselves

In the preceding chapters I have discussed some of the issues involved in collecting and selecting evidence of children's learning and considered some ways in which teachers can make sense of that evidence. But before the act of assessment even begins, other factors are at work; these must now be considered in their turn.

When we look at children and try to understand their learning, we do so supposing, for the most part, that we see what anyone would see. But this is an illusion. What we see is deeply affected by what we bring to the act of seeing. The radiologist described by Jane Abercrombie (quoted in the last chapter) brings to each X-ray he examines his knowledge of radiographs, throats – and buttons. His professional training, his experience, his expertise, help him to see what he needs to see. But when we look at learning, we bring to the task more than a professional training or an authoritative understanding of some aspect of learning; we bring the whole of ourselves. Underlying the very act of seeing for each of us is a whole set of beliefs and values about the world and the people in it, values that we rarely make explicit, still less rarely explore and critically examine.

Much of the time in our working lives there seems to be no need to examine these values; we tend to assume that our colleagues share the same value base, and, often, this assumption is justified. But sometimes we discover that one and the same incident has elicited very different responses from a number of people. These differences could be explained by postulating errors of judgement, bad understanding, misinterpretations by all but one of those involved. Such is the power of egocentric thought, even in mature adults, that this explanation does have certain attractions. It is sometimes tempting to say to oneself, as it were: 'If all these people disagree with me, it is because my judgement remains unclouded while theirs is partial, confused, incomplete.' But a more parsimonious explanation would refer to the hidden value systems of all those who disagree.

For example, when an adult sees a baby sucking a dummy, a variety of responses is possible. When I show a photograph of a baby sucking a dummy to a group of early years educators and ask them what they see, typical responses include:

- a baby who is being comforted
- a baby who is neglected
- a baby who is spoiled
- a baby whose language development may be impaired

None of these interpretations is necessarily right or wrong; all of these judgements tell us something about the speakers' values, and give us some insight into their expectations of very young children.

During the development and trialling of the multi-disciplinary pack *Making Assessment Work* (Drummond *et al.* 1992) the authors showed photographs of children in a variety of circumstances to groups of early years educators in order to stimulate an enquiry into the value systems that inform our impressionistic judgements. The photograph shown below (figure 6.1) evoked strongly differentiated responses. For example, two of my own colleagues commented variously:

Figure 6.1

'What a sad child, doomed to a life of that kind…'
'Lucky little devil.'

Are these errors of judgement? Gross misunderstandings? Blind prejudices? Or are these two adults simply expressing, in a roundabout way, some of their dearly held beliefs about what young children should do and be, and about what the young child's relationship with the material world should or should not involve? All of us have beliefs and values of this kind, which have been forming since our childhood, when we too were little children, and adults spoiled or neglected or comforted us. For all that we rarely express our values, we hold them very dear. For all that we rely on our values in making sense of the world, we rarely question their naturalness or inevitability.

In the development of *Making Assessment Work*, the educators who were shown the photographs were asked to respond quickly – a gut response – without striving for a more professional impartiality. In discussion, many educators reported how they could, and would, and did, override their gut response when working in a professional context. But they also conceded that the gut response, which they had been encouraged to express in this exercise, was still a part of their thinking, even if it was masked, or overlaid by a more professionally 'correct' interpretation.

In another section of *Making Assessment Work*, educators are asked to read a passage from *Pre-School in Three Cultures* (Tobin, Wu & Davidson 1989) which describes a four-year-old boy, Hiroki, in a Japanese kindergarten. Hiroki started his school day with a flourish by pulling out his penis from under his shorts and waving it around during the morning welcome song. The workbook session that followed was enlivened by Hiroki's constant running commentary, as he worked quickly and accurately on his task of colouring-in. He answered all the teacher's questions and made many spontaneous contributions of his own; he entertained his class-mates with songs, favourite cartoon themes, dancing and more penis jokes. When he came close to other children, he punched, poked and wrestled with them, even leaving his post as monitor at the organ during the pre-lunch song to wrestle with a child nearby. After his dinner he enjoyed roughhouse play with a small group of boys and disrupted a card game by throwing the cards over the balcony to the ground below. As fast as the cards were collected, Hiroki sent them flying again, and in the midst of this mêlée deliberately stepped on a younger boy's hand, making him cry. At clean-up time,

Hiroki disrupted the group by rolling on the cards and putting them in his mouth. And so the day goes on until:

> during the free playground period that ends the day, Hiroki played gently with a toddler and more roughly with some of the older boys. He was finally picked up shortly before 6.00 by his father, making him one of the last children to go home.
>
> Tobin *et al.* (1989) p.21

I have led discussions of this case-study material in a variety of groups, with a large number of teachers and other educators. What distinguishes these discussions are the passion and fervour of those involved, not their logical rigour or analytical excellence. Sympathies run very high, sometimes for Hiroki, sometimes for his teacher, sometimes for the horrified American educators whose response to the videotape made in Hiroki's kindergarten is also documented in the extract under discussion. Even the authors, filming and observing, record their emotional response to what they saw; there were moments 'when it was all we could do not to drop our camera, and our posture of scholarly neutrality and tell Hiroki to cut it out' (p.23).

There is clearly more at stake here than a choice of strategies for working with a particular child in a far-away kindergarten. What is at issue is the whole set of values that surrounds the Japanese concept of 'Kodomorashii kodomo', a child-like child. Tobin, Wu and Davidson record Japanese, Chinese and American educators' views of this concept, which goes far beyond individual characteristics, aspects of personality, or typical behaviours. These authors show clearly how the whole pre-school curriculum in the three cultures represented in their book is deeply imbued with taken-for-granted understandings of what young children in each culture should do and learn and be. For example, the Japanese attitude to fighting and violence seems very unfamiliar to Western educators. The director of Hiroki's pre-school, Yoshizawa-sensei, explains:

> If there were no fights among four-year-old children, that would be a real problem. We don't encourage children to fight, but children need to fight when they are young if they are to develop into complete human beings... Ten or fifteen years ago...the prevailing trend in pre-school education and in child-rearing became too sweet...The children were pampered in the wrong way; their school world became too safe, too calm. These children were never given the chance to fight. When children are pre-school age, they naturally fight if given the chance, and it is by fighting and experiencing

what it feels like to hit someone and hurt them, and to be hit and be hurt, that they learn to control this urge to fight, that they learn the dangers of fighting and get it out of their system. (p.33)

The authors report that most Japanese educators with whom they discussed this issue agreed that:

fighting is natural and has a place in the informal pre-school curriculum. For example, Assistant Principal Kumagai of Senzan Yochien told us 'as the year progresses we put fewer and fewer toys out during free play time, to give children additional opportunities to learn to share and to deal with the conflicts which arise'. (p.33)

On a less controversial issue, the place of spoken language in the learning of young children, there are substantial differences in approach across the three cultures:

In China, the emphasis in language development is on enunciation, diction, memorization, and self-confidence in speaking and performing. Chinese children learn in pre-school to recite stories and inspirational moral tales and to sing and dance both alone and in groups. American and Japanese visitors to Chinese pre-schools are invariably impressed by the self-possession and command of language of Chinese children who flawlessly deliver long, rehearsed speeches and belt out multiversed songs.

Language in Japan, both in and out of pre-schools, is divided into formal and informal systems of discourse. Children in pre-schools are allowed to speak freely, loudly, even vulgarly to each other during much of the day. But this unrestrained use of language alternates with periods of polite, formal, teacher-directed group recitation of expressions of greeting, thanks, blessing, and farewell. Language in Japan – at least the kind of language teachers teach children – is viewed less as a tool for self-expression than as a medium for expressing group solidarity and shared social purpose. Americans, in contrast, view words as the key to promoting individuality, autonomy, problem solving, friendship, and cognitive development in children. In American pre-schools children are taught the rules and conventions of self expression and free speech.

Tobin *et al.* (1989) pp. 189–90

What Tobin, Wu and Davidson are so vividly illustrating here is the value-infestation of the pre-school curriculum. And if the curriculum is infested with values, so too must be those who plan, implement and evaluate it. These conclusions are not confined to pre-school contexts. Everyone who works with children is as value-infested as Hiroki's teachers, and their critics. Understanding children implies understanding ourselves. If we want to increase our understanding of children's learning, we will have to take into account the connection, however deeply buried it may be, between the people we are and the judgements we make.

Madeleine Grumet, the American feminist curriculum theorist, puts the case even more strongly; she emphasises the closeness of the connection between the people we are and the curriculum we teach. In her memorable phrase: 'we are the curriculum' (1981). Fictional stereotypes of teachers endorse Grumet's argument. Mr Gradgrind *is* the curriculum, in Grumet's phrase, for Sissy Jupe and Bitzer in Dickens' *Hard Times*. The novel opens with his famous declaration:

> 'Now, what I want is, Facts. Teach these boys and girls nothing but Facts. Facts alone are wanted in life. Plant nothing else, and root out everything else. You can only form the minds of reasoning animals upon Facts: nothing else will ever be of any service to them.'

The identity between person and curriculum is so close that the man's very name, Gradgrind, has become synonymous with a knowledge-heavy, assessment-centred curriculum, and with the 'empty vessel' theory of children's learning. In Gradgrind's school, the master surveys 'the inclined plane of little vessels then and there arranged in order, ready to have imperial gallons of facts poured into them until they were full to the brim.' Mr Gradgrind's own children are part of the system too.

> There were five young Gradgrinds and they…had been lectured at from their tenderest years; coursed like little hares. Almost as soon as they could run alone, they had been made to run to the lecture-room. The first object with which they had an association, or of which they had a remembrance, was a large blackboard with a dry Ogre chalking ghastly white figures on it.
>
> Not that they knew, by name or nature, anything about an Ogre. Fact forbid! I only use the word to express a monster in a lecturing castle, with Heaven knows how many heads manipulated into one, taking childhood captive, and dragging it into gloomy statistical dens by the hair.
>
> No little Gradgrind had ever seen a face in the moon; it was up in the moon before it could speak distinctly. No little Gradgrind had ever learnt the silly jingle, Twinkle, twinkle, little star; how I wonder what you are! No little Gradgrind had ever known wonder on the subject, each little Gradgrind having at five years old dissected the Great Bear like a Professor Owen, and driven Charles's Wain like a locomotive engine-driver. No Gradgrind had ever associated a cow in a field with that famous cow with the crumpled horn who tossed the dog who worried the cat who killed the rat who ate the malt, or with that yet more famous cow who swallowed Tom Thumb: it had

never heard of those celebrities, and had only been introduced to a cow as a graminivorous ruminating quadruped with several stomachs.

When Mr Gradgrind finds his two eldest children, Louisa and Tom, peeping in at the back of the circus tent, his lofty astonishment is complete: 'I should as soon have expected to find my children reading poetry.' The child-like Gradgrind knows nothing of circuses or poetry. And yet,

> Mr Gradgrind, though hard enough, was by no means so rough a man as Mr Bounderby. His character was not unkind, all things considered; it might have been a very kind one indeed, if he had only made some round mistake in the arithmetic that balanced it, years ago.

He is not a malevolent teacher, or an unloving father, but his value system has no place for anything but its own furniture of facts: 'Stick to Facts!'

Mr Gradgrind is not the only educator in Dickens; there are subjects for admiration as well as for satire. David Copperfield attended Dr Strong's:

> Doctor Strong's was an excellent school; as different from Mr Creakle's as good is from evil. It was very gravely and decorously ordered, and on a sound system; with an appeal, in everything, to the honour and good faith of the boys, and an avowed intention to rely on their possession of those qualities unless they proved themselves unworthy of it, which worked wonders. We all felt that we had a part in the management of the place, and in sustaining its character and dignity. Hence, we soon became warmly attached to it – I am sure I did for one, and I never knew, in all my time, of any other boy being otherwise – and learnt with a good will, desiring to do it credit. We had noble games out of hours, and plenty of liberty; but even then, as I remember, we were well spoken of in the town, and rarely did any disgrace, by our appearance or manner, to the reputation of Doctor Strong and Doctor Strong's boys.

This description starts with the person; through the person of Dr Strong we are shown the curriculum of his school. It is the man's values, rather than his pedagogy or his syllabus, that we are invited to admire. Meanwhile, at Blimber's Academy, poor little Paul Dombey is on the receiving end of a different set of values: the ancient and classical.

> They comprised a little English, and a deal of Latin – names of things, declensions of articles and substantives, exercises thereon, and preliminary rules – a trifle of orthography, a glance at ancient history, a wink or two at

modern ditto, a few tables, two or three weights and measures, and a little general information. When poor Paul had spelt out number two, he found he had no idea of number one; fragments whereof afterwards obtruded themselves into number three, which slided into number four, which grafted itself on to number two. So that whether twenty Romuluses made a Remus, or hic haec was troy weight, or a verb always agreed with an ancient Briton, or three times four was Taurus a bull, were open questions with him.

'Oh, Dombey, Dombey!' said Miss Blimber, 'this is very shocking. '

Miss Blimber expressed her opinions on the subject of Paul's uninstructed state with a gloomy delight, as if she had expected this result, and were glad to find that they must be in constant communication. Paul withdrew with the top task, as he was told, and laboured away at it, down below; sometimes remembering every word of it, and sometimes forgetting it all, and everything else besides: until at last he ventured up stairs again to repeat the lesson, when it was nearly all driven out of his head before he began, by Miss Blimber's shutting up the book, and saying, 'Go on, Dombey!'

It was hard work, resuming his studies, soon after dinner; and he felt giddy and confused and drowsy and dull. But all the other young gentlemen had similar sensations, and were obliged to resume their studies too, if there were any comfort in that. It was a wonder that the great clock in the hall never said, 'Gentlemen, we will now resume our studies,' for that phrase was often enough repeated in its neighbourhood. The studies went round like a mighty wheel, and the young gentlemen were always stretched upon it.

That wheel is of human design, and there are human hands turning it; the energy that propels it is derived from human values.

In order to understand learning, we build theories about learning; we try to delineate the characteristic features of our pupils' learning in a way that helps us to make sense of the bewildering complexities of the classroom. I am arguing here that we need to do more: that we need to think about teachers as well as learners. To understand learning, we must also try to understand teaching; to understand a particular child's learning, we must try to understand that child's teacher; we must try to understand ourselves, the people we are, and the values we hold most precious.

Most primary teachers of my generation, and many of those who started teaching in the 1970s and early 1980s, would include in a description of themselves, the people they are, some reference to the Plowden Report (CACE 1967). Suddenly revived from the history books in the winter and spring of 1991–2, when a fierce debate about primary education raged in the popular (and the professional) press, the Plowden Report appeared to have created two distinct types, indeed stereotypes, of 'Plowden teachers'. They were portrayed either as shining examples of excellence, or as the epitome of all imaginable weaknesses. At both extremes, every single primary teacher was seen as having been shaped, in one way or another, by the recommendations of the Report. Perhaps the most serious allegation, in terms of teachers' professionalism, was made, albeit in the conditional tense, by Alexander, Rose and Woodhead (1992):

> If Plowdenism has become an ideology, to which thousands of teachers have unthinkingly subscribed, it is necessary to ask why... teachers have stopped thinking for themselves, and have apparently become so amenable to indoctrination. (para 22)

This possibility – which, the authors emphasise, is only a possibility ('The word "if" is important') – seems to me to fly in the face of what we know about human beings and their capacity to hold on to the cherished values that lie at each person's core.

Kenneth Clarke, at that time Secretary of State for Education and Science, expressed his opinion in even more dramatic terms; the Plowden Report, according to Clarke:

> was no doubt well-intentioned. But in fact it has led to an all-embracing and dogmatic orthodoxy about how children should be taught... this orthodoxy threatens to stifle independent thought based on the realities of the classroom.
>
> DES (1991b) para 10

There are, we may note, no 'if's or conditional verbs in this passage. Nevertheless, neither of these commentaries on 'Plowdenism' seems to me to take account of the proposition I am advancing here. Neither allows for the centrality of a system of values, in working order, in the lives and minds of teachers. If we were to accept that the Plowden Report affected classroom practice, in specific, recognisable ways (and this is by no means universally accepted), we would still only be acknowledging the outward, visible expression of the internal, covert belief systems of the teachers who read Plowden, or parts of it, and found its values consonant with theirs. Some classroom practice has been interpreted, by its recent critics, as evidence of stifling orthodoxy; but this interpretation does not do justice, I believe, to the way in which all classroom practice is, in a sense, an expression of a personal value, or a set of values, more or less well-organised and integrated.

What *were* the values expressed in the Plowden Report? What would it mean to be a 'Plowden teacher', in terms of beliefs about children, about learning, about the purposes of education?

Witnesses to the Plowden Committee were asked about their perception of the aims of primary education; there was 'a wide general measure of agreement' but, the Report continues: 'general statements of aims, even by those engaged in teaching, tend to be little more than expressions of benevolent aspiration' with only a tenuous relationship to specific educational practices (497). The Committee adopted instead 'a pragmatic approach to the purposes of education' (501). Their first conclusion, in a paragraph that was first famous and later notorious, as the epitome of Plowdenism, was that schools must transmit values. The values that the Plowden Report is advocating are set out plainly enough:

> 505. A school is not merely a teaching shop, it must transmit values and attitudes. It is a community in which children learn to live first and foremost as children and not as future adults. In family life children learn to live with people of all ages. The school sets out deliberately to devise the right environment for children, to allow them to be themselves and to develop in the way and at the pace appropriate to them. It tries to equalise opportunities and to compensate for handicaps. It lays special stress on individual discovery, on first hand experience and on opportunities for creative work. It insists that knowledge does not fall into neatly separate compartments and that work and play are not opposite but complementary. A child brought up in such an atmosphere at all stages of his education has some hope of becoming a balanced and mature adult and of being able to live in, to contribute to, and to look critically at the society of which he forms a part. Not all primary schools correspond to this picture, but it does represent a general and quickening trend.
>
> CACE (1967)

Added to these fundamental requirements for the imaginary Plowden school are the virtues of 'neatness, accuracy, care and perseverance, and the sheer knowledge which is an essential of being educated' (506). In the Plowden school, the interests of the children are paramount:

> those interests are complex. Children need to be themselves, to live with other children and with grown-ups, to learn from their environment, to enjoy the present, to get ready for the future, to create and to love, to learn to face adversity, to behave responsibly, in a word, to be human beings. (507)

The characteristics of children's learning, its investigative and active nature, its playfulness and creativity, its concentration and emotional involvement, make demands on the teacher whose 'task is to provide an environment and opportunities which are sufficiently challenging for children' (533). This environment comprises all the classroom activities and materials, all the visits outside school, the spoken language in which classroom life is embedded, and the relationships between teachers and pupils. The chapter on children's learning, which sets out this position, is followed by a chapter on *Aspects of the Curriculum*, which goes some way towards indicating appropriate experiences and activities for children's learning in a number of curriculum areas. But the Report goes very little further in prescribing the teacher's task, insisting on the autonomy and decision-making powers of teachers and groups of teachers (507).

'The Plowden teacher', then, is unlikely to be a person whose professional behaviour has been learned as a set of prescribed practices in the pages of the Report. The Plowden teacher is, rather, a person who respects children's individuality, creativity and their power to love, to discover and to learn, a person who believes in equality of opportunity and in differences between children. This is hardly a portrait of a dogmatic, orthodox teacher, incapable of independent thought.

'The Plowden teacher' was not, of course, invented in 1967. The central elements of the Plowden Report, those that concern children, learning and the curriculum, are all to be found in its predecessors, the first and second Hadow Reports. The *Report on the Primary School* was published in 1931 and was followed two years later by the *Report on Infant and Nursery Schools*, where we find the same explicit emphasis on the freedom and power of the teacher...

> We have deliberately refrained from detail because the last thing that we desire to see is a standardised infant school. We believe that the interests of children will be best served by giving to the teacher the same liberty in planning and arranging her work that we claim for the children in these early years.
>
> Board of Education (1933) p.146

And we see again an emphasis on values, on the belief system that guides the teacher in wise decision-making in the interests of children: 'our whole conception of ... the teaching of the infant school depends upon the teacher; it will be successful in so far as she has faith in the underlying principles, and confidence in her ability to interpret them' (p.146).

Like Plowden, the Hadow Report acknowledges its debt to earlier educators, and to established practice and 'normal procedure' in many schools. But it makes one important claim to innovation: 'What we do desire to see is the acceptance of a different set of values from that which has been usual in the past' (p.123). Here is an explicit recognition of the value-infested nature of educational debate and development. The shared values of the Hadow Committee can be traced back through Froebel and Montessori to Pestalozzi and Robert Owen; equally, the influence of Susan Isaacs, with her interest in children's intellectual and emotional powers, is everywhere apparent. But a set of values does not amount to an orthodoxy, let alone a stifling orthodoxy.

The Hadow inheritance, handed down through Plowden, is still a powerful if unacknowledged influence on teachers and teachers' thinking. But just as Plowden identified the tenuous relationship between rhetoric and reality ('It was interesting that some of the headteachers who were considered by HM Inspectors to be most successful in practice were least able to formulate their aims clearly and convincingly' (p.497)), so other educators have described the gap between teachers' beliefs and their ability to embody those beliefs in well-constructed models of teaching and learning.

Brian Simon, for example, argues that the pedagogic romanticism of Plowden has had far-reaching and damaging consequences:

> By focusing on the individual child ('at the heart of the educational process lies the child'), and in developing the analysis from this point, the Plowden Committee created a situation from which it was impossible to derive an effective pedagogy (or effective pedagogical means). If each child is unique, and each requires a specific pedagogical approach appropriate to him or her and to no other, the construction of an all-embracing pedagogy, or general principles of teaching, becomes an impossibility. And indeed research has shown that primary school teachers who have taken the priority of individualisation to heart find it difficult to do more than ensure that each child is in fact engaged on the series of tasks which the teacher sets up for the child.
>
> Simon (1985) p.98

In an early study of the relationship between parents and the educators of young children, Gillian Pugh and Erica De'Ath (1989) have come to a similar conclusion about educators' understanding of their own work. They investigated the concept of partnership between parents and professionals across the whole range of pre-school provision then available in this country. They described a number of different types of parental involvement that might be the precursors of a fully-developed partnership, and set out the characteristics of 'Partnership Proneness', analysing the factors that help or hinder progress towards partnership. At this point, they identified a 'major stumbling block': the lack of clarity, in many pre-school settings, about aims and objectives, about the questions 'Why are we here?' and 'What are we trying to do?' Pugh and De'Ath suggest that this absence, this gap in practitioners' thinking, may have serious consequences. Without a coherent, explicit, and openly debated understanding of the principles of pre-school education, it is 'difficult to work towards a common set of purposes, and to look at whether the values underlying the work with children and with parents could be shared by all parties' (p.69). Put less diplomatically, what this conclusion amounts to is that partnership is impossible if educators do not know what they are doing and why.

> Lack of clarity about the aims and objectives was particularly evident in the difficulty that workers in many centres had in articulating what it was they were trying to do with children – what in nursery schools and classes might be described as the curriculum. Even when the staff had worked out a detailed programme, they did not find it easy to put their thinking into words and share it with parents. (p.70)

The lack of an explicit, well-constructed framework of understanding must be a severely limiting factor in the development of effective education and worthwhile parental involvement. 'Good' pre-school and primary practice must be built on a solid foundation of both conviction and rationale.

Teachers and other educators rarely pause for reflection before using the word 'good' in this way: the phrases 'good practice' and 'good schools' do not normally send us flying to our dictionaries. These 'goods' have come to be defined in a long and complex process that has included both some uncritical swallowing of the great tradition and some reflective and rigorous self-examination. But there can never be too much of the latter. Our values, our 'goods', are cherished ones, deeply felt, and so not often enough subjected to persistent 'Why?' questioning. Barbara Tizard's small research project 'Parental Involvement in Nursery Education' makes clear how this affects communication between educators and parents (Hughes *et al.* 1980). In five out of the seven nursery schools and classes involved in the project, the teachers made determined efforts to inform parents about nursery education. They succeeded – and they failed.

> Though during the year most parents had become well informed about *what* their children did in the nursery class or school, few understood *why* the activities were provided and how they were supposed to help the child.
>
> Hughes *et al.* (1980) p.192

Teachers who do not, themselves, ask – and answer – 'Why?' questions, will not be able to lead parents towards a full understanding of their purposes. This is not to say that parents do not postulate their own explanations:

> Many Asian mothers were baffled by the purpose of all the equipment except for books, although sometimes they produced ingenious explanations for them: 'Sand – all English people like the seaside; as it is so far away, they bring some to school, to remind them of the beach.'
>
> Hughes *et al.* (1980) p.193

This misunderstanding, though showing forgiveness, even indulgence on the parents' part, is unnecessary; there is an antidote. It is for teachers to become clearer about what kind of teachers they are, what they stand for, what they would go to the stake for, and, most importantly, *why*. To ask oneself, 'What kind of a teacher am I?' is a powerful exercise in making one's innermost values apparent; to ask oneself 'Why am I this kind of teacher?' is to take another even more important step towards connecting one's internal value system to the external realities of children's learning in primary schools. To learn about children's learning, it is at the same time inescapably necessary to learn about oneself.

The Plowden and Hadow Reports are not, evidently, the only influences on experienced teachers' perceptions of themselves. The work of Lawrence Stenhouse was, for many of the same generation of teachers, enormously influential in the development of their understanding of themselves, and what it is to be a teacher. Stenhouse (1975) distinguishes teaching from instruction, seeing teaching as 'the systematic promotion of learning by whatever means' (p.24). These 'means' are not to be confused with 'teaching methods', a term which suggests that teachers are to be trained in a variety of specific skills. Stenhouse uses instead the phrase 'teaching strategy', which 'hints more at the planning of teaching and learning in the light of principles, and…lay(s) more weight on teacher judgement' (p.24). An essential principle, for Stenhouse, is respect for the pupil, and so 'we need to develop teaching strategies which embody such respect' (p.32). But an even more important principle is that teachers should recognise the way in which their own development is intimately bound up with the learning of their pupils. The effective teacher will:

> cast himself in the role of a learner in his work, so that his life in his classroom extends rather than constricts his intellectual horizons. A good

classroom, by this criterion, is one in which things are learned every day which the teacher did not previously know. (p.37)

Where instruction-based teaching, according to Stenhouse, is based on a simple transmission model (from the learned to the ignorant, from the full to the empty, from Gradgrind to Sissy Jupe), in discovery-based teaching, the teacher, who is also a learner, can develop the pupils' capacity to think. 'The superficialities of the disciplines may be taught by pure instruction, but the capacity to think within the disciplines can only be taught by inquiry' (p.38). Stenhouse develops the concept of inquiry: the inquiring, thinking pupil will be taught by an inquiring, thinking teacher. The 'process model' of curriculum is supported by a 'research model' of teaching, of curriculum planning, implementation and evaluation. In the research model, the curriculum developer is not a prophet, or a missionary, but an investigator, an explorer. The curriculum that is developed in this way:

> is to be judged by whether it advances our knowledge, rather than by whether it is right. It is conceived as a probe through which to explore and test hypotheses... What we ask of a curriculum offering is not that it should be right or good, but that it should be intelligent or penetrating. Its dilemmas should be important dilemmas. Its shortcomings should reflect real and important difficulties. (p.125)

Chapter 10 of *An Introduction to Curriculum Research and Development* sets out this view of teacher as researcher in more depth. Stenhouse himself emphasises the connection between the betterment of schools and the development of the teacher researcher and insists: 'for me this chapter is of central importance' (p.142). He describes the subjective perceptions of teachers who research their own practice as 'crucial' and not to be abandoned in favour of an unattainable objectivity. Instead the teacher researcher develops 'a sensitive and self-critical subjective perspective...' (p.157). In later works, Stenhouse reiterates this crucial subjectivity, distinguishing the teacher as an artist, practising the art of teaching, rather than as an objective, neutral or value-free researcher of pragmatic fact.

> Through self-monitoring, the teacher becomes a conscious artist. Through conscious art he is able to use himself as an instrument of his research.
>
> Stenhouse (1985) p.16

Stenhouse specifically rejects managerial or industrial metaphors for the work of teachers in classrooms, and emphasises both the mastery and aspirations of the practising artist...

> if my words are inadequate, look at the sketchbook of a good artist, a play in rehearsal, a jazz quartet working together. That, I am arguing, is what good teaching is like. (p.97)

But in all this, his emphasis is not on the artist as performer, or in teaching as performance; his major concern is for what the artist learns through his art, and what the teacher learns through teaching.

> Thus the actor learns about life and people and moral dilemmas through participation in plays. And similarly, I learned through teaching literature and history something of what literature and history have to teach. Curriculum is the medium through which the teacher can learn his art. (p.98)

This learning by the teacher, the teacher who is also artist and researcher, is, for Stenhouse, at the heart of effective education. The 'good classroom' is where the teacher learns things every day: teachers in such classrooms learn about children, about children's learning, and, equally importantly, about themselves.

Another, very different, educator resembles Stenhouse in his interest in teachers' self-knowledge. Bruno Bettelheim was, for many years, the Director of the Orthogenic School in Chicago. In this school for severely emotionally disturbed children, which was opened in 1944, the staff adopted a mainly psychoanalytic approach, and Bettelheim (1950) explicitly acknowledges their corporate debt 'to the writings of Sigmund and Anna Freud, John Dewey, August Aichhorn, and all those other great educators from Comenius and Pestalozzi to the Buhlers, Montessori and Piaget...' But, as he goes on to say, it is not simply that these educators have important things to say about children: they also speak directly to the teachers themselves. Their greatness lies in the ways 'they have helped us to understand children and above all to understand ourselves' (p.22). For Bettelheim, the task of learning to work with the emotionally disturbed children at the School, is a complex one. Staff members have 'to learn to become part of a purposeful unity and also what may seem still more difficult – to preserve, at the same time, their personal uniqueness. In a word, they must learn to become more themselves...' (p.22).

For teachers on the staff of the Orthogenic School, this growing self-knowledge includes learning some attitudes that are very different from those of many other adults in contemporary society. For example, the staff of the School allow the children the freedom to waste and destroy food and other materials, and they approve of infantile activities that are supposedly below the child's age level (such as playing with stuffed animals and thumb sucking). They believe that children's 'emotional needs take precedence over material considerations' (p.41). The core value that these teachers express is the centrality of emotion in personal growth and development; their own emotional growth and increasing integration is a precondition of the children's slowly regained confidence and security. In Bettelheim's thinking, as for Stenhouse, teachers' growth and development runs alongside children's growth and development.

Similar values are strong in the important work of Janusz Korczak, the Jewish-Polish doctor who introduced progressive orphanages, designed as just communities, into Poland in the years before the second world war. He is chiefly remembered today for his final act of sacrifice, leading the children in his care out of the Warsaw ghetto and onto the trains carrying them to the extermination camp at Treblinka. But his life's work with children has more to teach us than the catastrophic horror of his death. Korczak's life was committed to the children he cared for and educated in a number of different settlements and institutions. He cared for their physical welfare, and, much like Margaret MacMillan in the slums of Bradford and Deptford a generation earlier, he clothed and fed and deloused the children, bringing them from a state of physical destitution to comparative healthiness. But his chief concern was with their moral welfare. In 1910 he abandoned his career as a paediatrician at the Children's Hospital in Warsaw to work for the Orphans Aid Society, who were just embarking on a project to set up an orphanage for Jewish children in a poor working-class neighbourhood of Warsaw. Korczak worked with architects and philanthropists to design and build the orphanage, which he saw as a children's republic.

> The underlying philosophy of the children's republic was: children are not the people of tomorrow, but people today. They are entitled to be taken seriously. They have a right to be treated by adults with tenderness and respect, as equals, not as masters and slaves. They should be allowed to grow into whoever they were meant to be: the 'unknown person' inside each of them is the hope for the future.
>
> ... In the process of working together, they would learn consideration and fair play, and develop a sense of responsibility toward others, which they would carry with them into the adult world. In helping his orphans to respect others, a first step toward gaining self-respect, Korczak was a pioneer in what we now call 'moral education'. He was concerned not with teaching

children their ABCs – they would go to public school for that – but with the grammar of ethics.

Lifton (1989) p.62

Korczak was greatly esteemed as a writer and broadcaster on educational matters; few of his works have been translated into English, but the brief extracts that Betty Jean Lifton cites in her biography give us glimpses of the principles that inspired his work. As early as 1896, while still a student working as a tutor to the children of wealthy friends and acquaintances, he wrote of the need for a pedagogic strategy that would help children to 'see, understand and love, as well as to read and write'. This strategy must be based, he came to see in his maturity, on the 'pedagogical love' that an educator has for his children, not a sentimental love, but one based on mutual respect. Korczak's emphasis on love, and on the emotional relationship between educators and children, did not blind him to the importance of other forms of understanding. Lifton illustrates his belief that theory and practice were simply different ways of doing the same thing, quoting from an article written in 1924: 'Thanks to theory, I know. Thanks to practice, I feel, Theory enriches intellect, practice deepens feeling, trains the will' (p.125).

One of Korczak's most influential works was *How to Love a Child* published in 1920. Designed as a short pamphlet for parents and teachers, it eventually grew to hundreds of pages.

> One of its main theses is that you cannot possibly love a child – your own, or another's – until you see him as a separate being with the inalienable right to grow into the person he was meant to be. You cannot even understand a child until you achieve self-knowledge: 'You yourself are the child whom you must learn to know, rear and above all, enlighten.'

Lifton (1989) pp.79–80

The importance of self-knowledge for the educator is plainly spelled out: effective educators are those whose work includes the study of themselves, their knowledge, their feelings and the frameworks within which they understand children.

What is it to be a teacher? What kind of a teacher am I? Stenhouse argues that teacher development, and teachers' self-awareness, are essential requirements for effective education. Bettelheim and Korczak (whose work Bettelheim greatly admired) both argued that being a teacher is, in a sense, little more than being profoundly and completely oneself. But to practise this belief, to *be* oneself, necessitates self-knowledge and self-exploration.

In this chapter I have been arguing that this self-knowledge is a pedagogical imperative for all teachers. I have drawn on the work of a variety of educators to support the contention that teaching the National Curriculum and the early learning goals in the early twenty-first century calls for self-knowledge just as demandingly as any other kind of teaching, in other times, other places, in orphanage, institution, primary or comprehensive school, or university department. In understanding our students' learning, I repeat, we also come to understand ourselves.

One aspect of ourselves that we will encounter in this process of growing understanding is our own early experience as learners, when teachers taught us, and assessed our learning. All teachers have first-hand experiences, as learners, of the assessment cycle that I have characterised as the movement between evidence, judgements and outcomes. All teachers know what it is to feel the teacher's eye upon them, and to be on the receiving end, for good or ill, of the teacher's judgements. Like Jason, all teachers have learned, at some time in the past, what it is to be a pupil and how to behave like a pupil. All teachers have learned, like the pupils in Mary Willes' study (described in Chapter 4) to enter into competition for the teacher's approval.

Madeleine Grumet's assertion that, today, in the present, 'we *are* the curriculum' is justified by reference to our experiences in the past:

> It is we who have raised our hands before speaking, who have learned to hear only one voice at a time, and to look past the backs of the heads of our peers to the eyes of the adult in authority. It is we who have learned to offer answers rather than questions, not to make people uncomfortable...
>
> Grumet (1981) p.122

When, as mature adults, we set about, in our turn, assessing pupils' learning, these experiences may not be strong in our conscious memories, but they have still played a part in making us into the people we are. Our assessment practices in the present are not dictated by phantoms from the past, but they are certainly shaped by our slowly forming understanding (in childhood) of how human beings treat one another – with respect or disrespect, with trust or mistrust, with admiration or scorn, with acceptance or rejection, with loving attention, or impersonal distance.

Understanding ourselves, I am arguing, is an important part of the task we set ourselves in assessing children's learning. But there is still more to think about. Understanding learning also necessarily involves, for adult teachers, understanding children. And this may be a good deal more problematic than we would wish.

The slogans of the child-centred tradition, and the famous (or infamous) one-liner from the Plowden Report ('at the heart of the process lies the child...') may have lulled us into thinking that the concept of 'the child' is self-evidently simple, that when we talk about 'the child' or 'children', we have no more to do than see what there is to see, and say what there is to say. But there is, as I argued earlier, always more to see, always more to learn.

Valerie Walkerdine (1984) writes convincingly of the damage done to teachers' thinking by the reified concept of 'the child', as if there was only one, an amalgam of Piagetian stage-theory, Froebelian growth and spontaneity, and a dash of noble savagery. This universal, all-purpose 'child' is, she argues, a 'powerful but impossible fiction'. She urges us to clear out of our conceptual cupboards all the constructions that educationalists have based on this fiction.

It is not just the singular 'child' who is a problematic figure in our thinking. The concept 'children', too, we can recognise as a cultural artefact, which at any given historical – or educational – period, has particular meanings and implications. Our perceptions of children, of child-like children, are coloured by our biographies, by our schooling, by our religious, psychological and political beliefs, by the attitudes of those around us, by the professional demands made on us in schools and classrooms, by the hidden curriculum of contemporary schooling.

A rose may be a rose, but children are not children. Children are a heterogeneous crowd of unique individuals, onto whom we project our understanding of what it is to be four – or seven – or 11 years old.

Teachers' perceptions of their pupils are shaped, first of all, by some simple contingencies of time and place. When I started teaching, four-year-old children were, first and foremost, of pre-statutory age: very few of them were to be found in infant or primary schools. Some were in nursery schools and classes: self-evidently pre-school children, in pre-school education, which is based on play, self-directed activity and independent choice. By the mid-1980s, most four-year-olds, for a variety of reasons, were admitted to primary or infant schools at some point during the academic year in which they turned five. They were then known as the reception class, then formally as Year R, and from 1988, while still of non-statutory age, they began their education within the provisions and structures of the National Curriculum.

Now these same four-year-olds have been repositioned. Since the introduction of the Foundation Stage in 2000, Year R is technically the final year of this new stage of education, which starts after the child's third birthday. They are working towards the early learning goals (QCA 2000) and will, in principle, become National Curriculum pupils only in the September after the fifth birthday, when they enter Y1. Seven-year-olds are in an equally confusing variety of positions: some of them are the oldest pupils in an infant school, trusted and respected as senior members of the school community; others are Year 2 pupils in a primary school for pupils from Year R to Year 6, roughly halfway up the ladder of primary school progress; and some seven-year-olds are the youngest members of a 7–11 junior school, treated very much as the babies of the school family.

There are other more complex forces at work when teachers look at children and think about what they see. Beyond the context of the school itself, beyond the accidents of school uniform or the organisation of year groups, are unspoken expectations of what children of any age should do, think, be and feel. Many authors, in different disciplines, have explored the theme of changing perceptions of childhood. Philippe Ariés' *Centuries of Childhood* (1962, English version 1973) traces the origin of modern ideas about the family and childhood from the twelfth century onwards, in a richly illustrated demographic history, covering topics such as children's dress, their games and pastimes, and their education. His work, and particularly some of his more extreme conclusions (for example: 'in mediaeval society the idea of childhood did not exist') initiated a continuing debate about the 'invention of childhood'. Peter Coveney examines childhood from a literary perspective in *The Image of Childhood* (1967) and follows key themes, such as innocence, sinfulness, sexuality and freedom through the work of western authors from Rousseau to Blake and on to James Barrie, Mark Twain and D. H. Lawrence. Each of these writers, argues Coveney, held a particular view of childhood. Each of these writers can contribute, if we choose, to our present personal understanding of what it is to be a child, what it ought to be, and what it might be.

From the disciplines of sociology and psychology too, come diverging formulations of appropriate frameworks for the study of childhood. Richards (1974) and Richards and Light (1986) have rejected the mono-culturalism of developmental psychology, which claims to be based on universal laws, as failing to take account of the social context in which psychological processes take place. Their new paradigm emphasises that childhood is socially constructed; biological immaturity is indeed a universal and natural feature of human groups, but ways of understanding childhood and children vary from place to place, from time to time, from culture to culture.

In *Visions of Infancy* (1989) Ben Bradley sets out to 'probe the foundations of child psychology by looking at what scientists say about babies'. He attempts to account for differences between various scientific studies of infancy (such as Darwin's and Freud's, as well as Piaget's and Chomsky's) by the personal and historical conditions of those who conduct them. One of the most arresting sections of the book is an illustrated description of the large centrally heated box, with a picture window, in which the behaviourist Skinner placed his second daughter for much of her childhood. There are comparable surprises in a series of papers, edited by Alison James and Alan Prout, *Constructing and Reconstructing Childhood* (1990), that range from Disneyland to the ghetto streets of Asuncion, the capital city of Paraguay, in search of new insights into the culturally specific sets of ideas and practices that constitute working theories of childhood.

These papers by professional psychologists and sociologists may seem remote from the interests of practising primary teachers. An account of children's involvement in the labour force in Norwegian village communities, or a study of children's daily life as patients on a terminal cancer ward are, at first sight, unlikely to be the stimulus for a teacher's critical enquiry into children learning in a British classroom. The arresting images of children around which some of these authors weave their arguments may even serve to reinforce a taken-for-granted sense of normality in our professional perceptions of the children whom we educate. The unforgettable photograph of Skinner's daughter in the 'Heir Conditioner' box will certainly astonish early years educators in Britain today; surely, no-one in their senses would ever consider housing a naked two-year-old in a centrally heated box. But this justifiable astonishment, reinforced by resistance to Skinner's forceful advocacy of his own invention, may prevent us feeling a comparable astonishment at any of our own practices in early childhood care and education.

I am arguing that when, as teachers, we look at children's learning and seek to understand it, our understanding of children is an important part of the picture. A description of the normal child, or the ideal child, or the child-like child, is not usually made explicit in the process of assessment.

Nevertheless, I maintain that as we set about assessing our pupils, we do have, deep in our minds' eye, some dearly held beliefs about what we are looking for. We would be as surprised to see a boy of three in a long dress with leading strings attached to it, as to see a boy of seven wearing a man's hat and a sword; but Louis XIII, the little Dauphin of France, whose daily life the doctor Heroard recorded in his diary, was dressed in just this way, conforming to the strictest expectations of the child-like child in the early seventeenth century. He started to learn the violin at 17 months, began archery practice at four, and at five was taken to join the King in the ballroom to see the dogs fighting the bears and the bull. At just over a year old he was engaged to the Infanta of Spain, and at 14 married, and put, almost by force, into his 13-year-old wife's bed (Ariés 1973). The intensity of our present day response to these practices may indicate the intensity with which we hold to our own conceptions of the child-like child.

The concept of the normal child, held implicitly as part of a teacher's construction of the world, may help to explain Jason's predicament. It is possible that, at some stage, Jason's teachers have been deceived by his conformity to certain norms of childhood as they conceive it. Jason's obedience, his passivity, his willingness to follow instructions, are desirable characteristics in a pupil, and will have been welcomed by his teachers. But these thoroughly normal behaviours may have led his teachers to believe that his learning is normal too, an acceptable variation on the universal seven-year-old theme. They may have used other words to describe him – a disadvantaged child perhaps, or a slow learner, or a language-deprived child, or a statemented child, or a willing child, who gives no trouble. These phrases, too, describe normal children, whom every teacher recognises. Jason's teachers probably did not consider questioning the categories they used to describe him, or admit the possibility that some labels conceal what they purport to describe. Somehow Jason's crucial lack of understanding was hidden from his teachers, and I suspect that it was his acceptable appearance as a pupil that disguised the unacceptable state of his mathematical development.

These suggestions are speculative; but they stand as an illustration of a very real possibility for all primary teachers. We all face the possibility that what we think we know about children may prevent us from seeing what we more urgently need to know. What we most urgently need to know is how our schools, our practices, our attitudes and our beliefs are affecting each child and all children, their learning and their development, for good or ill. We may be able more completely to understand this process if we examine our beliefs about children, as well as our beliefs about effective pedagogy.

A poem by Vladimir Nabokov, 'An Evening of Russian Poetry', depicts the poet lecturing to an audience of schoolgirls, who madden him with their insensitive questions.

> Why do you speak of words,
> When all we want is knowledge, nicely browned?

Nabokov (1977)

Teachers today teach and assess their pupils in a world where knowledge is, by statute, a desirable and necessary outcome of their work. The forms of this desirable knowledge are prescribed in a variety of official documents. But knowledge, however nicely browned, can never be the whole story. Teachers teach themselves, as well as the contents of the documents on their desks or in their cupboards, and they assess children's learning with the whole of themselves, not just with a list of targets or goals. The concepts that are strong in us, the images we have learned to store in our mind's eye of the desirable pupil, our memories of the children we once were, or the children we were told we were, all have their effect on the assessment process. We can see some of these values and beliefs about children and childhood expressed very plainly in many of the baseline assessment schedules that, before 1997, proliferated in schools and local authorities all over England. These schedules offer interesting insights into the conceptual systems of those who devise them. Some of the more bizarre examples suggest that teachers sometimes regard the behaviour of young children starting school as deviant and disruptive, behaviour that must be minimised if the child is to become a properly functioning pupil. One such schedule, an 'infant rating checklist of educational difficulties' offers descriptions of five different levels, ranged from left to right, for each of 18 categories, such as motor skills, language, behaviour, play, attitude to learning and personality. Those descriptions printed down the lefthand side of the page are the levels that are assumed to be signs of educational difficulties. They include the following:

ATTITUDE TO LEARNING	Completely uninterested. No concentration.
PLAY AND SOCIAL DEVELOPMENT	Withdrawn, unable to play with others.
BEHAVIOUR	Constantly attention seeking. Disruptive. Uncontrollably aggressive.
PERSONALITY MATURITY	Very immature, cries easily, unstable.
INTELLIGENCE OUTWARD EXPRESSION	Dull, unable to understand. No problem solving skills.

These phrases are not, in my opinion, descriptive, but severely condemnatory. They are not entries in a pupil's profile, but extracts from a character assassination. They are by no means unique.

Another schedule devotes a page to a 'personality record' of the child with categories that include:

Amenability
1. Wishes to please and is most willing.
2. Helpful and cooperative fairly often.
3. Over anxious to please.
4. Frequently uncooperative and unresponsive.
5. Refuses actively to cooperate.

Attitudes to Adults (Authority)
1. Consistently helpful and obliging.
2. Mostly satisfactory – sometimes rude, etc.
3. Unreliable and unpredictable.
4. Defiant, challenging, pleases self.

Other People's Attitude to Him (sic)
1. Quite popular, better liked than most.
2. Accepted by others who are generally friendly.
3. Others take little or no notice of him.
4. Disliked and rejected by others.

Application

1. Active, applies himself reasonably well.
2. Willing but needs constant prodding.
3. Easily distracted by surroundings and events.
4. Cannot apply himself – restless, overactive.
5. Inactive, slow, ineffective, helpless.

Categories such as these seem to me to presuppose that young children starting school will present their teachers with problems; they seem to embody a view of children as wilfully difficult, grossly unsuited for the smooth running of the classroom; helpless or defiant or dull pupils must be marked out from the start. Another example reveals a similarly simplistic approach; normal children will be at the right-hand edge of the scale, problems on the left.

DEVELOPING SKILLS

	1	2	3	4	5
7. *Gross Motor Movement*	Clumsy, uncoordinated, Tends to fall over or bump into things.		Developing coordination, no apparent problems.		Well coordinated, agile, responds quickly.
8. *Fine Coordination and Manipulation*	Experiences great difficulty in manipulation – small objects, pencils.		Appropriate competence.		Dextrous, highly competent.
9. *Drawing*	Very limited development Drawing or scribble barely recognizable. Would need explanation.		Recognizable. Usually self-explanatory.		Very well executed, great attention to detail, little explanation needed.

APPROACH TO LEARNING

14. *Attention and Concentration*	Very short attention span. Unable to concentrate, easily distracted.		Can settle to a set task for a short period.		Works well on set task for a long span. Not easily distracted.
15. *Organization*	Disorganized, rarely completes set task, confused by expectations.		Can organize self with some additional assistance.		Is capable of organizing self with no additional assistance.

16. *Involvement*

| Avoids learning. Few or no interests. | Willing to become involved in most activities. | Keen, enthusiastic, with wide range of interests. |

17. *Type of Response*

| Little or no response without supervision. | Works steadily, acceptable progress being made. | Responds quickly, and accurately, enjoys demonstrating new skills. |

Since it seems unlikely that the teachers who wrote these descriptions were at heart anything but well-intentioned towards their prospective pupils, the best way of explaining the negative values that are here being projected onto some children is by invoking these teachers' own experiences as children, and as pupils, which may have been very damaging. They themselves may not have been treated respectfully, with trust and loving attention. We need not, however, in sympathising with them, go on to adopt their approach.

Assessment practices, I am arguing throughout this book, are based on the personal value systems of the teachers who make the assessments. I have given some examples here that reveal aspects of teachers' value systems that are not in the interests of children. A value system that rejects young children's tears as immature is not respectful of children's grief. A value system that interprets a child's lack of interest in an assigned task as evidence of possible learning difficulties is mistrustful of children's appetite and capacity for learning. In effective assessment, which works for children, we draw on a coherent set of values that are truly respectful and trustful. We may need, in the process, to struggle to understand our own past experiences, and if necessary, outlive them, in the interests of the children we work with today. If our well-intentioned assessment procedures reveal, on close inspection, an element of rejection, disrespect or retribution, we have work to do in reaffirming the basic human virtues that our adult lives are intended to express. The moral dimension of assessment is inescapable, however nicely browned the knowledge we are choosing to assess.

CHAPTER 7

Trying to Understand: Making it Work

It is possible to distinguish between different kinds of assessment in terms of their different purposes. Broadly speaking, we can separate assessment used as part of the process of accountability, from assessment used to differentiate between pupils; these are both distinct from the evaluative purpose, when assessment is used to provide the evidence against which to review curriculum, teaching styles, learning opportunities and educational achievements. When assessment became a statutory requirement, for the first time, the prestigious Task Group on Assessment and Testing (DES 1988) described a set of four purposes for assessment: formative, diagnostic, summative and evaluative. Much of the energetic debate that has continued to follow the publication of this report has been concerned with the possibility or, as it is more often argued, the impossibility, of devising forms of assessment that would simultaneously serve all four purposes.

This debate has distracted our attention from an important distinction that must be made between purposes and outcomes, which are not synonymous organising categories. Purposes are, essentially, expressions of hope, however well-founded that hope might be. A description of purpose in any human enterprise cannot be an adequate description of what actually happens. Hundreds of thousands of well-intentioned teachers enter their classrooms every morning replete with benevolent purposes for their pupils' learning. The outcomes of the lived curriculum may be very different. If we wish to understand assessment as it really is, we must critically examine its outcomes as well as its purposes. We may choose to match outcomes to purposes as part of this critical examination, but we must not allow the expression of a purpose to pass as the equivalent of its realisation.

With this distinction in mind, we can see how defining and designing assessment procedures with purposes in mind, as the TGAT Report did, so helpfully, at the time, may prevent us from seeing the undesirable outcomes of particular practices. For example, the statutory assessments that are now a taken-for-granted event in the educational histories of six- and seven-year-old children, have, we are repeatedly assured, entirely beneficial and laudable *purposes*. Anxiety about statutory forms of assessment at the end of the Key Stage One should not be allayed by these assurances, because it is the *outcomes* of the procedures that are potentially damaging. Statutory assessment, including the requirement to ascribe pupils' achievement to numerical levels, is intended to serve all four of the purposes proposed by TGAT. But there may be other outcomes. Assigning young children to one of three (or four) levels of achievement has had, as we have now seen, the very undesirable outcome of creating a new category of underachievement: the 'Level One Child'. The purpose of compiling numerical data on every child's performance on each attainment target may be to achieve accuracy and objectivity (which may well prove to be illusory); but the outcome may be a rigid stratification of pupils based on the string of numbers they carry round with them in their record folders and that go forward to be used in league tables, and in setting targets for future years.

Kenneth Clarke, Secretary of State for Education and Science at the time, went so far as to identify this possibility as a welcome outcome of National Curriculum assessment, and to recommend it as a desirable practice, with undisputed benefits.

> For many schools, there must be scope for organising their teaching in classes grouped more closely with their attainments in the subjects of the National Curriculum. We have introduced a clear framework of assessment and monitoring such performance. We must use the benefits which that framework provides.
>
> DES (1991b) para 36

The evaluative purpose of statutory assessment procedures may go as badly awry. It would be quite possible for a school staff to conclude from a disappointing set of SAT results that the curriculum provided did not give enough emphasis to the learning being assessed. 'Teaching to the test' would be the natural outcome. Equally a set of unexpectedly high SAT results might play a disproportionately important part in the exercise of a school's accountability to its governors, parents and the community, suggesting that all was well, meantime masking some real deficiencies in the school's curriculum. To judge assessment practices by their purposes is to limit one's professional judgements to the land of good intentions. The real effectiveness of assessment can only be judged by its outcomes. Does the process make the school more fully and more effectively accountable? Does the process enable teachers to attend to individual differences between their pupils in ways that are supportive and truly educative? Does the process enable teachers to shape a curriculum that enriches individual children's learning? Does the process stimulate an evaluation of curriculum that extends learning opportunities for all pupils? Does assessment create a continuity of learning at every stage of education? Does assessment *work*, for the benefit of all?

Some of the authors discussed in earlier chapters have much to show us here. First, let us return to Chris Athey, whose study of children's cognitive schemas is set resolutely in the context of her contention that early childhood education is short on theory to describe the relationship between teaching and learning. In her words:

> not enough attention is paid to how children learn most effectively, and consequently, how teachers can teach most effectively.
>
> Athey (1990) p.8

The key word is 'consequently'. Studies of young children's learning, Athey is arguing, hold the key to worthwhile education. When we understand learning, we will be able to understand teaching. The educator's observations and assessments are the means by which educational provision becomes more effective, more closely attuned to individuals, and richer in opportunities for all. The educators whose observations reveal children's cognitive schemas are uniquely well-placed to shape the curriculum (resources, activities and interactions) to support and extend children's cognitive growth. The outcome of these educators' assessments is an enriched curriculum.

Athey emphasises that such an enriched curriculum will not result from an interest in the content of children's thought, but from an understanding of its associated cognitive form. She appreciates that educators have, in the past, focused on content, rather than form, because of our lack of understanding of what might constitute cognitive form in the thinking of young children. So, for example, she cites Victor Lowenfeld's (1957) advice to teachers about extending children's thinking by talking to them about their drawings. A child who draws an aeroplane, suggests Victor Lowenfeld, should be asked questions about the plane, such as its size, where it lands, who is on board and so on. The limitation of this approach is that these questions stimulate 'associative rather than conceptual thinking, in that the child is encouraged to associate content with content' (p.42). More rewarding for the child's learning is the approach of the educator who perceives the cognitive form of a child's interest and responds sympathetically and encouragingly to the child's prevailing concern. An illustration makes the distinction abundantly clear:

> In the following example from Katz and Katz (1936), the difference between 'content' and 'structure' (or 'form') can be illustrated. The 'cognitive form' is *seriation of size*. The 'content' or 'stuff' of thinking is that of natural science, more specifically, 'elephant', 'mouse', 'snail' and 'flea'. The child is an intelligent and experienced five-year-old who is having a conversation with his father, who is a natural scientist:
>
> Child: The elephant is the biggest animal and the mouse is the smallest.
> Father: The mouse isn't the smallest.
> Child: No...it's the snail.
> Father: There are still smaller ones.
> Child: The flea is of course the smallest.
> Father: There are still smaller ones but you don't know them. They live in water.
> Child: I know them but I don't know what they are called.
>
> If this conversation took place in class, the teacher might decide to ask questions on where elephants live, how a snail protects itself or what kind of food a mouse eats. These questions may interest the child and they are worth asking, but they have a 'hit-or-miss' quality. The responses the father gave show that he is aware of the prevailing concern of the child, which is *size*. A size continuum is an invariant cognitive structure that links individual objects in the world with each other. Schemas and concepts facilitate a cognitive organization of disparate content.
>
> Athey (1990) pp. 42–3.

The task for the educator attuned to children's cognitive schemas then, is to use the knowledge gained through observation and monitoring of children's spontaneous activity to good effect. Athey predicts that a curriculum for young children that was shaped in this way would be greatly more stimulating and challenging than the arbitrary content-led curriculum of the traditional nursery teacher, who selects topics and themes for their surface features or for their association with the time of year. Tadpoles, fire-stations, pancakes and hedgehogs are all typical items in an attractive nursery curriculum, but for these experiences to become part of a child's developing conceptual framework of coordinated schemas, there must also be an arresting or challenging cognitive form available to him or her. For example, children who are absorbed in an *enveloping* or *containing* schema are unlikely to be inspired by baking sessions dedicated to rock cakes, but, Athey suggests, may respond enthusiastically to other more adventurous forms of cookery.

> There are great opportunities in early education to introduce children to various foods *en croute* (French), lamb cooked in paper and stuffed cabbage leaves (Greek), samosas (Indian), eggs stuffed with various mixtures... Frugal cookery as well as many of the great cuisines of the world consists of wrapping up food in various ways. (p. 196)

Throughout Athey's long and challenging *Extending Thought in Young Children*, we can see how a knowledge of young children's schemas, when used by educators as a working tool in assessment, contributes to the worthwhile outcomes of that assessment. It contributes to increased accountability, as parents and educators come to know and understand each other more fully; it allows educators to differentiate between children by identifying their different pressing cognitive and emotional concerns. And it enables educators to provide a curriculum that fully supports children's learning, a rich curriculum for one and all.

Bruno Bettelheim's work with emotionally disturbed children in the 'totally supportive environment' of the Orthogenic School was briefly described in the previous chapter; here we will turn our attention to his fascinating study of children learning to read (Bettelheim & Zelan 1982). The story starts with the familiar observation that many children teach themselves to read, 'being children who have acquired a love of reading as they were being read to. The child who enjoys being read to learns to love books' (p.8). The authors contrast these children, 'who learn to read from texts that fascinate them', with children who learn to read only in school, by 'being drilled in skills of decoding and word recognition from texts devoid of meaningful content that are demeaning to the child's intelligence' (p.10). But this book is significantly more than a transatlantic contribution to the 'real books' campaign, or another nail in the coffin of the advocates of basic readers. From their discussions with children about their graded primers and early readers the authors learned a great deal about the children's emotional response to the basal reading texts they had been offered as beginning readers:

Without exception, the children complained about how stupid the stories in their basic readers had been, and said how much they had hated having to read them. With venom they spoke of 'all those sweet little kids in the stories,' furious that the stories assumed they were so simple-minded as to believe that children were like that... When asked why they had not expressed their opinions about these readers before, the answer was that nobody was interested in their true thoughts on this matter; everybody wanted only to hear that they liked the stories. One mature fourth-grade girl remarked: 'In none of the stories does anybody ever say his true opinion, so how could we?' (pp.14–16)

Building on this insight, Bettelheim and Zelan began to speculate that many of the difficulties that children encounter in learning to read, and many of the errors they make as they read aloud to their teacher, are due 'not to an inability to decode or understand the text, but often rather to their understanding the text quite well, sufficiently so to reject it for what seemed to them valid reasons' (p.64). They transferred the psychoanalytic principle, that the analyst must be ready and able to see the world through the eyes of his or her patient, taking the patient's perspective on all things, to the teaching of reading. They set out to explore the consequences of accepting the children's view of the reading material set before them, and of trying to see the underlying meaning of their so-called difficulties and mistakes. Observations were made of the reading performance of some 300 children, over a period of four years, in eight schools, seven public and one private, each 'the best in their respective systems according to school administrators, knowledgeable members of their communities'.

The report of their investigation comes to some startling conclusions. Bettelheim and Zelan did not treat the children's misreadings as mistakes, or as deviations from the ideal; they tried to take them seriously, and to learn from them something important about the child's understanding of what he or she was reading, and about the child's understanding of him or herself. For example, a first grader described by her teacher as 'brilliant and quite a competent reader', made consistent errors with the phrase 'terrible shot' while reading a story called 'My Father is a Terrible Shot'. She substituted 'trouble shot' and 'trouble shooter'; after some discussion, she continued to misread the phrase but now corrected herself every time she made the substitution.

All this began to make sense when the teacher remembered that the child's father had recently left the family... since the story's content centres on an inadequate father, this had reminded the girl of the ways in which her own father was inadequate.

In her reading of this text, she was being exposed to a treatment of a theme, which was, to her, of supreme personal importance, the site of fierce inner conflict. Her misreadings, Bettelheim argues, illuminate her thinking around this conflict:

> Finally she explained: 'Oh it's "terrible shot"...Why can't he do it?...I could do it.' It made no sense to her that the text portrayed adults as less proficient than children: in fact this idea aroused her indignation...As if to make her message absolutely clear, she said; 'That's stupid...the father is not very smart.' In this way she criticized a text that made no sense to her and, at the same time, her father's recent behaviour. (pp.105–6)

Bettelheim speculates about the effect of this reading experience on the child. If she had been listened to by a teacher assessing her accuracy, or her ability to make self-corrections without prompting, her performance would have been considered as inadequate. If her misreading had been continuously corrected, and not accepted as valid, she would have learned that in school, no attention is paid to what is most important in her life.

> Fortunately this girl had the experience that, contrary to her expectations, reading even a 'stupid' story had helped her to understand better what was going on in herself, because she had been encouraged in her efforts to endow the story with personal meaning. Although previously she had strongly preferred recess to reading, she now wanted to continue reading, even though it was time for recess. Reading had become a highly significant activity – something deeply meaningful in terms of her personal life. (p.107)

Bettelheim and Zelan pile up the evidence; they describe children reading complex and emotionally demanding stories, like the one above, children reading from their basal primers (in a chapter called 'Empty Texts – Bored Children'), and children reading lists of isolated words, out of context. A highly intelligent first grader who refused point blank to read the programmed texts his teacher offered him, eagerly read all 30 pages of *The Bear Detectives* by Stan and Jan Berenstein.

> But a few days later, once more this boy's workbook required him to read a list of words out of context, which, when read one after the other, made no sense. He then read 'dump' for 'jump'. Responding to the feelings this misreading expressed, we asked: 'Who wants to dump this?' referring to the workbook. The boy immediately reread 'jump' correctly. He nodded a

pleased assent to our remark that it seemed he wanted to dump the workbook. And when we asked him why he wanted to dump it, his unhesitating reply was 'cause it's garbage' (p.91).

The authors' case is a compelling one. They have shown us that, when we choose, if we listen carefully, and take children seriously, we can learn from the children themselves what it is important for us to know about their learning. If the outcomes of assessment are to include an enhanced curriculum and improved learning opportunities for all children, we would be foolish to exclude their voices from our selection of evidence on which to work. What children can tell us about their learning and about the provision we make for that learning has an important part to play in making assessment work.

Bettelheim's interest in children's emotional involvement in their reading material is an important reminder that cognitive growth is only one aspect of learning. Athey's preoccupation with cognitive form should not persuade us that cognitive form is all there is. Other authors emphasise the connectedness of intellect and emotion, of thought and feeling. Winnicott (1964), for example, writing of children's play, and of how children enrich themselves through their play, gradually enlarging 'their capacity to see the richness of the externally real world', identifies the emotions associated with play. It is easy to see that children play for pleasure but, Winnicott argues, it is harder to accept that children play to master anxiety: 'Anxiety is always a factor in a child's play, and often it is a major factor' (p.144). This insight suggests that the emotional set associated with learning is not one of unadulterated pleasure, but includes some element of dissatisfaction, of internal disturbance. Piaget used the phrase 'cognitive dissonance' to describe the internal state that drives the processes of accommodation and assimilation; we can safely assume that cognitive dissonance has a corresponding emotional effect on those who experience it.

Building on Athey's work, a small-scale study by Janet Shaw (1992) suggests that a description of young children's cognitive schemas, identified through close observations of their patterns of thought and activity, is incomplete if it excludes the emotional and symbolic functions of children's behaviour. Shaw's account of young children's learning is multi-layered, showing how the outer form of children's activity, their words and actions, can best be understood as expressions of cognitive, symbolic and emotional concerns, and not as simply one of these, taken singly, in isolation. Shaw concludes that all cognitive activity in young children has associated emotional form, and that young children's emotions play a part in shaping their cognitive concerns.

This association of cognitive and affective processes in children's learning has important implications for the practice of assessment. If the effectiveness of our assessments is to be evaluated by their outcomes, then we must be attentive to the emotional impact of assessment on our pupils. If assessment is to work for pupils, in terms of practical outcomes (and not just good intentions), we must not ignore the part that pupils' feelings play in the process. When we examine the practical outcomes of our assessment practices we must note increased or decreased motivation, enhanced or shattered self-esteem, positive or negative attitudes towards learning, an enlarged or diminished desire for understanding. In Simone Weil's words: 'in human effort the only source of energy is desire' (1986, p.265).

Studies of individual children by practising teachers can tell us a great deal about the effect of accumulated assessment upon a child's learning and development considered as a whole. In one such study, Shelagh McDonald reported an eight-year-old child remarking, during a discussion of his achievements at school, 'Well, what else can you expect of one of Mrs C's children?' Mrs C was the teacher who withdrew groups of children for extra support in reading and writing, and it seems as if the mere membership of this group was enough to teach this boy a disabling lesson about his own capacity to learn. In a group of teachers working for an Advanced Diploma in Educational Studies, McDonald's case-study was discussed in detail. A teacher admitted to a strong sense of identification with the boy's feelings. 'After all,' she said, 'I've always been a C, so I should know.' For some children the step between being assessed as a C (whatever that might mean), and 'being a C', seems alarmingly short.

Margaret Prosser, a primary teacher in Cambridge, carried out a study of her class of eight- and nine-year-old children, investigating the possibility of self-assessment by these pupils and hoping to understand more about their perceptions of their own learning. She began a class discussion by asking the children why it was necessary for teachers to assess their learning. The children immediately identified an impressive range of purposes which she grouped as follows:

Formative
So you can plan the right work for us.
So you can work out what we do each day.
So you have a picture in your head where to move us to next.

Because one job you have to do is decide what we should learn next and you have to do that by looking at our work and seeing what we're ready for next time.

Summative
How good we are at certain things.
So you know what people are good at.
If I'm good at reading.

Diagnostic
Like in maths, if I can't do it, you know you have to show me again how to do it.

Evaluative
So you can choose our project for next term.
So you can see if we need more certain types of books and things.

Informative
So you can let our parents know we are doing all right.
So you can tell our parents if were not getting on or if we're naughty.

Prosser went on from this preliminary discussion to ask her pupils whether they thought the teacher's assessment of a child's learning and behaviour should be open to the child concerned.

There was an immediate and unanimous chorus against this idea. I asked why they should be secret and the replies included:

to save embarrassment;
so people's feelings aren't hurt;
it might be unkind to tell someone they aren't very good at something if they think they are;
supposing it's someone who's a slow learner. Think how they would feel if you said so.

What is remarkable in this discussion, is not that these eight- and nine-year-olds are aware of the possible emotional impact of assessment; it is that they regard that impact as inevitably negative. There are no references to the motivating power of positive feedback, or any recognition of the possibility that the assessment of achievement might enhance children's feelings of success and self-esteem. Their perception is of the potential hurt to children's feelings, and they seem to have excluded the possible rewards of praise and celebration from their account. This discussion, in itself, was enough to suggest to Margaret Prosser, the children's teacher, some worrying possibilities. Did the pupils' comments mean they had never experienced motivating praise, or reassuring assessments? Were her comments, her informal assessments, really so hurtful and damaging? How did they know, so confidently, how badly children can feel about themselves? What did they know about their teacher's assessments of their learning?

Margaret Prosser decided to take her investigation one stage further, by exploring this final question. She asked the group:

> 'Do you think then that some of you think you are good at something when you aren't really good at it at all in my view? Do some of you really think my views about you are quite different from your own view of yourself?' There was lively discussion at once of the possibilities of a mismatch between their perceptions and mine, with some children thinking silently and hard on the issue, while others began noisy arguments with each other, and several children insisted over everybody else's heads that they didn't know what I thought of them.
>
> (After further discussion and a show of hands) the results were: ten children (out of 22) believed they knew just what their teacher thought of them. Seven children said they had no idea. Five children said they couldn't make up their minds. They thought they knew but they weren't very sure.

This discussion surprised and alarmed the teacher. It seemed that for more than half the class:

> issues of identity are so blurred, that they must lack any reference point from which to begin to think through, to evaluate and eventually define, their own role in learning.

In follow-up interviews with individual children, Prosser investigated the complex thinking that surrounded the children's statements, and revealed some surprising inconsistencies. For example, a tape-recorded interview with Chris included this exchange:

T: Chris, aren't you really sure what I think about your work?
Chris: I know you think I'm good at maths. I am good at maths but I should be. My Dad's a maths teacher. But I don't really know about the rest of everything.
T: Yes, you are very good at maths.

Chris:	But I'm useless at reading.
T:	Chris, what a ridiculous thing to say. You're super at reading.
Chris:	(Very animated and interrupting me) My Mum says I'm useless. I know you say I'm good at it but my Mum says I'm useless.

Prosser's study, though small in scale, alerted her to ways in which her children seemed to be losing out on possibilities for learning about themselves; she was forced to consider what effect her assessments were having on the children themselves, and their views of themselves:

> The kind of image conflict apparent in Chris was later mirrored in other conversations with individual children. Whatever the foundations for such conflicts, however, the fact remains that more than half the class are beset by confusions over self-image and identity which must sit very uncomfortably on small shoulders…For all these children, such issues may impede or inhibit learning.

She also noted that the children seemed to believe very firmly that assessment was something that was done to them, by an adult. The earlier discussions had showed how they thought this assessment was best not revealed, and half the class had admitted that the nature of the teacher's assessments was unknown to them. To redress the balance in favour of pupil involvement in assessment, she invited the class to devise a self-assessment schedule, to which they gave the title, 'What makes me, ME?' As they worked in small groups to determine the categories for this schedule, Prosser was encouraged by the children's motivation, interest and awareness of the issues. But once individual pupils began to complete the schedule in its agreed format, she was disagreeably surprised to observe the pupils' anxiety about whether they had fulfilled the task 'correctly', asking the teacher several times if what they had written down was 'right' or 'true'.

> My feelings were dramatically underlined by the following exchange:
>
> | David: | Shouldn't you write down on this if you agree with what we've written? |
> |---|---|
> | MP: | I don't think so. It's what you think that matters, not what I think. |
> | David: | But we might be wrong. |

David has been learning, throughout his schooling, that whatever this particular eccentric teacher may say about the importance of the pupil's point of view, it is, in the end, the teacher who distinguishes right answers from wrong. In self-assessment, as in any classroom inquiry, the pupil must defer to the teacher. Assessment practices that reinforce this view are, effectively, denying children's autonomy and individuality as learners; they cannot be in the best interests of children. Assessment that works in the interests of children will enhance their ability to see and understand their learning for themselves, to judge it for themselves and to act on their judgements.

Among the outcomes of effective assessment are, I have suggested, ways of seeing the differences between pupils that will enable teachers to understand and support the learning of individuals. This suggestion might be interpreted as implying that the process of differentiation is necessarily an enabling one, in which teachers create optimum learning conditions for each child. But the concept of differentiation is a great deal more complex than that. Furthermore, the application of the concept in classrooms may have extremely undesirable consequences. As some of the examples already given have shown, the identification of differences between pupils ('one of Mrs C's children') may have severely disabling effects.

In a challenging paper Susan Hart (1992) reviews the current debate around the practice of differentiation and concludes that its uncritical use may encourage a damaging tendency to locate learning difficulties inside particular pupils, rather than somewhere in the constellation of classroom events, teaching styles and curriculum content that surrounds all pupils. Differentiation, at its most extreme, may be a process of labelling, and eventually, condemning those pupils whose learning is sufficiently different to cause concern. When differentiation reinforces and perpetuates existing inequalities, it cannot be in the interests of children. Hart argues the need for 'a *critical* alternative to differentiation as a framework for providing "appropriate" educational opportunities for all children' (p.131). She calls on teachers to 'reformulate "difficulties" as a problem for the *curriculum* rather than a problem of the child' (p.136). 'Learning difficulties' (for example, in copying from the blackboard) 'can perform an important service on behalf of all children by drawing attention to possibilities for development which might otherwise pass unnoticed.' The provision of appropriate and equitable learning opportunities for all depends on the teacher using the differences between children, as observed in their interaction with the curriculum, as a way of evaluating that curriculum. Perceived individual differences can be useful in alerting the teacher to inappropriate elements of provision, materials and teaching styles, elements which are inappropriate for all pupils.

Equally, I would argue, the observation of individuals and the differences between them can serve to reinforce our respect for the rights of children to learning that is personally meaningful to them. In Chris Athey's nursery project, children's rights in this respect were recognised and provided for; they were given freedom of choice in selecting curriculum content that was appropriate for the invariant patterns, the cognitive constants, of their thought and behaviour. In the High/Scope nursery, the concept of active learning is used to ensure that each child's chosen activity leads him or her into experiences that foster meaningful learning. In Stephen Rowland's class, closely observed by Michael Armstrong, the freedom of choice given to all pupils for at least some of each day, allowed individuals to allocate time and energy to different activities. Observations of these individual differences enabled Armstrong and Rowland to see and understand each individual's learning more clearly. Their own learning about children's learning helped them to support it more appropriately.

Mary Rosenberg carried out two studies in her Norfolk primary classroom of 32 children, aged seven and eight. In the first, she examined the writing of Katey, aged seven and a half. She found that this child, quiet and often tearful, showing many signs of insecurity, both in her friendships and in her cautious approach to unfamiliar tasks, was most completely at home in this one area of the curriculum, her writing. In writing Katey finds the security and the isolation that she seems to need; she works at a table with five other children, who sit where Katey directs them to sit. The three boys in the group sit opposite Katey, so that she can control their behaviour, to some extent, by her directions (which, to the teacher's surprise, they obey). The two other girls sit either side of Katey, so that she can give them the help they often ask for with reading and writing. In this apparently safe environment, that she has arranged to her own satisfaction, Katey sits and writes.

Mary Rosenberg's collected examples of Katey's writing illustrate the range and power of this child's learning – about the world, herself, and the relationships between the two. Like four-year-old Shazia and her friends, playing at wolves, doctors and nurses, Katey explores the world around her in its emotional as well as its material richness, investigating her own feelings of vulnerability, fear, triumph, loneliness and pride. In one particularly moving story, she seems to be investigating the tension between dependence and independence.

Once upon a time there was a little boy called Johnny and all he would do was gardening. His mum tried to make him do other things but he simply would not leave the garden. So his mum gave it up. One day at dinner time his mummy said to him:

'Johnny, go out and play football with the other boys.'

'Alright,' said Johnny, but after he had had his dinner he went straight to the garden till teatime. So when teatime came John came indoors with very muddy hands.

'Johnny,' said his mother, 'you've been gardening again.'

Then his mum had an idea.

'Johnny,' she said, 'go round Peter's house after tea please.'

'Yes, mum,' he said.

At Peter's house there was a garden. John was pleased. He started gardening and he found a bird in it. Johnny picked it up and took it home. His mother washed it, then made a nest for it.

'You can keep it,' she said to Johnny. Johnny kept it and looked after it and he doesn't garden quite so much as before.

Mary Rosenberg comments:

This was maybe her fullest expression of uncertainty about the outside world, enigmatic and beautiful...in the final twist, Johnny's dependence on his familiar surroundings is transformed into a bird's dependence on him, maybe reflecting the strength which Katey derives from her own group of friends.

In another case-study of her own class of pupils, Mary Rosenberg surveyed a large collection of children's drawings made over one term. The variety of the collection is astonishing, and the children's interest in their teacher's interest is intense. Her data includes long transcribed interviews with the children about their drawings, which told her more than she ever imagined she could learn from them. Two children stand out in this study: Max and Daniel. Max draws at home as well as at school:

Well what I do at home is, I get a piece of paper and just put something and then make it into something. Like a squiggle, and then I look at it for about a quarter of an hour and think of lots of things what it could be, and then I just draw. I did a straight line once, and it ended up to be a Viking ship, which is hanging, which is on our wall.

Both Max and Daniel are confident that it is their favourite activity, and Max knows why:

You can put a lot of life into drawings if you try. Then it feels as though it's really happening, if you get into drawing, it feels as though it's really happening.

Like Shazia's play, and Katey's writing, Max's drawing is the domain where his imagination makes things 'really' happen. School and home are real too, of course, but when 'you get into drawing, it's really happening'. Both Max and Daniel use writing and drawing as parts of the same process, of building an imaginative world of their own.

Max: I draw my pictures before I start writing.
Daniel: Me too.
Max: So then I can write about my picture.
MR: Does it help you to write stories?
Max &
Daniel: Yes.
MR: Do you think you could write a story without drawings?
Daniel: I think I could – probably.
Max: I don't think I could do it *properly*, without a drawing by the side.

But the most convincing evidence of the importance of drawing to their intellectual and emotional well-being, to their lives and learning, is in this passage from a long taped interview, when their teacher asks:

MR: What would you say if you were told you could never, you were
              never allowed to do any more drawings?
Daniel
& Max: (as if in pain) Oh!
Daniel: Leave school.
Max: I don't know.
Daniel: I would go, er . . .
Max: I don't know, but I just wouldn't do anything else. I would get very
              upset, and start shouting at whoever said that.

Mary Rosenberg's two studies of children's learning, of one child's learning through writing, and two others' learning through drawing, show very clearly that the appropriate educational opportunities for all children, for which Susan Hart (op. cit.) calls, can be equitable without being identical. Within the undifferentiated curriculum that their teacher is offering, Max, Daniel and Katey have exercised their right to be different and to make their learning meaningful to them. Their teacher is acting responsibly in safeguarding this right. Whose interests would be served if Katey were obliged to draw pictures to go with her writing, or Max and Daniel were forbidden to draw when they should be writing? The equitable curriculum maintains equality of opportunity while recognising and respecting children's right to be different in ways that are worthwhile.

And so, in effective assessment, teachers learn to understand learning, they learn about individuals and about groups of children; they learn about the impact of their teaching and about the value of the curriculum they offer. They use their assessments to enhance the learning of all children, individually and collectively. Recognising differences in children's learning does not entitle teachers to label or denounce these differences; trying to understand difference rules out rejecting or pathologising it; respecting difference also entails maintaining fiercely egalitarian principles. The difficulty and complexity of this task does not reduce its importance.

An interesting insight into how this educational task looks from outside the world of education can be found in an essay by D. W. Winnicott (1964). In 'Educational Diagnosis', Winnicott discusses the diagnostic purpose of assessment. 'What is there that a doctor can usefully say to a teacher?' he begins, asking his readers what in teaching corresponds to the diagnosis on which the whole of a doctor's work is based.

> ...I feel bound to say that I can see but little in teaching that is truly equivalent to the deliberate diagnosis of doctors. In my dealings with the teaching profession I am frequently disturbed in mind by the way in which the general mass of children are educated without first being diagnosed. (p.206)

Winnicott goes on to distinguish between the varying *intellectual* capacities of children and their varying *emotional* needs (his italics), arguing that to treat all children as if their emotional needs were identical is, at the very least, strange. 'A doctor's suggestion is that more could be done than is being done at present along the lines of diagnosis' (p.207). The doctor's suggestion that follows is, at first sight, bizarre, and on closer inspection, completely unacceptable. Winnicott suggests classifying children into two groups and creating two different types of schools, planned to take account of the differences between children with satisfactory homes, who come to school because 'they want to learn lessons', and children with unsatisfactory homes who 'do not come to school to learn, but to find a home from home' (p.208). While we can confidently decline this suggestion, which, however, was certainly intended to be helpful, we may profitably note, and reflect on Winnicott's starting point: that the foundation of good medicine is accurate diagnosis. Accurate diagnosis on a scientific basis distinguishes the medical profession proper from faith healers and other quack cures (among which Winnicott includes the blind administration of antibiotics). The foundation of good education is, by analogy, the process of assessment, which is, among other things, diagnostic of individuals in purpose, and beneficial to the learning of individuals in its outcomes.

It is interesting to speculate how Winnicott would have responded to the work of Vygotsky (1978), and in particular to his description of the process that he calls 'dynamic assessment'. Winnicott's anxieties centre on the problem of 'the general mass of children (who) are educated without first being diagnosed'. Vygotsky's argument is based on a different premise: that teachers do 'diagnose' children, but that the diagnosis is unhelpful because it focuses on the past, on what has already been learned, and not on the future, on learning that is yet to come. Teachers have, according to Vygotsky, concentrated their efforts in assessment on establishing each child's actual developmental level, and the functions that have already matured. Vygotsky suggests an alternative: 'Imagine that I do not terminate my study at this point but only begin it' (p.86). His assessment will be of the 'zone of proximal development', of the cognitive functions that are in the process of maturing, of the learning that is just about to take place. Enlightened by this form of assessment, the teacher is in a good position to support each child's learning as it happens. 'Learning which is oriented toward developmental levels that have already been reached is ineffective from the viewpoint of a child's overall development. It does not aim for a new stage of the developmental process but rather lags behind this process' (p.89). Assessment that focuses, not on the past, but on the immediate future, is the key that opens the door to the next steps in learning. In the case-study that follows we will be able to see glimpses of this approach in action.

This observation was made by Jenny Colls, class teacher in a unit for four-year-old children in a primary school in Bedfordshire. As part of the evaluation of the expansion of early years education in that county, teachers in six of the new four-plus units were asked to monitor the learning of four targeted children over the academic year. Guljeet is one of those children, and this observation is taken from a much longer account of her learning throughout the year.

Figure 7.1 Guljeet's drawing and writing

Observation of Guljeet – June 1990

G is working with the hollow blocks with L – they make a long slide with steps going up to it.

G organises children to go in a line, and invites the teacher to take a turn too. 'Everyone get in a line.'

'I'm going to make a photo of her on the slide.'

(fetches paper and pencil).

The teacher encourages her to look at the shapes of the bricks she has used.

G: 'I can't see it when people are on it' (waving people off). She sits down with paper and pencil.

'Make a rectangle round there to make a photo.' Draws the slide (1), then goes to get another piece of paper and draws human figures (2).

G: 'Like the lady did outside with girls and boys.'

A photographer had taken the class photo recently.

G continues drawing: 'We have to put the boys at the bottom so they don't get mixed up...Now I'm going to get scissors and cut it out...Now I'm going to stick it and then I'll make tickets to go on the slide...I'll cut the tickets and you (the teacher) must tell me how to write it. I want to write 'You can go on the slide'. (There has been a lot of ticket making/invitation writing going on recently in child-initiated play activities.) The teacher writes out the words at G's dictation and G copies it (3) forming all the letters correctly. Another child approaches – 'Can I go on the slide?'

G: 'I doing tickets. Wait!...' Another child tries to use the slide, 'Wait Raji!... Levi wait a minute!'

R tries again. G: 'Raji! *wait* a minute... When I say "ready" everyone can go. People can give the ticket back and more people can go on.' She has finished copying four tickets. She organises a ticket for each child waiting and stands by the slide. G: 'We're ready.' S, L, B and R get in line.

G: 'Ticket. Slide down.' She gives a ticket to M: 'What does it say?'

G: 'You can go on the slide.'

Unfortunately the play came to abrupt halt here with the appearance of a tray of biscuits!

In this observation we can see how the teacher's support for Guljeet's urgent purposes (writing the tickets) enabled her, in Vygotsky's words 'to do with assistance today (what) she will be able to do by herself tomorrow' (p.87). The teacher did not conclude from her observation that Guljeet could not write independently; on the contrary, she made a very positive judgement about Guljeet's developing mastery of the writing system, including her ability to use adult support to achieve her goals. She recognised in Guljeet's dependence upon the adult writer what Vygotsky calls the 'buds' or 'flowers', rather than the 'fruits' of development. Her disposition to look to the future of Guljeet's learning, and not just at what she had or had not already learned, was firmly in Guljeet's interests.

Furthermore, this case-study illustrates how the adults who worked in Guljeet's classroom built on what they saw, using their understanding of children's learning to shape a curriculum that offered both food and exercise to their developing powers. Children learning to write independently were given many and varied opportunities to write purposively, with support from others. Children learning to represent the world around them in a variety of ways were given rich experiences of different forms of representation. Children working for sustained periods, with concentration and intensity on a single activity, were given time to see their projects through to completion. Assessment worked for the children in this classroom.

Making assessment work is a project that occupies teachers in a number of different contexts: within the classroom, within the school as a whole, within the parent/teacher partnership, within the process of transfer from class to class and school to school. Similarly, early years educators strive to make assessment work in playgroups, day care, family centres, family group care, as well as in nursery schools and classes, before children reach the statutory age of education. As children move from one educational setting to another, even if it is only a short distance along a corridor, from Year R to Year 1, or from Key Stage One to Key Stage Two, how can assessment work for them?

Solving this problem in teachers' assessment practice is likely to be at least as difficult as any other, if not substantially more so, since between our genuine aspirations for good practice and its realisation falls the shadow of professional mistrust.

When teachers discuss, on in-service courses and at staff meetings, the ways in which their assessments of children's learning are received and made use of by others, in other settings, their comments are often reproachful, even bitter. Often the story is one of feeling unwanted, undervalued and unappreciated; the Key Stage Two teachers show no interest in the lovingly compiled portfolios of three years' learning in Key Stage One; or the secondary school staff have asked for a summary of each child's learning given as quantifiable test results. Early years educators have been heard to complain that their detailed assessments are tidied away into cupboards in the reception classroom, never to be seen again. Every teacher has anecdotal evidence to recount of the way in which his or her judgements were discounted, over-ruled, ignored. Many staff groups will have had the frustrating experience of being asked to provide assessments in forms that they do not think appropriate.

A directive from the junior school up the road arrived one day in the infant school where I was working, requesting the following information at transfer *and nothing more* (junior headteacher's italics); for each pupil, date of birth, day-time phone number of parent(s) and reading age (Young's group reading test). The emotions aroused in the infant school staff by this diktat did a great deal to harm professional relationships between the two staff groups.

But when the focus of discussion shifts to the ways in which teachers themselves receive and make use of assessments made by others, then the shoe is on the other foot. Teachers on the receiving end are at pains to point out their independence and strength of judgement, their neutrality and impartiality, and the corresponding likelihood that the judgements of others will be misguided. On the receiving end, teachers have been known to stress the importance of starting with a clean slate, making up their own minds, taking it with a pinch of salt, and allowing for exaggeration. They are likely to refer to their previous experience of 'that' nursery, 'those' children, and 'some' teachers.

Incidentally, there is some evidence that this is not a problem confined to England and Wales; the report by HMI of practice in a small group of French schools (DES 1991a) described the use of the *Dossier Scholaire*, a cumulative record of each pupil's achievements. Two conditions are attached to its use: first, the parents of the pupils are not allowed to see the *Dossier*, and, secondly, the receiving teacher is not allowed to read it until after Christmas, that is, until after one-third of the school year has already passed. The assessments recorded in the *Dossier*, then, can only work for pupils in the remaining two-thirds of the school year. When the receiving teacher does see the records, after Christmas, the impact and relevance of what was written, at the very least, five months previously, is likely to be minimal.

Practice in this country is not yet centrally regulated in this way, nor perhaps so arbitrarily and absolutely fixed. But there are similarities between the French approach and the English primary teacher who insists on making up his or her own mind before studying pupils' records and assessments. The common factor is professional mistrust. The assessments of other teachers, other educators, are treated with caution, even with suspicion. The assumption seems to be that the judgements of the receiving teachers, meeting a group of pupils for the first time, are likely to be more accurate and better informed than the judgements of teachers who have worked with these pupils over the previous academic year. It is very difficult to see how such an assumption can be justified.

Assessment cannot be made to work for the benefit of pupils if teachers mistrust one another's judgements. There is little hope of achieving continuity for each child's learning if there is a break in professional confidence at points of transfer, from year to year, or from school to school. Assessment will only work for pupils when mistrust gives way to trust, and when teachers treat each other's judgements with respect, confident that they can all contribute to a shared understanding of children's learning. Underlying effective practice in the transfer of assessments and records will be a relationship between teachers based on trust and respect. But these attitudes cannot be set in place at the stroke of a pen on a policy document, or by an imperative from the senior management team.

Trust and respect for each other's judgements will only develop when there are opportunities for open dialogue between teachers in different settings, opportunities for genuine debate and disagreement, as well as for agreement and accord. The dialogue will be concerned with the principles that underlie effective assessment as well as with the day by day practices. Teachers who engage in such a dialogue will explore the relationship between their principles and their practices, as well as listening to other teachers' accounts of their own explorations into making assessment work.

CHAPTER 8

Practices and Principles

In Chapter 2, I suggested that the complex process of assessment could most simply be described by using a simple model made up of three elements: evidence, judgement and outcomes. Each of these three elements has been discussed and now it is time to examine the more elusive part of the process, the way in which we move, in our assessment practice, from element to element within the model. How do we, as teachers, move from evidence to judgement, from judgements to outcomes? What kinds of choices are we making as we do so? What kinds of practices are involved? Can we describe our choices simply in terms of practices, or are there other kinds of choices to be made? What connections can be drawn between the external events of the classroom and the internal conceptual structures that help us to shape and understand those events? What sort of correspondence is there between the inside of a teacher's head and the outside world of schools, classrooms and pupils?

In reflecting on these questions we need to distinguish between classroom practice as it actually is, as fairly and fully as we can describe it, and classroom practice as we would ideally like it to be. These two versions of events are not just different, I will argue, but sometimes in opposition. Some characteristics of schools and classrooms, as we know them today, make it highly unlikely that our ideals can ever be realised.

One such characteristic is the inertia of the daily routine in an institution such as a school. Minor interruptions and disruptions are commonplace in every school and classroom, but they are normally absorbed without any difficulty: only major disturbances have any power to affect the apparently inexorable order of things. On the whole, one day is very much like another, one week very much like the one before and the one after; the successive terms bring their own rituals, but Christmas follows Christmas and summer follows summer in a highly predictable pattern. This pattern certainly contributes to a sense of purpose and stability for all the members of a school community; a school where nothing was predictable would be unendurable for teachers, pupils and parents. Knowing roughly, or even precisely, what is going to happen next is a very powerful human strategy for reducing anxiety and conflict, and increasing control and harmony. And yet, in the inertia-bound classroom, which I have baldly and exaggeratedly represented in figure 8.1, there is, in addition to a sense of security, a sense of sterility. What happens today can be seen as the sum of what happened yesterday, plus the available resources (what there is in my cupboard), plus the amount of personal energy remaining, plus the requirements of other powerful individuals (headteacher, Secretary of State) plus National Curriculum requirements, plus the ordinary routines and rituals of the school (what happens anyway, in spite of everything).

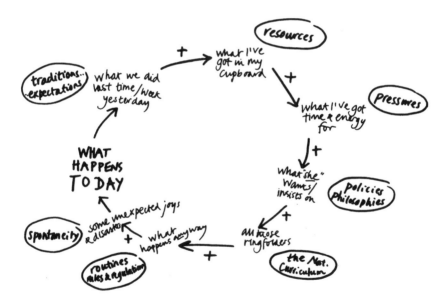

Figure 8.1 The inertia model

The inertia-bound classroom is characterised not just by its predictability, but by the absence of questions. There is no need to ask any, since the answers are already given in the elements of the cycle.

Practice can be reduced to the sum of its parts: the provision, the timetable, the programmes of study, the traditions and expectations of a particular time and place. The inertia-bound classroom is deeply resistant to change and development. The ideals and aspirations of the teachers who work there are somehow split off from the daily cycle of events. We can represent life in such a classroom, even more simply, as the relationship between three worlds:

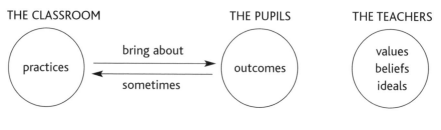

THE CLASSROOM   THE PUPILS   THE TEACHERS

Figure 8.2

In this crude diagram, 'practices' represents everything that teachers and pupils actually do in the school or classroom, and 'outcomes' represents the learning and development that ensue, including the negative, undesirable and unintended outcomes, which may then modify the practices themselves. The teachers' beliefs, values, ideals and aspirations play no discernible part in the daily pattern of events.

This pessimistic caricature does, I maintain, represent some inescapable realities in primary education: the force of inertia, the tendency not to question taken-for-granted practices, the pressures experienced by teachers from outside themselves (from educational publishers and manufacturers as well as from central and local government, professional bodies, and powerful individuals in the school community).

Another characteristic of primary schools that contributes to the difference between what teachers believe and what teachers do is the emphasis given to planning classroom events, as opposed to reviewing and evaluating them. It is not uncommon for teachers, working individually, or in teams or year groups, to plan a series of topics for up to a year ahead. These long-term plans are normally supplemented by both medium- and short-term plans: in the last of these it is sometimes possible to read how every pupil in the class, frequently assigned to one of three or more so-called ability groups, with tasks differentiated accordingly, will spend every minute of his or her school week – week after week, month after month. Enormous quantities of time and energy are expended by teachers and their support staff in this way. And yet some of this planning activity may, in the long term, be counter-productive. Planning is essentially a forward-looking activity; it is carried out in the future tense; it is a way to express one's ideals and aspirations; it can be very satisfying – and sometimes dangerously remote from reality. There is a danger that, in schools, planning becomes a vivid description of the world as we would like it to be, rather than an action plan for how we might make it happen. Figure 8.3 is an attempt to illustrate this danger.

This is not to suggest that we can dispense with planning; but rather to argue that unless planning is tied to a rigorous process of review, it remains in the domain of wishful thinking, hope-for-the-best. And the land of good intentions is not good enough for our pupils.

Too frequent a use of the future tense can lead us to neglect the present tense, the reality of the moment, the only curriculum that our pupils ever experience. And to understand that present, we need to interrogate it, to find the piercing questions that will help us achieve a quality curriculum. Questions about everyday life in classrooms are the essence of review – and it is only questions like those on the right-hand side of the diagram (figure 8.3) that can turn planning into a force for reality, rather than fantasy.

PLAN –	OR	– REVIEW
looking ahead	or	looking back
good intentions	or	what actually happened?
'wouldn't-it-be-lovely'	or	well, was it?
wishful thinking	or	factual descriptions
aspirations	or	analysis
theories	or	evidence
hope-for-the-best	or	real understanding

Figure 8.3

Only when the process of review is at least as painstaking and meticulous as the process of planning can we expect that the curriculum that pupils experience will reach the quality we aspire to. And in the process of review, one of our most powerful professional strategies will be the practice of assessment, the practice in which, first, we come to understand what and how our pupils learn, and then put that understanding to good use.

There is still another element to be added to this analysis. I have suggested that classroom practice should be driven by critical review as much as by optimistic planning; but reviewing and planning cannot reliably generate effective practice unless they are rooted in and informed by principles, principles that have themselves been shaped by our most deeply held values and beliefs. The extent to which we can articulate our values, our sense of what we believe to be good and worthwhile, have a direct bearing on the cycle of classroom events. Our values can lead us, if we take the trouble to explore them and understand them, to formulate the principles by which our classroom practices are to be both planned and reviewed. Our on-the-spot choices and instantaneous decisions during the hurly-burly of classroom events, can be informed, if we so desire, by a framework of principles that express our deepest understanding of the purposes of education. A representation of this possibility is shown in figure 8.4.

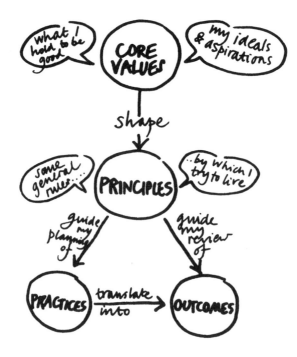

Figure 8.4

This diagram represents a teacher's core values, a teacher's sense of 'what I hold to be good', as shaping the principles that guide practices. This representation seems to suggest that personal values are the starting point of a teacher's enquiry into teaching and learning: in fact, it is much more common, in my experience, for the intellectual journey to be undertaken in the opposite direction, from practice, to principle, to value.

Substantial experience of in-service courses on the topic of assessment over the last ten years has shown me that this journey is, for many teachers, well worth making, arduous though it may sometimes be. When discussions of assessment practice take place at the practical level, with teachers exchanging formats and record-keeping systems, they can serve a very comforting and useful function. Teachers who support each other in this way appreciate the chance both to be helpful and to be helped. But being helpful is no substitute for thinking. A discussion of practices that leads to principles being established is likely to be more challenging, but, in the long term, more worthwhile. A discussion of principles that discloses core values is likely to be still more challenging and still more worthwhile. These propositions have been used as the basis for part of a discussion pack on assessment in the early years (Drummond, Rouse & Pugh 1992). In one of the activities in this pack, early years educators are offered, for discussion, a handout giving a set of principles extracted from a variety of policy documents on assessment (see figure 8.5).

The purpose of this activity is not simply for each individual to declare a position on each statement, nor yet for the members of the group to identify a number of statements on which they agree. Rather, it is for the educators to have the experience of establishing *why* they would hold to these principles. The process of persistently asking 'why?' about a set of statements that seem at first sight to be self-explanatory, has proved to be a valuable one for those who took part in the trialling of the pack.

For example, a group of educational psychologists worked together to explore their understanding of the principle shown in item 14 in figure 8.5. Their thinking proceeded slowly at first:

Assessments made over a period of time should be used to review and evaluate the provision made for the children during that time.
Why?
Because assessments form the basis for further assessments.

Do You Agree?	Strongly	Agree	Disagree	Strongly
1 Parents should be involved in the assessment of their children.				
2 All the adult staff should be involved in the process of assessment.				
3 Children should be involved in the assessment of their own progress and development.				
4 We should only assess those aspects of children's learning and development that we believe to be truly important.				
5 To assess effectively we need to be certain of the kinds of learning that we value most.				
6 Assessments of children of nearly school age should match the assessment practice used by the school as the children enter Key Stage One of the National Curriculum.				
7 Records should show the development of each child's social relationships and attachments.				
8 Assessment must be based on detailed observations of what children do and say.				
9 Written records should include factual evidence, sensitive interpretations and tentative judgement.				
10 Written records should not show isolated incidents but selected observations that demonstrate progress and development.				
11 When appropriate, assessments of bilingual children should be made in the child's home language by a person who understands the child's culture.				
12 Assessment must take account of the possible effects of the context on the child (e.g. the language used, the child's previous experience, the child's emotional state).				
13 Assessments of individual children should be used in planning activities for those children.				
14 Assessments made over a period of time should be used to review and evaluate the provision made for the children during their time.				
15 Please add…				
16 …some more…				
17 …of your own				

Figure 8.5

But Why?
Because we use the knowledge we gain about children to plan the future.
But Why?
Why do we want to use this knowledge to help in planning?
Because children are different, at different times, in different places, with different educators.

But gradually the group began to use their stream of why questions to force them to articulate their implicit understanding:

But Why?
But why do we say children are different at different times?
Because one-off assessments can be very misleading.
But Why?
But why do we think these assessments are misleading?
Because children are affected by changes in external factors – relationships, environment, resources, everything around them.
But Why?
Because children are a product of their constantly changing environment.
And so...everything that educators do has an effect on children and their learning.
And so...Assessment is part of everything that educators do...
And so...Assessment must work for the benefit of children.

In this discussion, these educators were moving towards the expression of a statement of value: they have articulated their belief that children's interests are paramount in the practice of assessment, and will now be able to go on to clarify what they mean by 'children's interests'. They will be able to think about their aspirations for children's learning, defining for themselves the learning and development that they value most highly. In the process they have drawn, and will draw, on other dimensions of their professional expertise – on their understanding of children's learning and behaviour, and their knowledge of contextual and motivational factors in learning.

This example of discussion between experienced professionals who practise assessment in their daily work illustrates clearly the benefits of reflective and challenging self-questioning. The experience of this group, working in this way, is not unique. During one in-service course, I worked with a group of early years teachers and nursery nurses from three primary schools, using the format shown in figure 8.5. The group spent some time discussing a number of the principles that they would draw on in their assessment practice. Like the group in the previous example, they worked hard to uncover the core values that gave life to and sustained their principles. The principle of parental involvement in assessment, for example, was discussed at length, in an attempt to discover why it was held to be so important; the concepts of partnership, dependence and interdependence were examined. By the end of the discussion a firm link had been established between what these teachers believed to be centrally good in human relations, and their desire to express the core values of respect and trust in the process of involving parents in the practice of assessment. During the discussion the teachers clarified and articulated the connection between their values and their principles.

At a subsequent session of the same in-service course, the teachers and nursery nurses were invited to describe one particular aspect of their assessment practice. They brought with them to the session a variety of formats and examples of their work: portfolios, tick-sheets, reading records, annotated collections of children's drawings, end-of-year reports, and so on. They talked for some time about the ways in which they used these formats, giving practical details and noting the benefits and limitations of each practice. But the discussion came to an abrupt halt when we tried to discern the principles that underlay the practices. After a brief but awful silence, the group began to discuss, rather disconsolately, their sobering awareness that there was no connection to be made between the principles they had discussed so attentively the week before, and the practices that were occupying them now. It was as if, like Mother Hubbard, they had suddenly found 'the cupboard was bare'.

After further discussion, and some mutual reassurance, this group of educators came to see the urgency of establishing connections between their inner and outer worlds. It was not that these educators lived without values, or acted in unprincipled ways; the cupboard was not, after all, as bare as Mother Hubbard found it. But they did appreciate that they had neglected to establish and maintain a living link between belief and practice, between ideal and reality, between aspiration and action. They saw the inadequacy of a model of teaching and learning that is confined to the practical domain, where practice and outcomes are split from the educator's idealism and conviction. They recognised the need to reaffirm their belief in themselves as people with the power to think, as well as people with the power to do.

At the heart of effective assessment, at the heart of worthwhile teaching and a proper understanding of learning, is the power of teachers to think, not just about pedagogical issues, but as moral beings. The power to make moral judgements about what is good and worthwhile is added to the power of teachers to act, in classroom practice, to bring about the learning that is judged to be good and worthwhile, the expression of the ideal they are striving for. Teachers who see themselves in this way, with their power to do governed by their power to distinguish and define the good, can escape from the inertia model and from the wishful thinking of planning and hoping for the best. Teachers who recognise their moral discernment as the force that guides their pedagogical choices will not suffer from the Mother Hubbard syndrome, or fail to see the connections between children's interests and their own moment-by-moment choices in the classroom.

This moral awareness will, furthermore, remind them constantly of their fallibility, of the essential provisionality and imperfection of the art of teaching. Their sense of what is good, and what is to be aspired to, will not delude them into assuming that they can always achieve that good. They will not confuse quality with perfection, or the process of striving to do better by their pupils with the unimaginable condition of having arrived at an unsurpassable best. These teachers will welcome opportunities to move beyond questions of what and how to teach, and questions of what and how children learn, to sterner questions that uncover their core values. 'Why?' questions about teaching and learning can only fully be answered by reference to a system of moral beliefs about what it is to be a human, and, in Aristotle's terms, what it is to lead 'a virtuous life'.

Aristotle maintained that the good and virtuous life included the practice of self-understanding. Coming to know and understand oneself and one's values is, in itself, a constituent of the 'good life'. Aristotle says, of his own enquiry into ethics, 'We are enquiring not in order to know what virtue is, but in order to become good' (Lear 1988, p.159). Teachers coming to understand themselves and their core values, as part of the process of coming to understand the world in which they work, and the children whom they educate, will also come to understand what it is to 'become good'. They will learn to articulate their vision of the kinds of people, good people, they intend their pupils to be. They will be able to identify, with confidence, those elements of 'good practice' that contribute to these ends. It is teachers' moral understanding that drives effective teaching and worthwhile learning. Without an apprehension of the good that is striven for, and the outcomes to be desired, the act of educating becomes a series of random, unprincipled, more or less pragmatic decisions, which may or may not be in the interests of children.

Robin Alexander (1992) has critically explored the relationship between teachers' value systems and the problematic concept of 'good practice'. His model, shown in figure 8.6, represents 'good practice' as lying, conceptually, at the intersection of five dimensions. Political, pragmatic, empirical and conceptual considerations stand alongside the teacher's value system in the formation of 'good practice'.

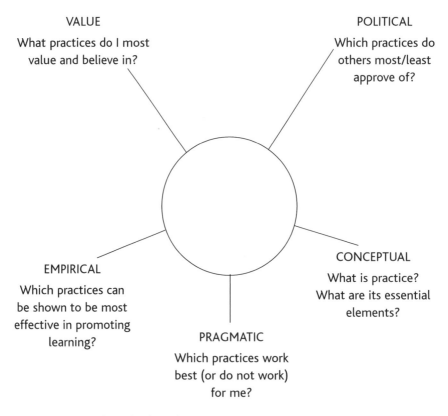

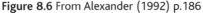

Figure 8.6 From Alexander (1992) p.186

This model seems to me to miss the full meaning of the term 'good', and to ignore its power to define and qualify the four other dimensions that Alexander identifies. For example, the pragmatic consideration, 'Which practices work best for me?' begs the question of what it means for a practice to 'work', let alone 'work best'. The criteria by which such a judgement might be made are not neutral, or value-free. Rather, the pragmatic enquiry into practice is value-infested, since the phrases 'work for me' and 'work best' are philosophically equivalent to 'bring about that which I hold to be good' or 'bring about the development of the good pupil', whatever the term 'good' might represent to a particular teacher. The pragmatic consideration cannot be separated, as in Alexander's model, from the value dimension. In the same way, the empirical consideration is informed by moral judgements about what constitutes worthwhile learning.

The political dimension too is open to a similar qualification, since teachers are unlikely to achieve 'good practice' at the behest of those whose authority they do not accept. If the 'others' who exercise influence and control over the teacher's practices are conceptualised as using a just and justifiable authority, they may well exert a telling influence on practice. But if their authority is seen as unjust, or their value systems are perceived as in opposition to the teacher's, there will be at the very least, resistance to their imperatives, if not outright opposition. A teacher's view of what is good cannot be dictated by a person who does not share the teacher's understanding of the good. Teachers' practices may be manipulated, coerced, laid down by statute, and rewarded by promotion, but only their practices, not their moral judgements; whatever legislation may exist or be brought to bear, teachers retain their moral freedom.

Teachers' values are not, as Alexander suggests, one single isolated element in a web of conflicting and constraining considerations. Teachers' values and beliefs are central in defining and deciding on the 'good' in good practice. Teachers who ask themselves the conceptual, political, pragmatic and empirical questions that Alexander's model illustrates are not operating from outside their value system, but within it. They cannot answer these questions without reference to their beliefs about what is in the best interests of children, beliefs that have been formed as the result of rigorous moral enquiry. Alexander goes on to use his model to warn of the dangers of relying exclusively on values and beliefs.

> Classroom strategy can never be merely an enacting or an extension of educational belief. Yet this is exactly how good practice has frequently been defined in primary education. First work out your 'philosophy', then construct your practice to fit it; if the philosophy is right, the practice will be sound. In this version of good practice, faith alone provides the justification and evidence becomes irrelevant.
>
> Alexander (1992) pp.188–9

Here Alexander represents the belief system of teachers as impervious or antagonistic to evidence and information from the world in which they work for the benefit of children.

And, indeed, an unbridled belief in the superiority of one's unsubstantiated opinion would be an inappropriate element in a teacher's value system. Alexander illustrates the danger of relying on 'faith alone' by quoting one of his respondents in the evaluation of the Leeds Primary Needs Programme who told him, 'I don't care what the ILEA research shows: the integrated day is right for me and right for my children.' I believe that this teacher is expressing an exclusively and unreasonably pragmatic position and not a position of value at all. This teacher seems to me to represent a different danger – the danger of treating one's practices with exaggerated respect, as if they were one's core values, instead of trying by persistent and discomfiting 'why?' questions to arrive at the hidden values that underpin them. The teacher Alexander quotes seems to me to stand in need of a severe dose of 'why?' questions, questions that would enquire into the underlying reasons for each element in his or her definition of the practice of 'the integrated day'. Not until this teacher arrives at some kind of statement about what it is to be educated, or what a 'good' education makes possible for pupils, could we be said to know anything about his or her value system.

Alexander's work, here and elsewhere, is concerned with primary practice as a whole. The practice of assessment is only one constituent part of that practice. But my argument about the relationship between value, principle and practice is independent of the dimensions of the territory within which values and principles operate. Our values alone can give us the moral criteria for formulating principles by which to work. Our knowledge and understanding of children's learning can give us pragmatic and empirical guidelines to follow in the pursuit of our ideals, but our values alone can be held up alongside the outcomes of our practices, as we evaluate the effective implementation of our principles. The process of evaluation is, essentially, a process of making public the value base of our actions, and using that value base to judge our effectiveness.

An example may help to make this relationship clear. A group of early years teachers was working together to develop an assessment format to use as three- and four-year-old children entered nursery and primary school. One of their principles, already established in the group's discussions, was that parental involvement is one necessary element in effective assessment. The values that underlay this principle were respect, trust, and equality of regard. Using this principle and these values as yardsticks, they reviewed and discarded a number of published formats as being, variously, culturally insensitive, exclusive of parents, teacher-dominated, patronising and inflexible. They gradually came to realise the need to involve parents themselves in the process of devising a more appropriate format. They realised too the necessity of committing themselves to a regular and democratic review of their practice, in which parents would have an important voice. They abandoned the search for the ultimately perfect solution, and recognised the need for a format representing 'work in progress'. In this way they were able continually to draw on the insights of the parents, whose interests were affirmed by their original principles, and whose egalitarian involvement was stipulated and respected by their basic value position.

Their values did not dictate or determine the details of their eventual practice; as Alexander himself argues, 'values...provide no recipe for action, only the broad criteria by which we judge (whether) what we do is right' (p.188). But without an established core of agreed values, these teachers would have been unable to discriminate between different possibilities, except by the most limited of pragmatic considerations. There are many aspects of our daily lives where we are entitled to make unprincipled decisions and choices – whether or not we eat gooseberries, for example, as I have suggested elsewhere (Drummond, Rouse & Pugh 1992). But in the process of assessing children's learning, a process that essentially contributes, as we have seen, to an evaluation of our whole educational practice, we cannot operate without a basis of principle and value. The evaluative function of assessment depends on the existence, coherent and articulate, of the assessor's value system.

The absence of such a coherent system may well have been at the root of the indignities suffered by Jason, whose experience we considered in Chapter 1. Here pragmatic and political considerations stood in the place of any principled understanding of the purposes of assessment. Jason's performance on this test represents and reveals the value that his teachers apparently place on conventional, conforming pupil behaviour; his mathematical understanding – or lack of it – represents and reveals the lack of value that his teachers seem to place on trying to understand each learner's thinking. The value these teachers seem to attach to one particular manifestation of learning (high test scores for some pupils) is not compatible with a value system based on equality of opportunity and regard. Jason's mathematical learning will not be enhanced by the use of a different maths test, or even by the disuse of maths tests completely, but only by a revived commitment from his teachers to the essential value and importance of each individual's learning, however far it seems to fall short of desirable levels of attainment. If Jason's teachers were encouraged and supported in evaluating both their practice, and Jason's learning, they would come to see the need to re-examine the value system that sustains their practice. Their massive responsibilities to Jason's learning, they would come to see, cannot allow them the right to value Jason himself so little.

This chapter began with a series of questions about the nature of teachers' choices in the sequence of considerations that I labelled evidence, judgements and outcomes. I have argued that choices guided by pragmatic and political considerations, caricatured in the 'inertia model' (figure 8.1), cannot constitute responsible pedagogy. The responsibilities of the teacher include the responsibility to think, as well as to do. The powers of the teacher include the power to make moral judgements as well as to make practical decisions. The external events of the classroom can only fully be understood by reference to the internal moral and philosophical acts of the teacher.

CHAPTER 9

Rights, Responsibilities and Power

In the last chapter I examined the relationship between external events in schools and classrooms, and the internal conceptual structures that help to shape those events; I argued that the inside of a teacher's head can be read as a conceptual map of the outcomes striven for in everyday practices. In this chapter I consider three of the concepts that I believe play an important part in the development of effective practice, including the practice of assessment. They are the concepts that were introduced in the discussion of Jason's learning in Chapter 1, the concepts of rights, responsibilities and power.

My experience of in-service work with teachers and other educators over the last 20 years has convinced me that for the vast majority of them, the concept of responsibility is strongly developed. When experienced teachers look back at their earliest experiences, as beginning teachers, this sense of responsibility is centrally present, and is typically described, at least in retrospect, as daunting, awesome, even, for some, overwhelming.

The youth, confidence and optimism of beginning teachers may enable them to shoulder their responsibilities lightly, at least some of the time, but my own experience suggests that feelings of self-confidence and achievement are few and far between in the first years of teaching. The burden of responsibility certainly seemed at that time to be heavy enough to balance any tendency to self-congratulation; however hard one worked, it would never be hard enough. As the responsibilities of teaching became more familiar, the burden seemed to lighten, and anxiety to decrease (a little). At the same time, my increasing awareness, acquired over the years, of the complexities of teaching and learning, underlined again and again the enormity of the enterprise that I and my colleagues had signed on for. The range of our responsibilities grew too, as new areas of professional expectation opened up to us. Curriculum developments over the last 30 years have massively increased the scope of teachers' responsibilities. Working with parents, working with bilingual pupils, the introduction of micro-technology, the development of multicultural and antiracist principles, the growth of health and sex education, and developments in oracy and literacy: these concerns are only a few examples of the steadily increasing extent of primary teachers' responsibilities.

During in-service courses, when the concept of responsibility is being discussed, I often ask teachers and other educators to identify some elements in the complexity of their work with children and families for which they are *not* responsible; many of them find this very difficult. They are so much more accustomed to listing the vast range of responsibilities that they do shoulder, daily, that the suggestion that there are areas of experience outside their personal responsibility is, for some, extraordinary, and, for a few, quite unacceptable. One educator wrote: 'The minute I say that something isn't my responsibility, I begin to feel guilty about it,' and another commented, as the group discussed their written replies, 'You do feel that you are responsible for everything, even though you know it's impossible.'

It is, of course, entirely appropriate that teachers and other educators should appreciate the full extent of their professional responsibility. But, ironically, such an appreciation may sometimes act dysfunctionally, making us less effective in meeting the responsibilities of which we are so painfully aware. Some years ago a primary headteacher represented this possibility to me very vividly; as a member of a group of teachers studying for an Advanced Diploma in Educational Studies, she had been invited to contribute to a group discussion by bringing in a photograph or symbolic representation of some aspect of 'being a teacher'. She brought a full page spread from a tabloid newspaper, a dramatic aerial photograph showing the ferry boat 'The Herald of Free Enterprise' lying capsized in Zeebrugge harbour. This tragedy, still fresh in people's minds with its appalling loss of life and horrifying accounts of the scenes on board, had, naturally, affected everyone in the group, especially those who had recently travelled by ferry with their families. But the connection with the world of the primary school seemed obscure. We asked the headteacher to explain; her moving description of her thinking in selecting this image centred on the concept of responsibility, on the absolute and inexorable nature of the teacher's responsibility, which was, she suggested, ultimately quite as much a responsibility for life and death as the ferry boat captain's. She was not, she explained, thinking only of the physical safety of the pupils in a primary school, although teachers do, inevitably, take this part of their responsibilities very seriously. The headteacher told the group that she was, in a sense, haunted by her feelings of responsibility for the spiritual safety of the pupils, and by her self-imposed commitment to their educational well-being, and to every aspect of their human growth and development.

Her views were listened to attentively and respectfully; no-one attempted to persuade her that she was exaggerating. The group of teachers seemed to accept the gravity of her insight, and to endorse her expression of the seriousness of their chosen profession. The unexpected image, so powerful a reminder of the fragility of human life and the ubiquity of human error and failure, startled this group of teachers into a fresh sense of the extent of their responsibilities. But as the discussion continued, we became aware of the possible – even probable – cost of this gain in understanding. We identified another imperative, which would be needed to complement the concept of responsibility: the need to affirm our ability to meet our responsibilities to the height of our professional powers. If an awakened sense of responsibility were to cause an increase in feelings of incompetence and powerlessness, our last state would be worse than our first.

Looking back at my notes of this discussion after an interval of five years, I saw a missed opportunity; I wished I had gone on to discuss more openly with the group their feelings about this way of conceptualising their power. Responsibility levies an emotional toll as well as a professional one.

In subsequent work with early years educators from a variety of settings, I have made up for that missed opportunity. Using a discussion activity from the pack *Making Assessment Work* (Drummond, Rouse & Pugh 1992), I have explored with teachers, headteachers and other educators the cluster of concepts that concern us here: rights, responsibilities and power. In an activity called *Judge and Jury* we explore the distance, in terms of power, between the assessor and the assessed, and the rights and responsibilities associated with this relationship. The crude analogy, suggested by the title of the activity, between the judge on the bench and the teacher in the act of assessment, can be justified as a reminder of the relative powerlessness both of the prisoner in the dock and of children in schools and classrooms.

The discussion starts with group members working on a set of incomplete sentences, shown in figure 9.1. I have collected the responses of over 150 teachers and other educators to this activity, and in the process, I have gained, I believe, some important insights into their thinking. The responses to the sixth and seventh sentences are very clear indicators of the extent of teachers' sense of responsibility. There are, first of all, persons to whom teachers feel responsible: to the 'whole child', to the children, to their parents, the headteacher, other staff, and 'myself'. Looking even more widely, one reply includes...'and future generations'. But the majority of responses to these two items do not use nouns or proper names, but active verbs, describing the deeds of the responsible teacher or early years educator.

Judge and Jury

1. When I am assessing a child's learning, I feel...
2. When I write something down about a child, I feel...
3. When I think my judgements can help a child, I feel...
4. If I thought my judgements could harm a child, I would feel...
5. The word 'power' makes me think of...
6. As an early years educator/as a teacher, I have a responsibility to...
7. This responsibility makes me feel...
8. As an early years educator/as a teacher, I have the right to...
9. This right makes me feel...
10. I do *not* have the right to...
11. Children are powerful when...
12. Children have the right to...
13. If I knew what a difference my assessments might make in 20 years' time, I...
14. The best way to describe my relationship with the young children I work with is...

Figure 9.1

The replies reveal a whole range of ways of conceptualising this responsibility. A number of verbs cluster together around the idea of a benevolent, enabling teacher; for example, many replies refer to the responsibility to reassure, nurture, encourage, care, provide for, reinforce, support and enable children. A smaller number of more emphatic replies refer to the responsibility to empower, enhance, stimulate, stretch and 'open doors'. The theme of the future is continued in reference to children's potential which is to be tapped into, developed, and extended. Children's emotional development is to be attended to, particularly their self-confidence, which must be increased. A small minority of replies refer to happiness as an important and desirable outcome of the teacher's professional responsibility ('to make school happy', 'to give them a happy start'). A larger minority focus on learning and opportunities for learning, but a substantial majority do not include this concept in their replies. The words 'development', 'capabilities', 'abilities' and 'progress', which are frequently mentioned, can in a sense be read as substitutes or synonyms for the word 'learning', but it is worth remarking that over 80 per cent of this sample do not immediately respond to a question about their responsibility by referring to children's learning.

This curious absence is reminiscent of the primary headteacher's remarks, so mercilessly recorded by Sharp and Green (1975) in *Education and Social Control*:

> We are here to look after the children – it's their welfare that concerns me and I'd put that as a priority. I don't see the prime aim of the school as a learning institution although I realize that I'm paid to do this...and I have an obligation to see that my children become literate and numerate...but I feel that the child himself, his well-being and his welfare must be our first concern. (p.49)

I am not suggesting that the teachers in my sample take their responsibilities lightly. On the contrary, the responses that I have collected in investigating this concept add up to a picture of teachers' responsibilities that is, indeed, overwhelming, because of its extent and diffuseness. Responsibility for everything, and for everyone, for the whole of time future, does seem a massive undertaking. I am struck that not one of my respondents has taken a limited short-term view, describing a responsibility to particular children in his or her classroom now; there are no references to Jason, or Guljeet, no references to responsibility for 'what happened today' or yesterday, or what will happen tomorrow. Perhaps these responses indicate that, professionally, we are setting our sights too wide. A tighter, narrower definition of our responsibilities, here, in the present, to this or that particular group of children, whose learning is our central concern, might make the teacher's task seem less overwhelming. Recognising that some children, like Jason, though undoubtedly learning, do not learn what was intended by their benevolent teachers, might sharpen our appreciation of our responsibility to monitor the quality of each individual child's learning, asking ourselves persistently – 'Is this learning worthwhile? In what ways? How do I know?' The concepts of quality and worthwhileness were not mentioned by the teachers and educators in my sample, in their responses to item no. 6 (figure 9.1), 'As a teacher/educator, I have a responsibility to…'

The argument of this whole book has been that the act of assessment requires us to see, to understand, and to apply our understanding of each child's learning. If we could be as acutely aware of specific, individual, particular responsibilities as the respondents I have quoted seem to be of vaster, more shadowy enterprises, the practice of assessment might, perhaps, become more effective; perhaps teachers might feel more confident and secure in their undertakings, and even communicate some of their confidence and security to pupils like Jason. As it is, the feelings that are described by my respondents as being part of their sense of responsibility are serious and sombre. A very few find their responsibilities exciting (but also daunting, according to one, and panicky, according to another). The most positive response includes the words 'fulfilled, proud, happy and worried'; this worry is nearly universal, in all its degrees, from a milder 'anxiety' and 'concern' to feelings of 'being overwhelmed' by panic and fright.

Teachers' feelings are strong on this issue, there is no doubt, and their words are an encouraging reminder of the emotional strengths that teachers bring to their work. Feelings of pride and humility, of importance and inadequacy, feeling privileged and overawed, thoughtful, reflective and pressurised, creative and doubtful, full of awe and wary: these contradictions and tensions characterise the working lives of teachers, and constitute, I would argue, part of the case for teachers' emotional lives to be treated respectfully and seriously, throughout their careers, by the whole educational community.

The responses to the fifth sentence, revealing teachers' views of power, are, for me, much less predictable, and give me even greater cause for concern. These replies are overwhelmingly negative: there are references to Hitler, Saddam Hussein (the 1991 Gulf War had just ended when I was working with one group of educators), dictators, big brother, an overlord, bureaucracies, armed forces, authority, oppression, inequality and hierarchy. One teacher wrote: 'The word *power* makes me think of hierarchy' with a footnote '... of which I am no way near the top.' Another writes: 'Freedom taken from another individual, the victim of the power.' A student teacher on teaching practice recorded: 'Stone walls and vulnerability.' One headteacher wrote: 'The word power makes me think of "somebody else"', and another, 'imposition, unreality, doom, force, drive/driven, all enveloping.'

These responses are deeply disconcerting. If we as teachers are to act responsibly, putting into practice our commitment, our moral obligation to the interests of children, to children's learning and development, then I believe we must recognise and accept our power as teachers. We do have the power to educate, for a better world, the children in our schools; to deny this power is, by extension, to deny our real responsibilities to children. We cannot fulfil our widest educational purposes, or even our small-scale short-term projects for individual children, if we refuse to accept that we do have the power to act in the interests of children.

What might be the reasons for teachers' apparent readiness to disclaim their own power? A student teacher does seem to me to be entitled to a certain feeling of powerlessness, and hence, in her word, 'vulnerability'. But why a headteacher should use the words, 'doom', 'force' and 'imposition', is less immediately apparent. Hours of discussion, and repeated readings of the completed sentences on the activity sheets, have persuaded me that one of the reasons may be that these same teachers have an undeveloped sense of their rights. Replies to the eighth and ninth sentences have provided the evidence for this contention.

Some teachers openly and entirely disclaim the concept: 'I do not feel I have any rights.' A headteacher wrote: '... I have the right to nothing. I am paid to make decisions.' Others are more caustic: '... I have the right to make children jump through hoops.' Many replies make minimal claims. For example:

I have the right to do my best.
I have the right to make a fuss.
I have the right to spend the day with children.
I have the right to protest about gaps.
I have the right to change my mind.
I have the right to complain about too many children.
I have the right to make suggestions.
I have the right to some free time.
I have the right to a life of my own.

There are other, stronger, voices:

> I have the right to express my beliefs.
> I have the right to stand by my philosophy.
> I have the right to demand the best.
> I have the right to express differences of opinion.
> I have the right to question assessment at seven.
> I have the right to more positive recognition.
> I have the right to give an educational assessment.
> I have the right to have my opinions listened to.

But the number of responses that express a firm commitment to the teacher's right to act in the best interests of children is painfully small. What is more, these few responses are hardly forcefully expressed.

> I have the right to provide a wide range of experiences.
> I have the right to decide what's best for children.
> I have the right to guide, suggest, inspire.
> I have the right to plan and carry out appropriate teaching strategies.
> I have the right to provide ideas and direction for the children.

From this small sample, it does seem as if teachers' awareness of their right to think for themselves about their practice, and for their voices to be heard, is more fully developed than their awareness of their right to *act* forcefully, and consistently, in the face of opposition, if need be, in the interests of children. Only the right to act, and the power to act, can make our responsibility for children's learning work effectively, in their interests. Responsibility without rights or powers is a dead letter. Teachers who disclaim their rights are, indeed, 'doomed'; with powerlessness 'imposed' on them, they are 'forced' to fall short of their responsibilities to children. The headteacher's words take on a new and more coherent meaning when reapplied to teachers who perceive themselves as having limited or minimal rights.

Teachers' feelings about this question are illuminating too. For every response that finds something to be celebrated in the possession of certain rights, however minimal (for example, I feel energetic/crusading/happy/valued/proud/elated/privileged), there is another confessing a very different emotional set (for example, I feel angry/nervous/helpless/constrained/disappointed/anxious/frustrated/indignant/insignificant/useless). This emotional minefield cannot be the best working environment for dedicated teachers, committed to the complexities of teaching and learning.

This sentence-completion data has helped me to learn about the emotions that surround and invade the three key concepts of rights, responsibilities and power. The data has also, perhaps more importantly, illuminated for me the way in which these three concepts might be made to work harmoniously together. These teachers' responses have suggested the interconnectedness of the concepts I was exploring, indicating that a weakness, or lack of awareness in one area may have effects on teachers' thinking in another. In effective assessment, it seems to me, educators are fully aware of their responsibilities, their rights, and their power. This awareness includes an understanding of the educator's paramount responsibility for children's learning, of the educator's right to act in ways that will bring worthwhile learning about, and the educator's power to act wisely and lovingly in the interests of children. In the effective practice of assessment *responsible* educators acknowledge their *right* to use their *power* for the benefit of children.

Our responsibilities towards children and our right to work in their interests involve us in an extensive network of professional relationships outside the classroom. In these relationships too the concepts of rights and responsibilities play an important part. In the process of assessment, parents and professional colleagues have rights and responsibilities that are worth considering in more detail.

I argued earlier that the various purposes of assessment can more usefully be discussed in terms of a variety of outcomes, in terms of the actual impact of assessment practice on curriculum, on children, on children's learning, on groups and individual pupils, on parents, and on teachers themselves. Some examples of the outcomes of formative assessment were discussed in earlier chapters, where we saw how our knowledge of children's learning, acquired through observation and reflection, could be used to enrich and extend children's opportunities for learning. The outcomes of summative assessment, carried out at points of transfer of pupils, from teacher to teacher, or from school to school, are a more problematic area of enquiry. In trying to discern these outcomes, we are asking: what effect does one teacher's assessment have on another teacher's thinking? On another teacher's teaching? On another teacher's curriculum? We are exploring the relationship between two sets of professional judgements – the judgements of those who make the summary, and the judgements of those who receive it and work to put it to use. What part do teachers' rights and responsibilities play in this relationship?

In exploring this issue with teachers on in-service courses, I have invited them to begin by listing some of the comments they have heard colleagues make about the experience of being 'on the receiving end' of assessments made by other practitioners. Typical contributions to this part of the discussion include, for example:

I like to make up my own mind.
Start with a clean slate – that's my policy.
You can't be too careful.
Pupils can easily get labelled.
Teachers' views are always biased.
I leave the records alone till I've had a chance to see for myself.

Even allowing for an element of satire and exaggeration, some of these comments have alarming implications. Common to all of them is a pervasive sense of mistrust, a suggestion that other teachers' judgements are generally unreliable. Drawing on the law of miraculous exception, the receiving teachers seem to imply that wise, unbiased, objective and informative judgements are their sole prerogative. Other teachers' judgements are biased, prejudiced, subjective and misleading. These teachers seem to me to be suffering from an absence of professional trust and responsibility towards one another.

But this interpretation is not well received by the teachers who contribute the stereotypical comments I listed above. In discussion, teachers will earnestly and heatedly defend these positions as cautious, long-sighted, and entirely proper. Many cite their own experiences as pupils in defence of the clean-slate approach. Others have had more recent experiences as parents, which have given them grave cause for concern about the fallibility of teachers' judgements. Indeed, my own stepson was once given marks by a secondary school teacher for a subject he was no longer studying. The deputy head's explanation that a simple clerical error was to blame did little to reinstate the family's confidence in the school's assessment procedures. And yet, and yet... Effective assessment practice must surely be built on trust, not on mistrust; on the necessity for professional responsibility, not on an assumption of irresponsibility; on the principle of respect, not disrespect, for our colleagues. Teachers who write summative assessment documents have, I believe, the right to be trusted by their colleagues; they have in turn the complementary responsibility of trusting the assessments made by others.

The principle of trust need not be over-extended; I am not suggesting that teachers must commit themselves to swallowing unthinkingly every last word uttered by each and every one of their colleagues. They have, in order to earn the trust of others in their turn, the responsibility to examine the assessments they receive, both judgements and evidence, critically and sensitively. But their approach must be based on an assumption of good intent, and of professional expertise, in others as well as in themselves. Teachers' mistrust seems to presuppose that other teachers are out to deceive and mislead them. Does not this mistrust also suggest a weakness in our confidence in our own professional abilities? How can we justify the suggestion that our critical powers are so weak that they might be damaged by the inadequate and ill-informed judgements of others? Have we confused trust with gullibility? Do we mistrust trust? Are we projecting anxiety about our own fallibility onto the actions of others? Knowing my own professional weaknesses, do I hesitate to rely on the strengths of others?

For every practising teacher, these are not rhetorical questions, but practical ones, involving flesh and blood human beings, not the generic, anonymous 'teacher' of the educational book or paper. They are questions that can only be answered at the personal and individual level by the persons involved. The possibility of mutual trust in each other's professional responsibility can only become a reality after practical steps have been taken by the teachers concerned. In schools, or clusters of schools, where communication between the teachers of different year groups is minimal, this will be a tall order. Furthermore, improved communication is unlikely to begin with a full-scale investigation into the concepts I am discussing here. The unspoken questions 'Can we trust you?' 'Will you trust us?' may well be the motivating themes of any encounter between teachers who do not yet work together in teamship, but they are probably inappropriate starting points for the enterprise of building up trust and professional respect. On the other hand, practices already in place may play a part in effectively minimising the chances of improved, more trusting communication. The French system of a 'dossier scholaire' for each pupil (DES 1991a), referred to in Chapter 7, which remains, literally, a closed book for one-third of each academic year, is a salutory reminder of the power of silence and non-communication to limit the process of review and development. Until all teachers are ready, willing and able enthusiastically to create opportunities for working together on issues in assessment, they will not be fulfilling their professional responsibilities to one another or to their pupils.

The right to trust and be trusted is not confined to teachers. Parents too have rights in the practice of assessment, and the most effective procedures that teachers and other educators have developed in recent years have recognised these rights. Traditionally, for many years, assessment has been the province of teachers; they made the assessments, wrote the records, held the records and made the decisions about how to communicate which parts of what they contained and to whom. But this monopoly has been broken. The trail-blazing ILEA Primary Language Record was designed as a collaborative exercise in recording achievement. The development of the child's language – or languages – in the home is seen as just as important as progress in school, and so the contribution of parents is an essential part of the recording process (Barrs *et al.* 1988). The very first section of the record form is headed 'Record of discussion between child's parent(s) and class teacher'. This discussion takes place at the beginning of each academic year. The parents' perspectives are treated as valuable starting points for the teachers, a point at which they can begin to learn about their pupils, a point at which parents contribute significantly to teachers' understanding. The final section of the record is also designated for parents' use; here they reflect on what they have read on the completed record and here they are invited to comment, not only on their child's progress, but also on the teacher's account of that progress. The right of parents to contribute to the assessment process is fully recognised in this record format; parents are given the responsibility of contributing, and are assured that their contributions will be respectfully and trustingly received.

In early years settings, in playgroups and daycare, as well as in nursery schools and classes, there has been great interest in the developmental record *All About Me* (Wolfendale 1990). This is a small booklet, in which parents and educators together record anecdotal evidence that adds up to a vivid personal picture of many aspects of a child's development. Parents use the *All About Me* booklet to note down and record, from time to time, aspects of their child's development and progress in seven different areas: language; playing and learning; doing things for myself; physical development; health and habits; other people and how I behave; moods and feelings. It acts as a record for the family, and as a basis for discussion with each child's educators in nursery, family centre or playgroup. *All About Me* is based on an appreciation of each child's uniqueness; it does not require parents to tick boxes or answer closed Yes/No questions about their children, but to make comments in their own words under each different heading. The record does not lay down compulsory developmental milestones; it accepts that children develop at different ages and stages, and so there is plenty of space to record each child's individuality, rather than simply noting the age of reaching predetermined targets.

As parents and teachers come closer together, expressing the principle of respect in the act of trusting one another and one another's judgements, new understandings become possible. The Sheffield Early Literacy Development Project (Hannon *et al.* 1991) reports that when educators work with parents, describing and discussing the children's experiences at home, the outcomes are beneficial for all concerned. The parents involved in this project came to appreciate more fully the extent of their children's early literacy development. The educators involved gained insights into the children's activities at home that enriched their workplace observations and tentative assessments.

A full-scale development project is not, of course, necessary to stimulate teachers' awareness of the powerful contribution that parents can make to the practice of assessment. Ann Le Gassick, a nursery teacher on an early years in-service course, reported how she was discussing a particular child's learning with the child's mother. In the course of the discussion, the teacher commented that the child never used drawing materials in the nursery. The mother replied that he made many drawings at home and offered to show them to the teacher, who was pleased to accept the offer. She was not, however, prepared for the excitement of seeing the drawing (figure 9.2) that the mother produced next day, nor for the further excitement of talking about the picture with the child, who described and explained in detail every element of this amazingly complex representation. A whole new area of this child's learning had been opened up to the teacher by this casual conversation, which, she reported, had also transformed her understanding of the importance of involving parents in the assessment practice. Parents' rights to contribute can be fostered and protected by individuals as well as by institutions or authority-wide policies and practices.

Children too have rights in the assessment process, rights that go further than the right to be heard, to have a voice. The development of records of achievement, based on the continuous involvement of pupils in their own assessment, was briefly officially endorsed by the School Examinations and Assessment Council (SEAC 1991) for all primary schools. There were then dozens of local initiatives, many cited in the

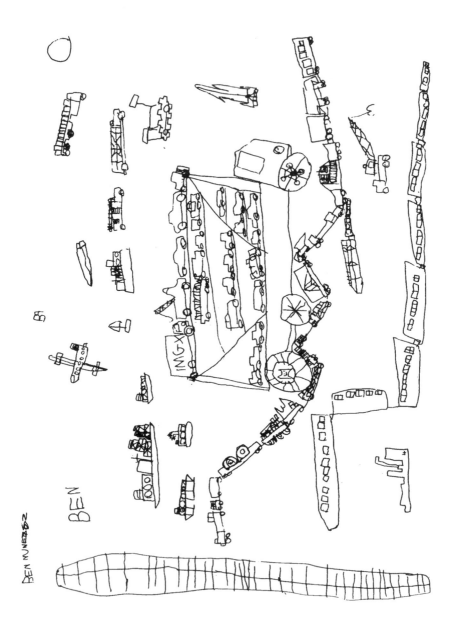

Figure 9.2

SEAC publication, which had in common the practice of giving the pupil a greater or lesser degree of control over what is recorded in the cumulative record.

But, as Stansbury (1992) promptly warned us, the label 'Record of Achievement' may be used to obscure the actual purpose of some forms of reporting. Some formats, including the National Record of Achievement, define success in terms of school subjects. The use of a standard format, as advocated over the last few years by some local authorities, can have the effect of enabling comparisons to be made more efficiently between the more and less successful pupils on standard measures. The idea of a single set of standards, now enshrined in the targets and levels of the National Curriculum, is gravely at odds with the diversity of human beings; records of achievement are, in themselves, no guarantee that the differences between pupils will be respected and valued. It is worth remembering the conclusion reached by the Hadow Report (Board of Education 1933), in discussing the outcomes of a pupil's two or three years in the infant school:

> In none of this should a uniform standard to be reached by all children be expected. The infant school has no business with uniform standards of attainment. (para 105)

Records of achievement that are truly respectful of pupils' rights will not be concerned with matching every pupil up against the same numerical scale; they will take account of each pupil's right to be different, to be a uniquely individual member of an equitable society.

Children's rights as persons to be assessed extend to the ways in which the assessment is to be carried out. The rights of bilingual children, for example, and of children who are learning English in school as a second or third language, have to be respected. There were early claims (Gregory & Kelly 1992) that this respect would not be readily compatible with National Curriculum assessment procedures, as they were first introduced. Bilingual children have been shown to develop different linguistic skills from monolingual children, and to show more flexibility and freedom in their use of language. These linguistic strengths are not tapped by language tests designed for monolingual children, on which bilingual children often make more grammatical mistakes than their monolingual peers. Recent small-scale studies suggest this pessimism was not ill-founded. Rose Elgar, a member of a group of primary teachers researching the impact of the National Literacy Strategy (Sheahan 2003), found that certain assessment tasks clearly disadvantaged some of her bilingual pupils.

Children's rights further include a right to a congruence between the curriculum they actually experience and the way in which their learning is assessed. All primary teachers face the need to establish this congruence, by monitoring the relationship between what they choose to teach and what they choose to assess. Teachers' choices will only be in children's interests if their forms of assessment match the curriculum they provide in every respect. Statutory forms of assessment match, by definition, the National Curriculum. If the National Curriculum is not to become the whole, instead of only part, of the lived experience of primary school pupils, assessment practice must match a wider and richer conceptualisation of curriculum than the core and foundation subjects laid down in Curriculum 2000.

The spelling test for six- and seven-year-olds introduced in the summer of 1992 was an early and telling example of the conflicts that responsible teachers face. The Teacher's Guide (DES 1992) states 'The Spelling Test must be used for all those children who have already attained level 3 or 4 in En4 (Spelling)' (that is, in English Attainment Target 4). The instructions for administering the test are very precise; the teacher reads a 'story' to the children, who are provided with test booklets containing the story, printed with 24 words omitted.

> You read the story to the children and tell them the missing words so that they can write these in the spaces...Explain to the children that, for this work, they should think of their own answers, and not discuss them with others. Collaborative work and copying should not be allowed.

The instructions to the children are equally precise:

> When we come to a space, wait for me to tell you the word and then write it in the space. If you're not sure how to spell it, just have a go and put in the letters you think are right.

This test was compulsory. Under the 1988 Education Reform Act, the Secretary of State had acquired the power to compel teachers to assess spelling in this way. As a consequence, the test was used in classrooms where the teaching of spelling had been approached in a completely different way, a way that emphasised collaboration and research. Thousands of children in this country had been taught (and I hope still are) that when faced with a question of spelling, there are several appropriate strategies available to them: they may decide to ask a friend, to discuss and confer, or to use reference material. This is hardly surprising, since these are the strategies used by fully literate, mature adults, when they are writing in contexts where correct spelling is important. But in this test, these strategies were forbidden. This test of spelling did not match the curriculum of spelling experienced by many children. Children who had learned to use dictionaries with confidence and accuracy, and who had learned to share their own knowledge with their peers, had that learning denied by this test. Their rights as learners, to have their learning respected, were denied. Their right to be assessed in a way that matched their curriculum was denied. The teacher's responsibility to match the method of assessment to the curriculum in all respects was denied.

It is, in my view, an insufferable burden for teachers to swallow these denials, and many others like them, that have become a normal part of the annual SATs procedures. Teachers are not blind to the damage that is done to childen's rights, and to their own powers as educators, but the juggernaut of statutory testing is not easily resisted. There are plentiful and persuasive arguments in favour of compliance with the testing regime, not least the long-term benefits of raised standards for all, an outcome universally ascribed to the continued use of testing. It remains to be seen for how long professional obedience, rather than civil disobedience, will rule the day. Maybe one day soon we will argue, as a matter of urgency, that our responsibilities to children's learning take precedence over our statutory responsibilities to assess in ways that are none of our choosing.

On the other hand, we may not have to wait for much longer to see some of the lasting effects on pupils of being assessed at level one at age seven, or level three at age 11: the vast literature from 30 years or more of research on students perceived and labelled as low achievers already suggests that the outcomes of the current regime will be anything but benign. For just one example, let us return to the pupils in Meek's challenging study (1983) of non-reading adolescents (briefly discussed in Chapter 2), who are perfectly and appallingly frank about their estimations of themselves as learners.

One of the teachers in Meek's group, Judith Graham, worked with a pupil, Trevor, aged 12.6 at the start of the study. By the end of his infant schooling he was reported to be 'backward'; five years on 'Judith chose Trevor (for this study) because he was the classic underachiever. He should have learned to read, but had mysteriously failed.' Trevor spent one tutorial session a week with Judith, stormy and emotional periods for both of them. During a lesson at the beginning of the second year, Trevor put up great resistance to reading at all. Judith Graham's account continues: 'I suggest that he is "giving up" which stings Trevor into the accusation, "it's a year now. Nothing's happened."' Trevor's outrage and despair are movingly described; his teacher can hardly muster the energy to 'start the long haul of re-establishing Trevor's image of himself'. Even in the act of doing so, she doubts her own judgement. 'By taking on so seriously – even somewhat emotionally – the task of building up Trevor's confidence, do I betray my own fear that I will not be able to teach him to read?' (p.158). Trevor, too, knows the meaning of fear. Three years into the study, Judith records Trevor's comments on his impending exams:

> 'What's the point of my coming in to do them? I can't even read the paper, and even if I can, I can't write quickly enough to answer the questions.'... I say 'These exams are five weeks away. Anything can happen in five weeks.' Then Trevor 'Oh yes miss, who are you kidding? I've been coming for three and a half years with you'... (p.216)

Three and a half years of failure in special reading lessons, on top of six years of failure in the primary school, have broken Trevor's spirit. Assessment practices that contribute, however minutely, to a learner's sense of personal failure cannot be justified. All pupils are learners; their rights to learn, and to feel that their teachers trust and respect their learning, are paramount. The teachers' responsibilities are plain. However constrained our assessment practices may be by Acts of Parliament beyond our control, we still have the right to use our remaining powers to act wisely and lovingly in the interests of our pupils.

Conclusion

In this book, I have identified three crucial questions that teachers and other educators must, I believe, ask themselves as they set about assessing children's learning. These questions are: when we look at learning,

- what is there to see?
- how best can we understand what we see?
- how can we put our understanding to good use?

I have tried not to suggest that there is only one possible set of answers to these questions. We would be deluding ourselves if we thought that these questions could ever be answered once and for all, or that assessment is a practice that can ever be perfected. But this lack of finality, this imperfection in our practice, should not cause us to feel shame or despair. To recognise that we cannot achieve absolute perfection in assessment is a first step towards recognising other characteristics of the process.

Throughout the book, I have tried to illustrate these characteristics by drawing on the assessment practice of other educators, past and present. Children's learning is so complex and various that the task of trying to understand it is necessarily complex too. The task entails trying to see and understand the whole, as well as the minutest parts; it requires us to appreciate the past, and analyse the present, as well as envisage and welcome the future; it obliges us to look for and attend to differences as well as similarities, individuals as well as groups, the unexpected as well as the intended outcome, absence as well as presence. It demands a broad vision and a narrow focus.

Above all, effective assessment requires educators to make choices, in the interests of children, that are based on a coherent set of principles, which are themselves an expression of each educator's core values. As these choices are made, and translated into daily classroom practice, teachers are exercising, as we saw in the last chapter, their responsibility for children's learning, their right to act in children's interests, and their power to do so wisely and well.

In effective assessment, teachers recognise the disparity of power between adults and children in schools and classrooms. David Smail, a psychotherapist writing of relationships between adults and children in the context of the family, takes a gloomy view of this disparity:

> We are approaching a state of affairs in which we simply do not know how to relate to one another except coercively and exploitingly…we have no articulate conception of the loving use of power.
>
> Smail (1987) pp. 115–16

But I believe that this inspiring phrase, 'the loving use of power', can illuminate, for teachers, some more optimistic possibilities. I believe that a full understanding of what it might mean, for teachers, parents and children, if we learned to use our power to educate *lovingly* (as well as effectively or efficiently) would transform our practice in assessment.

For all the pomp and circumstance of official policies and national initiatives over the last 15 years, for all the ferocity of the debate about assessment, and the passion of the arguments on either side, it would be foolish to suggest that the teaching profession has been facing an issue of recent invention, a new and unlooked for addition to their heavy load of responsibilities. Of course, assessment is no such thing. Teachers are not dumb beasts of burden; they have always been interested in learning and struggled to make sense of it. Trying to understand learning with intense professional commitment is nothing new. And in our cautious – and anxious – and, I hope, courageous responses to demands on us that *are* new, we will do well to turn back to earlier educationists, working within a very different set of values from those of today's legislators. Their work may help us to be clearer and more articulate about the values that permeate our chosen practices, and what we must do to live up to them.

Earlier in the book I quoted extensively from Susan Isaacs, not just because of her influential place in the history of British primary education, but also because of her influence on my own thinking. Her work has played an important part in my learning about learning; from her I have learned that there is always more to see, and I have tried, following her example, to see it more clearly. Another great educator, to whom I turn at moments of doubt and difficulty in these uncertain times, is Edmond Holmes. Remembered by some today as the stern and inspiring uncle of the irrepressible Gerard Holmes, author of *The Idiot Teacher* (1952), his professional position was, at his retirement, HM Chief Inspector of Elementary Schools. His most important book, published in 1911, *What Is and What Might Be* told, in his nephew's words:

> of how this experienced official, late in life, had come to realise that the whole system of teaching as practised in the schools of England was stultifying and repressive and destructive of the natural, spiritual and mental powers latent in young children. And it told of a real school where an altogether different and supremely successful method was practised by an enlightened woman.
>
> Holmes (1952) pp.20–21

In Edmond Holmes' own words, the central theme of the book is no less challengingly described:

> Does elementary education, as at present conducted, tend to foster the growth of the child's faculties?...the answer to the question, so far at least as thousands of schools are concerned, must be an emphatic No...The education given in thousands of our elementary schools is in the highest degree anti-educational.
>
> Holmes (1911) pp.143–4

But there are exceptions. The first half of the book – 'What Is' – is devoted to a scrupulous analysis of the ills of the current state of elementary education. The second half – 'What Might Be' – describes one of these exceptions, a village school of 120 pupils that Holmes names Utopia, and its headteacher, whom he calls Egeria. It is nevertheless a real school:

> in a very real village, which can be reached, as all other villages can, by rail and road...I have paid (this) school many visits, and it has taken me many months of thought to get to what I believe to be the bed-rock of (the headteacher's) philosophy of education.
>
> Holmes (1911) p.154

This philosophy is based on a highly original and distinctive analysis of the nature of children, an analysis that may remind us of the question we encountered in Chapter 6 of this book 'What is a child-like child?' In Egeria's philosophy, and in Holmes' own thinking, the child-like child is described in terms of the growth of six typical instincts 'which no-one who studies the child with any degree of care can fail to observe'. We may, today, with our more thorough biological understanding of the limitations of the concept 'instinct' beg to differ at this point; but it is worth continuing to read in order to appreciate the kinds of learning, growth and development that Holmes subsumes under these 'instincts', or 'instinctive desires' as he calls them elsewhere. His full description of them may be conveniently summarised in the form shown on page 179.

Edmond Holmes' educational philosophy, of which this is the barest outline, is characterised by the use of words, such as love, beauty and truth, that do not often appear in contemporary educational texts. Nevertheless his message reads at times as if it were written yesterday. For example, in the succeeding volume, *In Defence of What Might Be* (1914) he writes:

> The day is coming, if I do not misread the signs of the times, when the teachers of our elementary schools will have to choose between making a bolder use of their freedom and having it ruthlessly abridged.
>
> Holmes (1914) pp.227–8

But even if some of the terms of his argument may be unfamiliar or unfashionable today, there must surely still be a place for the human faculties that Holmes names so assuredly. Maths, English and Science, may, by statute, stand at the core of the National Curriculum, but at the centre of the education of young children, there must surely be more transcendent qualities. In Holmes' vision of 'What Might Be', at the heart of education as he saw it, is the human thirst for love, beauty and truth. In this book, I have been arguing that the practice of assessment bridges two main areas of concern: children's interests and teachers' choices. In the interests of children can we, as teachers, confidently choose to reject what Holmes is telling us?

(1) The communicative instinct – the desire to talk and listen, which develops into the desire to read and write.

(2) The dramatic instinct – the desire to play at make-believe, to imagine, to pretend, to identify one's life with others.

These may be grouped together as the *sympathetic* instincts – in and through which the child grows in the direction of love.

(3) The artistic instinct – the desire to draw, paint and model, which grows into a restless desire to express and delight in a perception of visible beauty.

(4) The musical instinct – the desire to dance and sing, to move and to express oneself with rhythm and grace.

These may be grouped together as the *aesthetic* instincts – in and through which the child grows in the direction of beauty.

(5) The inquisitive instinct – the desire to know the why of things, to understand how effects are produced, to discover new facts and pass on, if possible, to their causes.

(6) The constructive instinct – the desire to synthesise, to build things up, to put one's knowledge of the world to a practical use.

These may be grouped together as the *scientific* instincts – in and through which the child grows in direction of truth.

Afterword to the Second Edition

In preparing this second edition I have made some minor changes to the original text of the book, but I have kept these to a minimum because, to be blunt, I have not changed my mind about any of the issues that I invite my readers to think about. I have seriously reduced the number of references to the 1988 Education Reform Act, still fresh in my mind at the time of writing. The years have passed and the provisions of the ERA have become part of history: for a whole generation of young teachers, they are now ancient history. There are many teachers and other educators working with children today who have themselves experienced, as pupils, the best and the worst of the National Curriculum and the statutory forms of testing that accompanied its introduction.

I have adjusted some references to extinct official bodies such as SEAC (the School Examinations and Assessment Council) and NCC (the National Curriculum Council) and included an acknowledgement of the work of the current successor to the role, the QCA (the Qualifications and Curriculum Authority). I have referred to the establishment (in England) of the Foundation Stage of education, for three- to five-year-olds, and to the requirement to assess every child's learning at the end of this stage with the Foundation Stage Profile. But I have not engaged in a detailed critical review of the QCA *Guidance for the Foundation Stage*, or the content and procedures of the Foundation Stage Profile, as I plan to do this soon elsewhere. I have not given an account of recent policy initiatives affecting primary and pre-schools, nor of new accountability procedures such as Ofsted inspections: this book is not a history of contemporary education, but an attempt to establish some enduring principles in assessing children's learning that are not subject to the contingencies of short-lived national pressures and policies.

Finally, I have not watered down my extreme anxiety about inappropriately mechanical and numerical approaches to assessment, nor wavered from my cautious optimism that educators can do better, in ways of their own invention. In this new Afterword I discuss some of the reasons for my continuing optimism, and present brief accounts of some of the work that is now available for educators to draw on as they construct their own best practice in assessment, and come to understand the principles that underpin its effectiveness.

Frameworks of understanding

In Chapter 5 of this book, I described some of the ways in which teachers and other educators have approached the work of trying to understand children's learning. I illustrated a range of different interpretations, including those of some contemporary writers: Chris Athey, Vivian Gussin Paley, Michael Armstrong, Kieran Egan, and some from the past: Susan Isaacs and Margaret Lowenfeld, for example. I suggested that it is unlikely that any one single model of learning will enable us to understand everything we see, and that we will do better to draw on a variety of frameworks in our search for meaning. Since the first edition of this book, the choices at our disposal have been greatly enriched by the work of the Assessment Reform Group, whose important and influential publications have made a substantial contribution to our current understanding of the power and purposes of assessment. The first of these, *Inside the Black Box* (Black & Wiliam 1998), presented overwhelming evidence, firstly that improving the practice of formative assessment raises standards, secondly that there is room for improvement, and thirdly that we already know a great deal about the ways in which assessment can be made more effective. Black and Wiliam went on to argue that if teachers were to implement these ideas in their everyday practice they would need considerable support in the form of 'living examples of implementation'. They sketched out an ambitious programme for development, which would enable teachers to reconstruct their current approaches to assessment in the interests of learning: assessment *for* learning rather than assessment *of* learning was to be the driving principle of this development work.

In a later publication (Black *et al.* 2002), the authors report on the progress of their programme. They describe the innovative practices in assessment that have been developed in selected secondary and primary schools and the evidence that this work did raise standards. This classroom work is described under four headings: questioning, feedback through marking, peer and self-assessment, and the formative use of summative tests. In all four of these areas, Black and his colleagues claim, teachers became more effective as they redefined their role in learning, relinquishing the delivery-recipient relationship of expert teacher/ passive learner, and repositioning themselves with their pupils as 'partners in pursuit of a shared goal'. For the teachers whose work is reported here, assessment *for* learning has become a dominant responsibility, a key principle that extends to the whole of their teaching. Further development work continues, under the auspices of the ESRC Teaching and Learning Research Project, in the form of the *Learning How to Learn* project, which is extending the earlier work on formative assessment into a model of learning how to learn for both teachers and pupils: this in time may offer teachers a powerful framework for examining and understanding both their own practice and their children's learning.

One striking aspect of the work of this research and development programme is that it is taking place in an educational milieu where the prevailing trends seem to be set in a very different direction. My own observations (over the last ten years) of children in the early years of school, suggest that the process described by Willes in 1983, by which active, enquiring and exploratory children quickly become submissive and obedient pupils, is still a lived reality for most children. As funding arrangements for four-year-olds have changed, many more children now enter primary school at the beginning of the year in which they turn five. But these children of below statutory age are, on the whole, conceptualised as pupils, and subject to stringent classroom control. As a substitute for my self-imposed task of collecting baseline assessment schedules, now rendered inoperable by the imposition of the standardised Foundation Stage Profile, I have started to record the lists of classroom rules that appear on the walls of Key Stage One and Foundation Stage classrooms. These do nothing to suggest that the principle of children as 'active learners who take responsibility for and manage their own learning' (Black *et al.* 2002, p.21) has any currency in the wider world, outside the 'Assessment for Learning' project schools. For example, in one classroom for children turning five I observed a list that read:

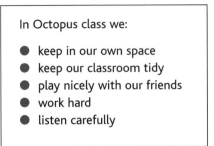

In Octopus class we:

● keep in our own space
● keep our classroom tidy
● play nicely with our friends
● work hard
● listen carefully

Figure A.1 Classroom rules

This is no recipe for an active learner, and no framework for understanding children's spontaneous acts of meaning-making and enquiry; under this rule of law, children are reduced and impoverished as learners, discouraged from exploring the world, from loving and quarrelling and peace-making, from engaging with interesting and exciting ideas that set them on fire with enthusiasm, from telling astonishing stories, or imagining new and impossible worlds. The model of assessment that accompanies this mindset towards learners is, I have come to realise, equally inappropriate. It is perhaps best characterised by the metaphor of the long jump.

In this approach, it is as if a narrow strip of land is marked out, a small slice of curriculum, so to speak; the educators divide up the strip with marking pegs at regular intervals and stand back to observe how far each child can jump. Some children fly swiftly through the air, clearing all the pegs in their path: some only travel a few inches. In the long-jump model of assessment, the educators' question of each child is 'How far can you jump?' There are examples of this approach in Chapters 1 and 5 of this book: what I have come to see more clearly is that our choices as educators include choices about the frameworks and metaphors we use to understand assessment, as well as those with which we examine learning. If we think of assessment in ways that do not do justice to the learning we are assessing, if we choose to calibrate children's progress with a tape measure (or by counting the number of stepping stones they achieve, in the QCA Foundation Stage model of assessment), we are unlikely to get close to their learning, or to understand it in ways that will help us to put our understanding to good use. The long-jump model does not lead to assessment *for* learning. Fortunately, there are other metaphors and other approaches available.

Learning from New Zealand

Since 1993, there has been intense interest in the early years community in England and Wales in the bilingual document *Te Whāriki* from New Zealand. The draft of these curriculum guidelines for early childhood services was widely circulated in this country, and many educators are now familiar with the officially adopted version (Ministry of Education 1996). The New Zealand approach to the early childhood curriculum is founded on four principles:

- **empowerment**
  the early childhood curriculum empowers the child to learn and grow
- **holistic development**
  the early childhood curriculum reflects the holistic way children learn and grow
- **family and community**
  the wider world of family and community is an integral part of the early childhood curriculum
- **relationships**
  children learn through responsive and reciprocal relationships with people, places and things

The vision for children that the *Te Whāriki* document sets out:

> is founded on the following aspirations for children: to grow up as competent and confident learners and communicators, healthy in mind, body and spirit, secure in their sense of belonging and in the knowledge that they make a valued contribution to society.
>
> Ministry of Education (1996) p. 9

These aspirations are summarised in the form of five strands that run through the document:

- belonging
- well-being
- exploration
- communication
- contribution

From the four principles and the five strands, each setting and centre for young children weaves its own curriculum programme: the Maori words of the title, *Te Whāriki*, refer to a traditional woven floor mat, with an infinite variety of patterns. From this starting point, educators in New Zealand have constructed an approach to assessment from which, in my view, we all have much to learn.

At the heart of their work are four mandatory requirements, derived from the four principles that underpin their curriculum document. Their model of assessment is thus tightly aligned with their understanding of curriculum, the experiences that they see as appropriate for young children. So, in New Zealand, assessment practices:

(i) enhance children's sense of themselves as capable people and competent learners
(ii) reflect the holistic way that children learn
(iii) reflect the reciprocal relationships between the child, people and the learning environment
(iv) involve parents/guardians and, where appropriate, Whanau (extended family).

Lee & Carr (2001)

At an international early years conference in the Netherlands, where Wendy Lee, Director of the Early Childhood Learning and Assessment Project, presented an account of this approach, an overhead transparency showing these four principles was greeted with some scepticism. She was asked, with some acerbity, how she and her colleagues could be so certain that these splendid aspirations would be realised in practice. Her reply was received in stunned silence: she explained that these principles are enshrined in the legislation; they have statutory force. There are no viable alternatives: the list above is not a wish-list but a statutory requirement. To fit these principles, Lee and her colleagues, in particular Margaret Carr, have devised an approach that they call *Learning Stories*, an approach fully and powerfully described in Carr's important book *Assessment in Early Childhood Settings* (2001).

Learning Stories are about children's developing identities as learners; they are written by their educators, with contributions from children, parents and extended family. They are public documents, much handled, much appreciated; they are favourite reading material in the early childhood settings, by both children and their families. *Learning Stories* take a credit, not a deficit approach to learning; their perspective is holistic, not atomistic. Learning is not subdivided and fragmented into areas, skills or aspects of knowledge; the *Learning Stories* record children's enterprises and enquiries over several days, ranging over every aspect of their experience. Perhaps most significantly, *Learning Stories* embody a coherent understanding of progression: over time, Carr demonstrates (2001, pp. 159–61) the *Learning Stories* become longer, deeper, broader and more frequent. The interests and dispositions they document become more complex; they appear in different activities in the programme; they extend over longer periods of time.

The New Zealand model of learning and assessment, and the narrative method at its core, have, I believe, enormous potential for educators in other places. In adopting the dominant metaphor of story, in place of the tape measure (or long jump), educators are committing themselves to taking each child's learning seriously as a process, with its own life and living landmarks. They are rejecting the whole set of product-based metaphors with which, in this country, we have grown familiar over the years, in which learning is described in terms of targets, levels, outcomes, goals (and most recently, stepping stones). All these product metaphors suggest that learning is time-bound, momentary and discontinuous; they suggest that learning is what children *have* (measured in terms of scores, grades, marks or levels) rather than something they *do*. The New Zealand approach emphasises learning as a moving event, dynamic and changeful, practically synonymous with living, a perspective with which I wholeheartedly agree. And I will also note, with a certain pride, but I hope without arrogance, that Carr's book (2001) is structured around my own definition of the process of assessment, as it appeared in the first edition of this book and as it still stands:

> the ways in which, in our everyday practice, we observe children's learning, strive to understand it, and then put our understanding to good use.
>
> Quoted in Carr (2001) p. 19

Learning from Reggio

New Zealand is not the only country to which teachers and other educators may turn in order to extend their understanding of children's learning, and in the search for frameworks that will support and enrich their practice. The work of early childhood educators in the region of Emilia Romagna, Italy, which has come to be known by the name of its principal city, Reggio Emilia, is internationally respected and renowned. In this country, hundreds of practitioners have visited Reggio and its preschools for children 0–6, or the travelling exhibit 'The Hundred

Languages of Children' that documents the approach; the publications of the organisation *Reggio Children* are becoming well known. The key text describing the approach is now in an expanded second edition (Edwards *et al.* 1998) and there is a growing number of related publications, many from the United States, notably *Bambini*, focusing on children under three (Gandini & Edwards 2001), and some home-grown (for example Gura 1997, Abbott & Nutbrown 2001, Valentine 1999).

The central concept of the Reggio approach is a particular construction of children as powerful and articulate learners, and of the pre-eminent place of the expressive arts in their learning. Carlina Rinaldi, until recently Director of Services for Young Children in the region, summarises their position:

> The cornerstone of our experience, based on practice, theory and research, is the image of children as rich, strong and powerful...They have potential, plasticity, the desire to grow, curiosity, the ability to be amazed and the desire to relate to other people and to communicate...(they are) eager to express themselves within the context of a plurality of symbolic languages, and...are open to exchanges and reciprocity as deeds and acts of love which they not only want to receive but also want to offer.
>
> Edwards *et al.* (1994) pp. 101–2

This view of children unequivocally excludes the possibility that because of their age and biological immaturity they are in any sense weak, needy, ignorant or lacking in ability. This construction of childhood in turn shapes the Reggio approach to pedagogy, which is based on the child as the one who, in relationships with others, constructs knowledge and understanding. Children are spontaneous and autonomous meaning makers in their own right: the Reggio educators honour learning over teaching and see the task of teaching as being to provide the conditions for learning. These conditions include an emphasis on the pedagogy of relationships, between child and child, between educators and children. Rinaldi explains it like this:

> The emphasis of our approach is...on each child in relation to other children, teachers, parents, his or her own history and the societal and cultural surroundings...The teacher must establish a personal relationship with each child and ground this relationship in the social system of the school. Children, in turn, do not just passively endure their experience, but also become active agents in their socialisation, co-constructed with their peers. (p. 105)

The reciprocity of teaching and learning is constantly emphasised; fundamental to the teacher's role is the documentation of children's learning. With this term, the Reggio educators refer to the whole variety of practices (video and audio recording, photographs, transcripts, observations, the preservation of artefacts, discussion, dialogue and representation) through which they make both their pedagogy and the children's learning visible – for the benefit of all: parents, families, children and their educators. Reggio educators never work single-handed, alone with a group of children; they always work in pairs and so are supremely well placed to enter into daily professional dialogue, reviewing, evaluating and documenting the learning that has been taking place before their eyes. The examples of the documentation process that are displayed in the Hundred Languages exhibit, and in Reggio publications available in English, such as *Shoe and Metre* and *Everything Has a Shadow Except Ants*, are magnificent and inspiring accounts of children's learning – in all its breadth, depth and complexity.

In the Reggio educators' professional vocabularies, 'documentation' has usurped the conceptual space occupied by 'assessment' in this country. They see no need to apply crude numerical measures of levels or standards, since they have at their disposal a much more powerful approach, which, according to Gunilla Dahlberg, an eminent Swedish educational philosopher and authority on the Reggio approach, provides them with a basis for changing and developing their pedagogical practice. The act of documentation becomes, in itself, a learning process for both educators and parents, through the reflective discourse to which it gives rise (Dahlberg & Åsén 1994). Documentation, as a pedagogical tool, both makes learning visible and contributes to the process of making it more effective, more engaging, more life-enhancing. Expanding these ideas in a more recent text, Dahlberg emphasises how documentation enables educators to take responsibility for creating their own meanings, and coming to their own decisions (Dahlberg, Moss & Pence 1999). Instead of being the servants of a locally imposed machinery for assessment, the Reggio educators, and those who follow their example, are masters of their own expertise and experience:

> What we document represents a choice, a choice among many other choices, a choice in which pedagogues themselves are participating...When we document we are co-constructors of children's lives and we also embody our implied thoughts of what we think are valuable actions in a pedagogical practice...[the documentation] enables us to see how we ourselves

understand and 'read' what is going on in practice... The awareness that we make choices... makes it easier to critically analyse our documentation and to find methods to counteract and resist the dominant regimes.

Dahlberg et al. (1999) p. 147

This description, it seems to me, comes very close to the position for which I argue in Chapter 8 of this book, in which the principles by which teachers try to live, in terms of teaching and assessing learning, are themselves the fruit of clear thinking and critical questioning of the teachers' core values and beliefs. The moral and philosophical work of assessment, as I have tried to present it in these pages, is beautifully exemplified in the Reggio educators' work of documentation.

Learning about the future

Since the autumn of 1999, I have been collaborating with colleagues at the Faculty of Education in Cambridge on a research project that we came to call *Learning Without Limits* (its earlier title, 'Anti-determinist approaches to pedagogy', though explicit, seemed to lack popular appeal). In this project we set out to document and theorise the practice of a small group of teachers who have rejected approaches to teaching and learning based on the concept of fixed, inherent ability, and whose pedagogy is constructed on a different premise: on the assumption that children's learning can be limited by a whole range of factors – emotional, social, pedagogical, environmental – and that the way to lift these limits on learning is to abandon ability labelling and ability-focused teaching, in all their guises, in favour of a commitment to enhancing the learning capacity of all children and young people. The experience of working on this project, and of contributing to the written account of our findings (Hart *et al.* in press), has immeasurably increased my present understanding of children's learning, and the imperative to conceptualise it in ways that are in the interests of children. The phrases I use in Chapter 2 to summarise the themes of this book – 'the interests of children and the choices made by teachers' – have come to have extended meanings for me, as a result of my membership of the *Learning Without Limits* research team.

One of the key concepts with which we sought to describe the thinking of the nine classroom teachers who collaborated with us was a particular relationship between the present and the future. As we studied these teachers' practice, we began to see more clearly how ability labelling, by even the kindest and most benevolent of teachers, inevitably imposes limits on children's learning in the present, by closing down possibilities for the future, by shutting the door on what might be. It seemed that the project teachers were able to lift limits on learning by focusing on a future that has not already been determined by some measure or perception of ability in the present. In due course we arrived at a formulation of this distinctive relationship between the present and the future in terms of the concept of *transformability*.

In ability-based teaching, children's futures as learners are already, to some degree, laid down. The upper limits of their achievement can be safely and accurately predicted. Nothing that can be done in the present will change the future that lies ahead. The concept of transformability defies these propositions. Inspired by a belief in transformability, teachers recognise that the future is constructed now, in the present. Everything that happens here and now, in schools and classrooms, today and every day, has a formative effect upon the future. For the teachers we worked with, the future of their children's learning was not fixed, but necessarily open. They saw children's futures as infinitely varied and unpredictable. One of them, Anne Reay, an infant teacher with whom I worked closely, and whose classroom practice I came to know well, often speaks of her class of five- and six-year-olds as 'people with futures', who each have their different way to go, their unique trajectories into the world. Anne is explicit and passionate about her determination to open up the world of learning to *everyone*, not just those children labelled, in other classrooms, the 'top table' or the 'high fliers'. For Anne there is simply no reason to predict how children will change and grow, or what form their learning will take in the future. The priority, in the present, is to continually extend and enhance learning opportunities, reduce and remove existing limits, consistently choosing the transforming options that will increase children's capacity to learn now *and* in the future.

The relationship between this way of making choices and forms of assessment that work for children is, I hope, transparently clear. If assessment is used to reinforce the limits that ability labelling can create for children's learning, then children's interests will be badly served. But if teachers are committed to a future that is essentially transformable and as yet unknowable, they are in a powerful position. They can use their acts of assessment, their seeing and understanding, to lift limits, to open the gate to children's futures as learners, rather than closing the door on them. When a child experiences a difficulty in learning, switches off or fails to connect, the teacher can choose how to interpret it: perhaps the reason is that the child is only at level 2; she or he is someone who will never go very far. Or perhaps the teacher reviews the possibilities of what might be limiting the child's learning: is it the language of the teacher? Or the experiences provided? Or the child's emotional state? Or earlier cognitive constructs? Or the nature of the task? Choosing to ask questions like these, in the process of assessment, must be in the interests of children. A commitment to the transformability of the future is, likewise, a choice in the interests of children.

Learning from the past

In the concluding chapter of the first edition, I describe, very briefly, some key ideas in the thinking of the former chief inspector of schools, the incomparable Edmond Holmes, who retired in 1910. Since I wrote this description I have read more widely and know and appreciate a little more of the enduring significance of his work. In particular I have studied his introduction to the fascinating early study of the work of Maria Montessori by a prolific American author Dorothy Canfield Fisher, whose novel *The Home-Maker* (1924) is an irresistible fictional account of one of the very first house-husbands, observed inventing and implementing Montessorian principles of early education with his demanding young child. Fisher's earlier book, *A Montessori Mother* (1913), in which Holmes' introduction appears, is in contrast a factual account of a visit she had recently made to Rome to see for herself what was going on in the Casa dei Bambini. Tempting though it is to report her observations, her emotions, her astonishment and her powerful interpretations of what she saw, it is Holmes' thinking that concerns us here. He identifies one key idea at the heart of Montessori's approach, one that she shares, according to Holmes, with 'Egeria', the pseudonym he gave to the teacher he immortalised in his 1911 text, *What Is and What Might Be*. 'What they both proved,' argues Holmes, is that 'self-education is the beginning and end of education – that the business of growing, *on all the planes of his being*, must be done by the growing child, and cannot be done for him by his teacher or by any other person' (italics in the original, Fisher 1913, p. xx). However, Holmes goes on to claim that the system of elementary education then current in England prevents any such thing from happening.

For what does education do to foster the growth of the child? If the child is to grow, he must do the business of growing by and for himself. He must himself digest and assimilate the food that is provided for him. He must himself exercise all his organs and faculties...In other words, he must be allowed to live and work in an atmosphere of freedom.

Now freedom is the last thing that education, as we know it in this and other 'civilised' countries, allows to the child. At every turn it closes in upon him with dogmatic pressure and constraint. From morning to evening, from day to day, from year to year, it does, or tries to do, for him most of the things which he ought to do for himself – his reasoning, his thinking, his imagining, his admiring, his sympathising, his willing, his purposing, his planning, his solving of problems, his mastering of difficulties, his controlling his passions and impulses, his bearing himself aright in his dealings with others. So complete is its distrust of the child's nature, that it will allow him to do nothing for himself which it can do, or even pretend to do for him; and it thus develops into an elaborate system for paralysing activity.

Fisher (1913) pp. xxii–iii

This is a chief inspector speaking, remember, who had been observing English elementary schools for 35 years. In short, times were bad. In his autobiography, *In Quest of an Ideal* (1920), he develops the theme: 'All this as I could not fail to realise, was as bad as bad could be. What was the remedy? The existing system was based on complete distrust of the goodness and capacity of children' (p. 120). But like the Reggio educators today, Holmes was not infected by this sense of distrust, nor convinced of the worthlessness and incapacity of children. The analysis continues and Holmes concludes:

A beginning would have to be made by giving the child some measure of trust and some measure of freedom. Trust first and then freedom. Freedom, because without freedom the child could not learn to do anything for himself. Trust, because without trust, one could not begin to set him free. (pp. 120–1)

The argument Holmes is making here is the one with which I close this Afterword. If we choose to distrust children and their learning, we cannot act in their interests. If we choose to clamp down on their freedom as active and spontaneous learners, they will not learn for themselves: they will become passive, obedient pupils; 'learning by swallowing' is Holmes' scathing, derisive description of the wrong kind of learning. But if children are offered trust and freedom, and invited to live and learn in a reciprocal relationship with their educators, as we have seen them do in New Zealand and Reggio in the preceding pages, then children's interests will be properly served. Offering children the gifts of trust and freedom is one of the ways in which educators can use their power lovingly, wisely and well.

Returning to Jason

Holmes' argument, now over 80 years-old, that children deserve, at the very least, both trust and freedom, calls for a contemporary illustration. As a conclusion to this edition, it seems appropriate to return to the child whose learning, or lack of it, stimulated my long-standing interest in the process of assessment and the tangle of rights, responsibilities and power that I see surrounding it. In Chapter 1 I analysed Jason's response to a formal mathematics test; here is Jason's work on an informal classroom spelling test, administered some months later.

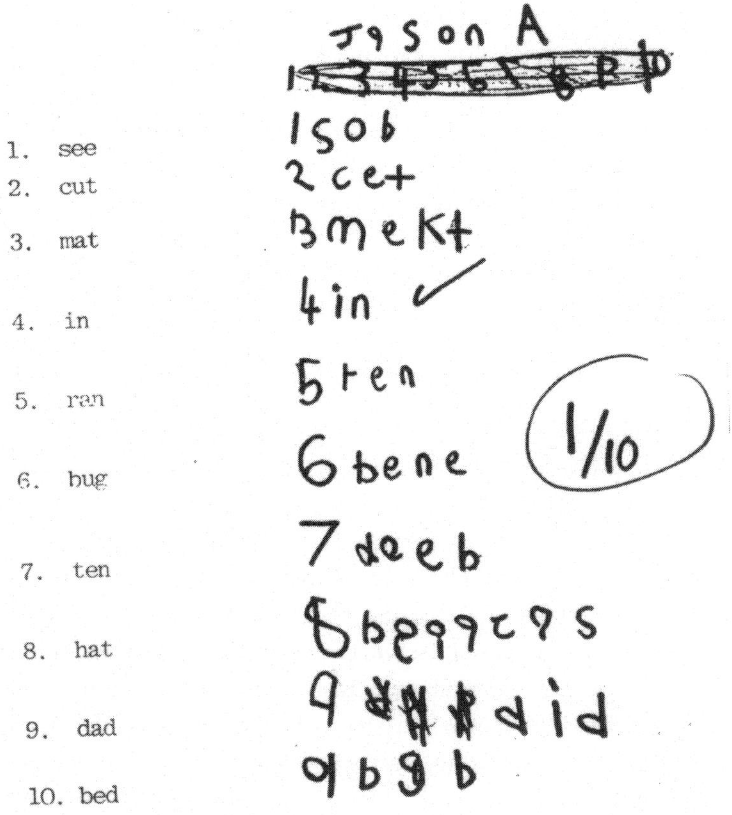

1. see
2. cut
3. mat
4. in
5. ran
6. bug
7. ten
8. hat
9. dad
10. bed

Figure A.2 Jason's spelling test

First let us consider what this test tells us about Jason and his learning and the choices his teachers seem to be making. The first instruction he is given is, apparently, to 'write down the numbers 1–10', which he does. But see how even in this simple direction there is room for ambiguity, confusion and, for Jason, getting it wrong and having to start again, writing the numbers *down* the page, in a vertical line, not just 'writing them down'. Now for the spellings themselves: in the first, Jason gets the first letter right, and in the next two the first and last: a small degree of achievement admittedly, but perhaps a promising sign that the mysterious process of transforming isolated spoken words into a sequence of written symbols is beginning to make sense to Jason. The fourth and fifth spellings both have two letters correct, and the fourth, being a two-letter word, receives the teacher's blessing and a tremendous tick. At the sixth spelling, Jason falters on his previous form and only achieves one correct letter; looking back up the list at the pattern so far, one may speculate whether Jason is using the letter 'e' as an all purpose vowel...maybe knowledge of the local accent would enable us to check out this possibility. However, at the seventh spelling, Jason goes completely off the rails as he hears the teacher utter the word 'seven', to indicate the seventh spelling, and then 'ten'. There is an almost audible crashing of mental gears as Jason fails to overcome the confusion that ensues. If this is a *spelling* test, he may well be asking himself, how on earth can I spell a *number*? And, in any case, I've already written '10' (twice). It is no wonder to me that the eighth spelling bears no resemblance to the target word 'hat', though I am not confident in my own reading of what Jason has written. But then Jason recovers himself; two letters are correct in the ninth word and all three in the final one, though with two reversals (three, if you include the reversal of the digits in 10 – is Jason left-handed perhaps?). But never mind the reversals, Jason is now back in pupil mode, responding to instructions as best he can, even when, as so often in his life as a pupil, it all makes very little sense to him. With a score of 1/10 boldly marked on his test paper, Jason moves on to face the next task, the next challenge, with a very negative evaluation of his worth as a speller made public, for all to see. This will not be the first time Jason has received such a low mark for his performance as a pupil: his teacher is unlikely to be surprised by it, and we can be fairly confident in assuming that she or he will use it to predict Jason's unsatisfactory and undistinguished future career as a learner.

Now let us imagine a different scenario, where Jason's future is shaped in a different way. In this imaginary but not impossible classroom, Jason is educated by teachers who are committed to the ideas I have been exploring in these pages, by teachers who reject the long-jump model of testing, who reject ability labelling, who believe that assessment must work for children, by promoting their learning. Suppose Jason to be educated by teachers who put their trust in him as a learner, who are committed to the Reggio construction of children as 'rich, strong and powerful'. Because they trust Jason's power to learn, these teachers give Jason the opportunities to exercise and strengthen his powers in ways that make human sense. They give him, for example, mathematical experiences that have meaning for him as a person, where his hitherto untapped capacity to think mathematically has relevance and impact. Jason's mathematics learning now takes place in the real-world contexts of shops, money, building materials, big blocks and planks of wood. Let us imagine, for example, that he works with a small group to build a rabbit hutch, and cooperates with his whole class to design a new gate in the playground fence (two illustrations borrowed from Carr's (2001) account of *Learning Stories*).

In this imagined classroom, Jason's teachers are equally convinced that Jason has emerging powers as a writer: again he is offered literary experiences that have real-world significance. He is given opportunities to write important notices, lists, letters, invitations, poems, secret messages, recipes, stories and magic spells, under his own direction. His teachers recognise the relationship between writing and the other forms of communication that the Reggio educators call the hundred symbolic languages of children (99 of which, they claim, are ignored in school). Jason's teachers do not ignore them: they give him opportunities to sing and dance and make music, to represent and express his thoughts in sound, paint, clay and, above all, in sustained, shared, purposeful talk.

Now Jason is daily engaged in many kinds of classroom talk that are a far more nourishing diet for his learning than any number of spelling tests. He joins in talk that sets the world to rights or solves a pressing social problem (in the playground or the toilets); talk that plans a new adventure or relishes an old one; talk that imagines the future and all the impossible things that might never happen; talk that remembers the past and all the amazing things that happened there. With this programme and more, Jason flourishes as a learner. From trusting him as a learner and giving him the freedom to act as a learner, setting off on his own inimitable journey, Jason's teachers take up their next responsibility: to document, in their assessment practices, Jason's unique and impressive learning story. I persist in my optimism for all the Jasons of the future.

April 2003

Bibliography

Abbott, L. and Nutbrown, C. (eds) (2001) *Experiencing Reggio Emilia: Implications for Pre-school Provision.* Buckingham: Open University Press.

Abercrombie, M. L. J. (1969) *The Anatomy of Judgement.* Harmondsworth: Penguin Books.

Alexander, R. (1992) *Policy and Practice in Primary Education.* London: Routledge.

Alexander, R., Rose, J. and Woodhead, C. (1992) *Curriculum Organisation and Classroom Practice in Primary Schools: A Discussion Paper.* London: DES.

Applebee, A. (1978) *The Child's Concept of Story.* Chicago: The University of Chicago Press.

Ariés, P. (1961) (English version 1973) *Centuries of Childhood.* Harmondsworth: Penguin Books.

Armstrong, M. (1980) *Closely Observed Children.* London: Writers & Readers.

Arnold, H. (1982) *Listening to Children Reading.* Sevenoaks: Hodder & Stoughton.

Athey, C. (1990) *Extending Thought in Young Children.* London: Paul Chapman Publishing.

Barrett, G. (1986) *Starting School: An Evaluation of the Experience.* London: Assistant Masters & Mistresses Association.

Barrs, M., Ellis, S., Hester, H. and Thomas, A. (1988) *The Primary Language Record Handbook.* London: ILEA/CLPE.

Bensley, B. and Kilby, S. (1992) 'Induction screening' *Curriculum,* 13(1), 29–51.

Bettelheim, B. (1950) *Love Is Not Enough.* New York: The Free Press.

Bettelheim, B. and Zelan, K. (1982) *On Learning to Read.* New York: Vintage Books.

Black, P. and Wiliam, D. (1998) *Inside the Black Box: Raising Standards through Classroom Assessment.* London: School of Education, King's College.

Black, P., Harrison, C., Lee, C., Marshall, B. and Wiliam, D. (2002) *Working Inside the Black Box: Assessment for Learning in the Classroom.* London: Department of Education and Professional Studies, King's College.

Blenkin, G. M. and Kelly, A. V. (1992) *Assessment in Early Childhood Education.* London: Paul Chapman Publishing.

Board of Education (1933) *Report of The Consultative Committee on Infant and Nursery Schools* (The Hadow Report). London: HMSO.

Bradley, B. S. (1989) *Visions of Infancy.* Cambridge: Polity Press.

Caldwell Cook, H. (1917) *The Play Way.* London: Heinemann.

Carr, M. (2001) *Assessment in Early Childhood Settings.* London: Paul Chapman Publishing.

Central Advisory Council for Education (1967) *Children and Their Primary Schools* (The Plowden Report). London: HMSO.

Coveney, P. (1967) *The Image of Childhood.* Harmondsworth: Penguin Books.

Dahlberg, G. and Åsén, G. (1994) 'Evaluation and Regulation: a Question of Empowerment' in Moss, P. and Pence, A. (eds) *Valuing Quality in Early Childhood Services: New Approaches to Defining Quality.* London: Paul Chapman Publishing.

Dahlberg, G., Moss, P. and Pence, A. (1999) *Beyond Quality in Early Childhood Education and Care: Postmodern Perspectives.* London: Falmer Press.

Department of Education and Science (1988) *National Curriculum: Task Group on Assessment and Testing: A Report.* London: HMSO.

Department of Education and Science (1991a) *Aspects of Primary Education in France: A Report by HMI.* London: DES.

Department of Education and Science (1991b) *Primary Education – A Statement by Secretary of State for Education and Science, Kenneth Clarke.* London: DES.

Department of Education and Science (1992) *KS1 Spelling Test.* London: DES.

Donaldson, M. (1978) *Children's Minds.* Glasgow: Fontana.

Drummond, M. J. (1991) 'Testing the science testers' *Nature,* **352,** 369–70.

Drummond, M. J. and Nutbrown, C. (1992) 'Observing and assessing young children' in Pugh, G. (ed.) *Contemporary Issues in the Early Years*. London: Paul Chapman Publishing in association with the National Children's Bureau.

Drummond, M. J., Rouse, D. and Pugh, G. (1992) *Making Assessment Work: Values and Principles in Assessing Young Children's Learning*. Nottingham: NES Arnold in association with the National Children's Bureau.

Early Years Curriculum Group (1989) *Early Childhood Education: The Early Years Curriculum and the National Curriculum*. Stoke-on-Trent: Trentham Books.

Easen, P. (1987) 'All at sixes and sevens: the difficulties of learning mathematics' in Booth, T., Potts, P. and Swann, W. (eds) *Preventing Difficulties in Learning*. Oxford: Basil Blackwell.

Edwards, C., Gandini, L. and Forman, G. (eds) (1994) *The Hundred Languages of Children: The Reggio Emilia Approach to Early Childhood Education*. Norwood, NJ: Ablex Publishing Co.

Edwards, C., Gandini, L. and Forman, G. (eds) (1998) *The Hundred Languages of Children: The Reggio Emilia Approach – Advanced Reflections*. Norwood NJ: Ablex Publishing Co.

Egan, K. (1988) *Primary Understanding*. London: Routledge.

Fisher, D. C. (1913) *A Montessori Mother*. London: Constable.

Fisher, D. C. (1924) *The Home-Maker*. New York: Harcourt Brace Jovanovich, reissued (1999) London: Persephone Books.

Fromm, E. (1942) *The Fear of Freedom*. London: Routledge & Kegan Paul.

Gandini, L. and Edwards, C. P. (eds) (2001) *Bambini: The Italian Approach to Infant Toddler Care*. New York: Teachers College Press.

Gardner, D. E. M. (1969) *Susan Isaacs: The First Biography*. London: Methuen.

Gregory, E. and Kelly, C. (1992) 'Bilingualism and assessment' in Blenkin, G. M. and Kelly, A. V. op. cit.

Grumet, M. (1981) 'Restitution and Reconstruction of Educational Experience: an Autobiographical Method for Curriculum Theory' in Lawn, M. and Barton, L. (eds) *Rethinking Curriculum Studies*. London: Croom Helm.

Gura, P. (ed.) (1997) *Reflections on Early Education and Care Inspired by Visits to Reggio Emilia Italy*. London: British Association for Early Childhood Education.

Hannon, P., Weinberger, J. and Nutbrown, C. (1991) 'A study of work with parents to promote early literacy development' *Research Papers in Education*, **6**(2), 77–97.

Hart, S. (1992) 'Differentiation. Part of the problem or part of the solution?' *The Curriculum Journal*, 3(2), 131–42.

Hart, S., Dixon, A., Drummond, M.J. and McIntyre, D. (in press) *Learning Without Limits*. Buckingham: Open University Press.

Hohmann, M., Banet, B. and Weikart, D. (1979) *Young Children in Action*. Ypsilanti: High/Scope Press.

Holmes, E. (1911) *What Is and What Might Be*. London: Constable.

Holmes, E. (1914) *In Defence of What Might Be*. London: Constable.

Holmes, E. (1920) *In Quest of an Ideal*. London: Richard Cobden-Sanderson.

Holmes, G. (1952) *The Idiot Teacher*. London: Faber and Faber, reissued 1977 Nottingham: Spokesman.

Hughes, M., Mayall, B., Moss, P., Perry, J., Petrie, P. and Pinkerton, G. (1980) *Nurseries Now*. Harmondsworth: Penguin Books.

Isaacs, S. (1930) *Intellectual Growth in Young Children*. London: Routledge & Kegan Paul.

Jackson, P. (1968) *Life in Classrooms*. New York: Holt, Rinehart and Winston.

James, A. and Prout, A. (eds) (1990) *Constructing and Reconstructing Childhood: Contemporary Issues in the Sociological Study of Childhood*. London: Falmer.

Lear, J. (1988) *Aristotle: The Desire to Understand*. Cambridge: Cambridge University Press.

Lee, W. and Carr, M. (2001) *Learning Stories as an Assessment Tool for Early Childhood*. Paper presented at the 11th European Conference on Quality in Early Childhood Education, EECERA Conference, Alkmaar, The Netherlands.

Lifton, B. J. (1989) *The King of Children*. London: Pan Books.

Light, P. (1986) 'Context, conservation and conversation' in Richards, M. and Light, P. (eds) (op. cit.).

Lowenfeld, M. (1935) *Play in Childhood*. London: Gollancz.

Mannheim, K. (1936) *Ideology and Utopia: An Introduction to the Sociology of Knowledge*, translated by L. Wirth and E. Shils. New York: Harcourt Brace.

Meek, M. (1983) *Achieving Literacy*. London: Routledge & Kegan Paul.

Meek, M. (1985) 'Play and Paradoxes: Some Considerations of Imagination and Language' in Wells, G. and Nicholls, J. (eds) *Language and Learning: An Interactional Perspective*. London: Falmer.

Ministry of Education (1996) *Te Whāriki Early Childhood Curriculum.* Wellington, NZ: Learning Media.

Nabokov, V. (1977) 'An evening of Russian poetry' in *The Portable Nabokov.* Harmondsworth: Penguin Books.

NFER (1984) *Mathematics 8.* Windsor: NFER-Nelson.

Nicholls, R. (ed.) (1986) *Rumpus Schema Extra.* Cleveland Teachers in Education (LEA).

Nutbrown, C. (1987) 'A case-study of the development and implementation of a nursery curriculum based on schematic theory'. Unpublished BEd dissertation, Sheffield City Polytechnic.

Paley, V. G. (1981) *Wally's Stories.* Cambridge, Mass: Harvard University Press.

Piaget, J. and Inhelder, B. (1956) *The Child's Conception of Space.* London: Routledge & Kegan Paul.

Pollard, A. and Tann, S. (1987) *Reflective Teaching in the Primary School.* London: Cassell.

Powys, J. C. (1974) *Letters to Nicholas Ross.* London: The Village Press.

Prisk, T. (1987) 'Letting them get on with it: a study of unsupervised group talk in an infant school' in Pollard, A. (ed.) *Children and Their Primary Schools.* London: Falmer.

Pugh, G. and De'Ath, E. (1989) *Working Towards Partnership in the Early Years.* London: National Children's Bureau.

Qualifications and Curriculum Authority (2000) *Curriculum Guidance for the Foundation Stage.* London: Qualifications and Curriculum Authority.

Richards, M. P. M. (ed.) (1974) *The Integration of a Child into a Social World.* London: Cambridge University Press.

Richards, M. P. M. and Light, P. (eds) (1986) *Children of Social Worlds: Development in a Social Context.* Cambridge: Polity Press.

School Examinations and Assessment Council (1991) *Records of Achievement in Primary Schools.* London: HMSO.

Sharp, R. and Green, A. (1975) *Education and Social Control.* London: Routledge & Kegan Paul.

Shaw, J. (1992) 'An investigation of parents' conceptual development in the context of dialogue with a community teacher'. Unpublished PhD thesis, University of Newcastle-upon-Tyne.

Sheahan A. (ed.) (2003) *Teachers Understanding Literacy Improvements in Primary Schools.* Cambridge: Faculty of Education, University of Cambridge.

Simon, B. (1985) *Does Education Matter?* London: Lawrence and Wishart.

Smail, D. (1987) *Taking Care: An Alternative to Therapy.* London: Dent.

Stansbury, D. (1992) 'A Loss to Comprehensive Education' *Forum*, **34**(3), 76–7.

Stenhouse, L. (1975) *An Introduction to Curriculum Research and Development.* London: Heinemann.

Stenhouse, L. (1985) *Research as a Basis for Teaching.* London: Heinemann.

Tobin, J. J., Wu, D. and Davidson, D. (1989) *Preschool in Three Cultures.* New Haven: Yale University Press.

Valentine, M. (1999) *The Reggio Emilia Approach to Early Years Education.* Dundee: Scottish Consultative Council on the Curriculum.

Vygotsky, L. S. (1978) *Mind in Society.* Cambridge, Mass: Harvard University Press.

Walkerdine, V. (1984) 'Developmental Psychology and Child-Centred Pedagogy' in Henriques, J. (*et al.*) *Changing the Subject.* London: Methuen.

Weil, S. (1986) 'Prerequisite to Dignity of Labour' in Miles, S. (ed.) *Simone Weil. An Anthology.* London: Virago.

Willes, M. (1983) *Children into Pupils.* London: Routledge & Kegan Paul.

Winnicott, D. W. (1964) *The Child, the Family and the Outside World.* Harmondsworth: Penguin Books.

Wolfendale, S. (1990) *All About Me.* Nottingham: NES Arnold.

Also available...

 **David Fulton** Publishers

The Art of Middle Management in Primary Schools
A Guide to Effective Subject, Year and Team Leadership

Peter Fleming and **Max Amesbury**

'Strong on management styles and getting the best out of people, the advice on performance management is timely.'

The Teacher

Contents: What is middle management? Different management styles; A look at effective school cultures; Getting the best out of people; Building your team; Effective communication; Meetings; Administration and resource management; Managing change and development; Performance management; Stress management and time management.

£16.00 • Pb • 176 pg • 1-85346-736-7 • 2001

Improving the Quality of Education for All
A Handbook of Staff Development Activities

| 2nd |
| Edition |

David Hopkins

This book provides many practical staff development activities and gives examples of specific changes which have taken place in IQEA schools, relating both to the progress of students and the professional development of their teachers. These training activities and examples demonstrate that improving the quality of education has many facets, not all of which can be measured and translated into league tables.

£25.00 • 144 pg • 1-85346-649-2 • 2002

Performance Management
Monitoring Teaching in the Primary School

Sara Bubb and **Pauline Hoare**

This book offers practical guidance on how to go about performance management. Based on experience of working with schools and running courses, and using the latest research on business strategies appropriate for education. Throughout, the purpose is to help schools and teachers to be more effective.

£17.50 • Pb • 144 pages • 1-85346-740-5 • 2001

The Effective Induction of Newly Qualified Primary Teachers
An Induction Tutor's Handbook

Sara Bubb

This is an excellent insight into the world of induction tutors. The book is optimistic yet realistic, sensitive yet uncompromising, and manages to provide up-to-date guidance on the support, monitoring and assessment aspects of the role. All issues are tackled thoroughly from both the NQT's and the induction tutors perspective, and pros and cons are explained carefully... The Effective Induction of Newly Qualified Primary Teachers will undoubtedly make induction tutors' lives easier and this book merits a wide audience from NQTs to headteachers.'

Managing Schools Today

£24.00 • 128 pg • 1-85346-684-0 • 2000

Teacher-Led Development Work
Guidance and Support

David Frost and **Judy Durrant**

The book

- demonstrates how secondary and primary teachers can contribute to the improvement of their school, whilst pursuing their own continued professional development and gaining accreditation through school-based work

- provides guidelines for school managers, higher education tutors, external consultants and LEA advisors establishing school-based support

- gives tried and tested flexible proformas, checklists and other practical tools that are ideal for training, INSET or a personal audit.

£25.00 • 160 pg • 1-84312-006-2 • 2002

Helping Teachers Develop Through Classroom Observation

| 2nd |
| Edition |

Diane Montgomery

'an essential practical guide for teachers and managers, which is easily read and balances theory, experience and practice.'

CPD Update

Contents: Performance management; Classroom observation methods; Case studies in appraisal using the formative system; Effective learning; Effective teaching.

£18.00 • Pb • 192 pg • 1-85346-872-X • 2002

Teaching Assistants
Practical Strategies for Effective Classroom Support

Maggie Balshaw and **Peter Farrell**

This practical book is intended to support schools and LEAs in developing effective strategies for working with teaching assistants. It is related to the DfEE's *Working with Teaching Assistants: A good practice guide* (2000). Suggested approaches are supported with real examples from practice, showing the reality of how schools can review and develop practice and so become more effective in their management and support of teaching assistants.

£16.00 • Pb • 144 pg • 1-85346-828-2 • 2002

Appointing and Managing Learning Support Assistants
A Practical Guide for SENCOs and other Managers

Jennie George and Margaret Hunt

Written specially for SENCOs and other managers, this book offers guidance on employing and managing LSAs and all those who support children in mainstream education (LSAs, TAs, SSAs or STAs).

£15.00 • • 112 A4 pages • 1-84312-062-3 • September 2003

David Fulton Publishers, The Chiswick Centre, 414 Chiswick High Road, London W4 5TF
Tel: 020 8996 3610   Fax: 020 8996 3622   E-mail: orders@fultonpublishers.co.uk
www.fultonpublishers.co.uk

To order...

David Fulton Publishers

If you would like to order any of our books, or would like to request a copy of our complete catalogue, just photocopy this page and send it to:

David Fulton Publishers, The Chiswick Centre, 414 Chiswick High Road, London W4 5TF

Alternatively you can telephone, fax, email or order online:
Freecall: 0500 618052   Fax: 020 8996 3622
E-mail: orders@fultonpublishers.co.uk   on-line: www.fultonpublishers.co.uk

ORDER FORM

Qty	ISBN	Title	Price	Subtotal

Postage and Packing: £2.50 for one or two books.
Postage and packing is free for orders of three or more books.

P & P	
Total	

Payment

☐   By credit card (Visa / Access / Mastercard / American Express / Switch / Delta)

☐   By cheque with order. Please make cheques payable to David Fulton Publishers Ltd.

☐   With invoice (applicable to schools, LEAs and other institutions)

Credit card number ☐☐☐☐☐☐☐☐☐☐☐☐☐☐☐☐☐☐☐☐☐☐☐

Expiry date ☐☐☐☐ (Switch customers only)   Valid from ☐☐☐☐ Issue number ☐

Name	Order No./Ref
Position	Date
School/LEA/Company	
Address	
Postcode	
Telephone Number	Signature